THE HEATH-CHICAGO
GERMAN SERIES

PETER HAGBOLDT, *Editor*

THE
TEACHING OF GERMAN

BY

PETER HAGBOLDT

Professor of German
The University of Chicago

D. C. HEATH AND COMPANY
BOSTON

TO

ROBERT HERNDON FIFE

**DISTINGUISHED CHAIRMAN
OF THE MODERN FOREIGN LANGUAGE STUDY
AND OF THE COMMITTEE ON MODERN LANGUAGES**

PREFACE

THIS BOOK has grown out of extensive teaching experience in high school and college, lectures given at various universities and at conventions on pedagogy of modern languages in general and of German in particular, and a large number of books and articles along these lines.

Naturally I have consulted all the works in this field that I could find, notably those by Bagster-Collins, Cole, Griebsch, Handschin, Prokosch, Michael West, and a score of others, but the conclusions I have reached are my own. It goes without saying that I have taken into careful consideration the main findings of the *Modern Foreign Language Study*, dwelling at some length on the brief course and its extremely difficult implications. Though some of my views involve disputed points, I have made an effort to be fair to those of contrary opinion. I have not avoided reiteration wherever it seems effective in driving home a point.

Articles of pertinence and value within the various chapters are often so numerous that I have simply referred the reader to appropriate sections in Oliver's excellent *Modern Language Teacher's Handbook*. If I have failed to mention specifically the contribution of some colleague, I beg the reader's indulgence, since not all the names and articles could be listed in the space at my disposal. Similarly I wish to point out that the special bibliographies following the *Note on Syllabi* make no claim to completeness, and are intended merely to be suggestive.

The following colleagues have read one or several of the eleven chapters: Professors Robert Herndon Fife, Erwin Escher, Paul B. Diederich, C. R. Goedsche, F. W. Kaufmann, Walter V. Kaulfers, Werner F. Leopold, V. A. C. Henmon, Clarence E. Parmenter, C. M. Purin, Holland D. Roberts, Curtis D. Vail, Ben D. Wood, and Berthold L. Ullman. To all of them I am indebted for many a helpful suggestion.

My good friend B. Q. Morgan has had the courage and the kindness to read the entire book. To him I am very grateful for much encouragement when I needed it most, for his thorough and critical reading as well as for many invaluable suggestions. He has also read carefully and critically the galley proof. Professor George J. ten Hoor of the University of Chicago had the kindness to do the same for the second half of the galleys.

I am indebted to Professors Robert Herndon Fife, the late Algernon Coleman, V. A. C. Henmon, C. M. Purin, and Ben D. Wood for permitting me to quote freely from their valuable books.

I take pleasure in expressing my appreciation to the following publishers who generously granted me permission to quote from their books: The University of Chicago Press, D. C. Heath and Company, The Columbia University Press, The University of Toronto Press, The Appleton-Century Company, Ginn and Company, George Allen and Unwin of London, and above all The Macmillan Company who published nearly all the volumes of the Modern Foreign Language Study.

I must not forget to pay my respects to Professor Henry C. Morrison whose wise and inspiring administration of the modern foreign language classes in the College of the University of Chicago during the first years of my activity there I recall with pleasure and gratitude.

To Dr. José Padín, Modern Language Editor of D. C. Heath and Company, goes my sincere appreciation for his careful reading of the manuscript, and to Miss Ellen E. Aldrich and her able assistants my thanks for their unfailing efficiency and courtesy and valuable help in seeing the book through the press.

PETER HAGBOLDT

TABLE OF CONTENTS

THE TEACHING OF GERMAN

THE TEACHING OF LANGUAGES FROM THE MIDDLE AGES TO THE PRESENT: A HISTORICAL SKETCH

THE WORD "sketch" is usually defined as an outline, a rough draft, or a memorandum hastily set down. It is in all or any of these connotations that I beg the reader to think of the following discussion. All sketches are fragmentary, and necessarily suffer from omissions. Yet even a brief survey of the history of language teaching drawn in bold and clear outlines will clarify our minds concerning the main thoughts and events of the past and give us a better appreciation of present and future problems. Therefore we shall attempt to describe succinctly the efforts of those outstanding scholars and teachers as well as committees whose work has been, and still is, of particular significance for all expecting to impart a knowledge of a foreign language.

After the fall of the Roman Empire, Latin persisted for a long time as a link between the nations of the West. Latin became the language of the school and the church and, as a medium for any higher education, it remained indispensable until about 1770, when the vernacular languages took its place.

Before and during the Middle Ages classical Latin gradually and imperceptibly changed to its later forms: first middle Latin and finally vulgar Latin. While these changes were taking place, Latin was a living language, and was acquired in a simple and natural way through hearing, speaking, and reading. Before the invention of printing, when manuscripts were rare and costly, instruction was mainly based on oral practice, oral examinations or disputations. "The pupil lived in a Latin-speaking atmosphere in which there was abundant opportunity for self-expression in the interminable controversies and discussions which formed . . . an essential part of medieval education." [1]

One of the most popular presentations of Latin grammar was written by AELIUS DONATUS during the fourth century A.D. His treatise on *De octo partibus orationis* constituted a brief Latin primer, became one of the most common of early printed books, and remained in use for more than a thousand years.[2] Yet the simple Donatus was forgotten as soon as the classics had been read again and again. Teachers leaned more and more toward the formal side of instruction, and grammar became more essential than the words of Cicero or Homer. Grammar was no longer a modest means toward an important end; it became an end in itself. "Out of the texts were dug the foundation stones of grammatical structure, artistic and symmetrical, so that finally a dead system of rules acquired independent value . . . Beginners in Latin sighed under its tyrannous yoke . . . and for several centuries it held undisputed sway . . . Language teaching became utter desolation, . . . heartily loathsome to youth." [3] Thus only "for a short period during the Renaissance the classical languages were presented in a vital way." [4]

[1] M. A. Buchanan and E. D. MacPhee, *Modern Language Instruction in Canada*, Vol. I (The University of Toronto Press, 1928), p. 2.

[2] Reprinted by Teubner as *Ars minor*, cf. H. S. T. Keil, *Grammatici Latini*, IV (Leipzig, 1864), 355. — Wilhelm Viëtor in *Die Methodik des neusprachlichen Unterrichts* (Leipzig: Teubner, 1902), p. 6, speaks of a *Donait françois* and of several *Donati* for English. An error against Donat became known as a *Donatschnitzer*, as the brothers Grimm report in their great dictionary. Donatus influenced the development of later Latin grammars (Lyly, 1515; Linacre, 1524; and many others) and the teaching of languages in general.

Viëtor's *Methodik*, a tiny book of 56 pages, contains four lectures on the history of teaching foreign languages, beginning with Louis the German and the Oaths of Straßburg up to and including Viëtor's own recommendations.

[3] Leopold Bahlsen, *The Teaching of Modern Languages*, translated by M. Blakemore Evans (Ginn and Company, 1905), p. 3.

[4] Buchanan and MacPhee, *op. cit.*, p. 3.

But note Professor Robert Herndon Fife's remark: "Most writers on the history of teaching grammar present a distorted picture of the position which grammar occupied in the schools after the Renaissance . . . As I look at it, the whole relationship of grammar to language teaching since the scholastic age has been a struggle against artificiality and the logical ballast of scholasticism. Ever since the beginnings of the humanistic reforms this struggle has gone on, and great progress has certainly been made. It is, however, still with us, in spite of all the efforts at reform." (Personal letter, May 4, 1938.)

There were exceptions nevertheless. A certain LUCAS DI MARINIS, a Sicilian, who devoted his life to letters and education in Spain, where he was named Lucio Marineo, was utterly dissatisfied with Latin instruction at the University of Salamanca. In his dedication to Queen Isabella "Marineo explained that he found his students . . . almost completely lacking in the first principles of grammar; he found that they stood in fear of bulky and verbose volumes of other grammarians; and that, thinking that his *discipuli* should be led to the enjoyment of Latin books and the mastery of smooth and practical speech in a shorter and easier way, he had prepared these *Grammatices compendia*, based on the Latin authors themselves." [1] The edition of 1532 was published in Alcalá under the title *Lucii Marinei Siculi Grammatica brevis ac perutilis*, as a small volume of sixty-seven pages, in beautiful and clear print, containing not more and not less than bare essentials. Since this grammar is very interesting in the light of present conditions, we shall quote from Marineo's Introduction:

> Judging these few things to be enough for beginners and the rest not necessary, I leave it to others fruitlessly to weary the minds of their students. For if, after they have made acquaintance with the form of words, they will spend that time which others spend on rules of grammar, in hearing the authors from whom those same rules are taken, they will certainly advance more, and become not grammarians but Latinists. Thus boys are being taught in Italy, thus in Germany. Witness of this in olden time is Quintilian; witness now in Germany is Erasmus . . . See to it then, I ask, nay I entreat, if you fear the judgment of God, you who teach boys grammar, that you do not place your own advantage above that of your students, and spread over five years what you could teach them in five months. [2]

Caro Lynn in her delightful and scholarly book continues: "This method did away with the learning by heart of complicated, singsong rules; it gave the student the essentials in a volume of hopeful size; it familiarized him by simple quotation with Latin authors; and it left the burden of language mastery on the use of language itself. It was a very modern method . . ." [2]

[1] Caro Lynn, *A College Professor of the Renaissance* (The University of Chicago Press, 1937), p. 98. [2] *Ibid.*, p. 99.

Emphatically in opposition to the purely formal approach to Latin, PHILIPP MELANCHTHON (1497–1560), too, had declared that grammar should never become an object in itself; MARTIN LUTHER (1483–1546) had insisted on "not too much drill on rules"; and WOLFGANG RATICHIUS (his real name was Ratke), the worthy predecessor of Comenius, had pointed back to the times when the student paid little attention to grammar, but instead, from the beginning of his study, had read eagerly and widely, soon becoming familiar with the language.[1]

The most interesting example of learning a foreign language during early childhood in a perfectly natural and effortless way is reported by MICHEL DE MONTAIGNE (1533–1592), who in his famous essay, *De l'institution des enfants*, describes the method by which he learned Latin easily and fluently. His father was a nobleman and a serious student of education. Anxious to provide the best possible training for his son, he intrusted him to the care of a competent tutor who spoke only Latin to him.

"As for the other members of my father's household," Montaigne tells us, "it was an inviolable rule that neither himself (*i.e.*, his father), nor my mother, nor man- nor maid-servant were suffered to speak one word in my company except such Latin words as everyone had learned to chat and prattle with me ... To be short, we were latinized that the towns round about us had their share of it. As for myself I was about six years old, and could understand no more French or Perigordine than Arabic ... and without books, rules or grammar, without whipping or whining, I had gotten as pure a Latin tongue as my Master could speak ... The best scholars have often told me that in my infancy I had the Latin tongue so ready and so perfect that they themselves feared to take me in hand." [2]

As we see immediately, this simple method deserves to be termed "natural," for it is, in fact, no more and no less than an exact and faithful reproduction of the process by which we learn our native language.

In the same essay Montaigne tells us that at the age of six he was sent to the college of Guyenne, at the time the best and most flourishing classical college in France. Latin was no longer spoken

[1] Bahlsen, *op. cit.*, pp. 2 ff. [2] *The Essays of Michael Lord of Montaigne*, translated by John Florio (London: George Roulette and Sons, 1885), p. 78.

in the schools, and Montaigne soon lost the facility to converse in it.

JOHN AMOS COMENIUS (1592–1670), born in Nivitz, Moravia, a leader and later a Bishop in the Moravian or Bohemian Church, through his extraordinary genius became a pioneer of modern education. For a short time he studied in Heidelberg, then in Amsterdam, where he spent the last days of an eventful life.

Finding the teaching of Latin altogether deficient, he experimented with a Latin grammar, and wrote several texts, which greatly simplified the teaching of Latin. In 1628 he completed his *Ianua Linguarum Reserata*, "The Gate of Tongues Unlocked," which, published in 1631, was immediately translated into sixteen different languages and for many generations remained a standard work. This book was based on several thousand words in common use, arranged in sentences, at first easy, then more complex, presenting a working knowledge of simple Latin. A hundred captions dealt with a wide variety of topics, from the "Origin of the World" to the "Providence of God." Grammar was not presented by rules, but by being applied; the skilful teacher was expected to present it through induction. Each word was used only once in one meaning and one construction. Nevertheless it was the first attempt to present grammar inductively.[1]

In 1632 appeared his *Magna Didacta*, "The Great Didactic," a truly prophetic work for his time and quite modern in conception. *Orbis Pictus*, "The World in Pictures," published in 1658, is the first significant and successful application of pictures for use in schools. Comenius' thesis was: *Nihil est in intellectu quod non prius fuerit in sensu*, "Nothing is in the understanding which has not previously been in the senses." According to this principle, each Latin word was preceded by an illustration.[2]

[1] For illustrations of inductive and deductive presentation of grammar, see Peter Hagboldt, *Language Learning* (The University of Chicago Press, 1935), pp. 70–75.

[2] C. H. Handschin in his article "Tests and Measurements in Modern Language Work," *Modern Language Journal* (Feb. 1920), pp. 217–25, does not approve of the use of pictures in learning vocabulary. Compare, however, Buchanan and MacPhee, *op. cit.*, pp. 53 ff., who report "that totally contradictory results appear in the studies to date," and also see the interesting monograph *Selection and Application of Illustrative Material in Foreign Language Classes* by Otto Koischwitz (Teachers College, Columbia University,

The most significant statement of Comenius is: "Every language must be learned by practice rather than by rules, especially by reading, repeating, copying, and by written and oral attempts at imitation," [1] but his wisdom seems to have been forgotten soon after his death.   Comenius had anticipated more than three centuries ago what we unwittingly ignore in modern times.[2]

JOHN LOCKE (1632–1700) in his essay on *Some Thoughts Concerning Education* [3] plainly shows the influence of Montaigne and Comenius.   He recommends French as a second foreign language for children, but "talked into" the child in a strictly natural way. He assails vigorously the foolishness and the pedantry of schoolmasters and protests against the teaching of Latin to pupils intended for a trade or for commerce.   Condemning the grammatical method of teaching Latin, he advises some easy and pleasant book, such as Aesop's *Fables*, "writing the English translation in one line and the Latin words just over it in another . . . The formation of the verbs first," he says, "and afterwards the declension of the nouns perfectly learned by heart, may facilitate his acquaintance with the genius and manner of the Latin tongue . . . Languages," Locke continues, "were not made by rules or art, but by accident and the common use of the people.   And he that will speak them well has no other rule but that, nor anything to trust to but his memory and the habit of speaking after the fashion learned from those that are allowed to speak by rote."   And as for grammar, "if his use . . . be only to understand some books writ in it, without a critical knowledge of the tongue itself, reading alone, as I have said, will attain this end, without charging the mind with the multiplied rules and intricacies of grammar." [4]

Stated in modern terms, the essence of Locke's argument is this: we do not learn a language by rule, but by use, not by committing to memory the conjugation of verbs and the inflection of nouns, but by applying the forms of language in whatever way we intend

1932).   On pp. 7–28, Koischwitz gives excellent arguments for the use of pictures.

[1] Bahlsen, *op. cit.*, p. 4.   [2] For a more detailed article on Comenius see Isaac L. Kandel and Paul Monroe in *A Cyclopedia of Education*. The Macmillan Company, 1928.

[3] London, 1693, see paragraphs on Reading, French, Latin, etc.   [4] Compare Buchanan and MacPhee, *op. cit.*, pp. 10 ff.

to use them. In other words, our individual aim and our individual and specific application and practice determine the result.

JOHANN VALENTIN MEIDINGER (1756–1820) published in 1783 a book with the alluring title: *Praktische französische Grammatik, wodurch man diese Sprache auf eine ganz neue und sehr leichte Art in kurzer Zeit erlernen kann.* Up to that time it had been customary to translate from the foreign into the native tongue. With Meidinger, translation into the foreign tongue became all-important. His sequence of instruction was (1) grammatical rule, (2) translation into the foreign language with the help of footnotes. In other words, the student manufactured himself the language he intended to learn, a process appropriately called *Meidingerei* by Wilhelm Viëtor.[1]

More in sympathy with Comenius, JAMES HAMILTON (1764–1829) issued his *The Hamiltonian System*, according to which he himself had learned German. His basic theory was that the student must be introduced from the beginning to the living language, and that he must gain the laws of language inductively. This was fundamentally the same theory which later was to gain general recognition through the German reformers. Hamilton's text was far too difficult for beginners, his system being based on the Gospel according to St. John.

Entirely in accord with Hamilton's basic idea, JEAN JOSEPH JACOTOT (1770–1840) wrote his *Enseignement universel* (1823), with Fénelon's *Télémaque* as the basic text. Both Hamilton and Jacotot influenced the *Unterrichtsbriefe* of Toussaint-Langenscheidt intended for self-instruction, popular to this day with mature students.[2]

JOHANN HEINRICH SEIDENSTÜCKER (1785–1817) attempted to avoid the obstacle of offering too difficult material to beginners. In his *Elementarbuch zur Erlernung der französischen Sprache* (1811) he limited himself to disconnected sentences. He succeeded in writing easy sentences, all containing the same grammatical phenomena, but failed in other vital respects. The same is true of JOHANN FRANZ AHN (*Französischer Lehrgang*, 1834) and of H. S. OLLENDORF (*Methode, eine Sprache in sechs Monaten lesen, schreiben und sprechen zu lernen*, 1783).[3]

---

[1] Viëtor, *op. cit.*, pp. 19 ff.   [2] *Ibid.*, p. 21.   [3] *Ibid.*, pp. 23 ff.

KARL PLÖTZ (1819–1881), to some an idol, to others the embodi-
ment of every linguistic malfeasance in language pedagogy,
dominated through his French and English textbooks the schools
of Germany until long after his death. He was an indefatigable
worker, a complete master of the language he attempted to teach,
and the last and most influential representative of the grammar-
translation method. Plötz, who attempted a correction of Ollendorf and who, according to Viëtor, only effected "a new infusion
of grammar," divided his texts into two parts: (1) rules and
paradigms; (2*a*) French sentences; (2*b*) German sentences. The
sole form of instruction was mechanical translation. The type of
sentences was:

> The garden is beautiful. The king has a black horse. The wall is
> black. I have a bread [*sic*]. Thou hast a book and a dog. The
> brother has got a beautiful gift. The horse of the father was kind.

In sum, it was "a barren waste of insipid sentence translation,"
as one writer terms it. There was seldom the relief of questions. "Committing words to memory, translating sentences,
drilling irregular verbs, later memorizing, repeating, and applying
grammatical rules with their exceptions — that was and remained
our main occupation; for not until the last years of the higher
schools with the nine-year curriculum did French reading come
to anything like prominence, and that was the time when free
compositions in the foreign language were to be written." [1]

Bahlsen, the author of the last lines, had been a student of Plötz
and assures us that whenever he and his fellow students were
obliged to write a letter, or speak in the foreign language, there
arose before their minds "a veritable forest of paragraphs," and
"an impenetrable thicket of grammatical rules."

In 1866 GOTTLIEB HENESS started a small private school of
modern languages at New Haven. He is the rediscoverer or reinter-
preter of the "natural method." His text *Leitfaden für den Unterricht in der deutschen Sprache* (1867) proved to be a healthy reaction
against the grammar-translation method of Ollendorf, Ahn, Plötz,
and others. Heness was joined a few years later by L. Sauveur,

---

[1] Bahlsen, *op. cit.*, pp. 10 ff.; also Viëtor, *op. cit.*, pp. 23 ff.

the author of *Causeries avec mes élèves* and *Petites Causeries*, and their undertaking flourished until about 1900. They founded a school in Cambridge, established summer schools of modern languages in various centers, and counted many outstanding personalities among their students, for instance, Eliot, Longfellow, and Gilman. "These summer schools were largely attended by modern language teachers, who were undoubtedly stimulated to try out in their classes at least some of the ideas they had gathered during the five weeks' intensive work." [1]

The lack of system is characteristic of the "natural method," and it is bound to lead to disappointment, unless combined with other methods, bringing system and order into natural disorder.

In 1867, the same year when Heness reinterpreted the "natural" method, CLAUDE MARCEL published his fascinating book on *The Study of Languages Brought Back to Its True Principles, or the Art of Thinking in a Foreign Language*.[2] This worthy treatise, written more than sixty years ago, retains its charm for any student seriously interested in the pedagogy of reading foreign languages. Marcel aims to impart a full mastery of the foreign language. First he trains the student's ear by having the teacher read extensively to him. Then the student begins to read simple, and if possible, familiar material, followed by more and more difficult discourse as he slowly progresses. The procedure is hearing, reading, speaking, and, finally, what Marcel considers the least desirable ability, writing. There is no formal training in grammar or translation. Marcel insists that grammar does not facilitate reading, since it fails to explain the meaning of words or phrases. Again and again he objects to grammatical comment on language, maintaining that reading is the best way of acquiring a large number of words and phrases. He recommends literal translation or indirect reading in the beginning as an introduction to direct reading, the student's ultimate aim. He is against the use of dic-

[1] E. W. Bagster-Collins, *The History of Modern Language Teaching in the United States*, reprinted from *Studies in Modern Language Teaching*, Vol. XVII, Publications of the American and Canadian Committees on Modern Languages (The Macmillan Company, 1930), 88 pp. See also Buchanan and MacPhee, *op. cit.*, pp. 23 f.

[2] xi + 228 pp. (Appleton and Company), translated from the French edition, Paris, 1867.

tionaries which, he says, prevent the student from reading more than twenty-five or thirty lines a day, or one volume a year, while in reality "twenty-five or thirty volumes at least should be read to secure the complete acquisition of the art of reading." [1]

Marcel quotes Benjamin Franklin's wise counsel: "If a book be worth reading once, it should be read twice." Then he goes on to say: "if, at an advanced stage, it is not worth reading twice, it ought not be read at all ... Productions of sterling worth afford new pleasures, and unfold new beauties at each successive reading; whilst those of inferior character scarcely bear a second perusal; they exhibit more imperfections, according as they are more frequently or attentively read." [2]

Claude Marcel was a pioneer. He has greatly influenced the teaching of foreign languages, particularly in the United States, since about 1920.[3] His fundamental argument equals the motto: "Learn to read by reading," an altogether sound doctrine, recently revived by Michael West.[4]

FRANÇOIS GOUIN in his *L'art d'enseigner et d'étudier les langues* [5] tells of his various endeavors to learn German, and of his experience with his son who inspired him with an idea that was to become the basis of his elaborate system. One day he observed his little son, who, in a series of carefully arranged steps, imitated a miller in his daily work: (1) The miller fills his bags with corn (sand, of course); (2) he puts a bag on his shoulders; (3) he carries it to the mill; (4) he throws it down; (5) he puts it into the mill; (6) the mill begins to grind. Gouin conceived the idea of developing this logical sequence of simple events for school use. His class procedure was: (1) the teacher explains in the vernacular the general content of the reading selection; (2) he enacts the events, describing at the same time what he does; (3) the single acts are then divided, and again enacted; (4) all this is done first orally, then in

---

[1] Claude Marcel, *op. cit.*, p. 54.   [2] *Ibid.*, pp. 64 ff.

[3] Compare "The Bond Reading Method" in Buchanan and MacPhee, *op. cit.*, pp. 490–99.

[4] Compare Peter Hagboldt, "The Work of Michael West," *Modern Language Journal* (March, 1938), pp. 411–19.

[5] Paris, 1880 (third edition, 1897), translated by Howard Swan and Victor Bétis under the title *The Art of Teaching and Studying Languages* (London, 1892).

writing. Here is an example from Gouin's *Erstes Übungsbuch für das Deutsche:*

Der Hund sucht. Er sucht und sucht. Er wittert eine Kette Rebhühner. Er tut eine Kette Rebhühner auf. Er steht. Er geht auf den Befehl des Jägers vor. Die Rebhühner bemerken (sehen) den Hund. Sie fürchten sich vor dem Hunde. Sie fliegen auf. Sie fliegen davon. Der Jäger sieht die Kette Hühner davon= fliegen. Er ergreift sein Gewehr. Er legt an (führt das Gewehr zur Schulter). Er zielt und zielt. Er drückt ab. Der Schuß geht los. Die Ladung trifft ein Huhn. Das Huhn fällt zur Erde.[1]

Throughout the course the foreign language is presented in systematic order by simple sentences, following each other in logical sequence. Each selection consists of 18 to 30 sentences. Fifty selections constitute one series. Several series combine to one general series. The five general series are equal to 2500 selections or 50,000 sentences. This elaborate and ambitious system is fully described by R. Kron, who also gives the literature that arose about the *Seriensystem*[2] as well as many enthusiastic commendations from various foreign countries.[3]

Gouin was little known in France. He had his greatest success in Germany. The new element which he brought into language teaching was that the student is forced to be intensely active with his whole being while dramatizing the single sentences of a given selection, an advantage hard to overestimate. Gouin's most vulnerable points were that he opposed phonetics, reading, and written exercises. Nevertheless to him belongs the distinction of having presented for the first time in flawless order and clear logic a consistent speech course which, unfortunately, was destined to fail through the very weight of its lofty ambition; for it was both too extensive, encompassing approximately 8000 words, and too one-sided, ignoring all phases of language except speech.[4]

[1] R. Kron, *Die Methode Gouin oder das Seriensystem in Theorie und Praxis* (Marburg, 1895; zweite Auflage 1900), pp. 22 ff.

[2] *Ibid.*, pp. 176 ff.　　　　[3] *Ibid.*, pp. 115–70.

[4] For a detailed discussion see R. Kron, *op. cit.* For a short and concise account, consult Erwin Escher's *Essay on the Sources and the History of the Direct Method of Teaching Modern Languages until Its Establishment in France and Germany* (University of Chicago unpublished Master's thesis, 1919), pp. 58 ff. Compare also *Report of the Committee of Twelve* (D. C. Heath and Company, 1900), pp. 20 ff.

Meanwhile, about the middle of the nineteenth century a new science had been born, "the science of speech sounds and the art of pronunciation," as it was called by Henry Sweet. ALEXANDER JOHN ELLIS published his *Essentials of Phonetics* (1848), E. BRÜCKE his *Grundzüge der Physiologie und der Systematik der Sprachlaute* (1856), ALEXANDER BELL his *Visible Speech* (1867) and his *Sounds and their Relations* (1882). HENRY SWEET, SIEVERS, TRAUTMANN, HELMHOLZ, PASSY, RAMBEAU, KLINGHARDT, and others untiringly developed this new science [1] to such an extent that today it has become an indispensable help in any language course. Archibald Sayce applied the newly founded science to the problems of language teaching, and WILHELM VIËTOR, at the time a lecturer in German at the University of Liverpool, after his return to Germany, issued in 1882 a pamphlet entitled *Der Sprachunterricht muß umkehren, ein Beitrag zur Überbürdungsfrage, von Quousque Tandem.*[2]

Viëtor's pamphlet acted like a trumpet call to arms. High praise followed violent attack. A considerable literature arguing for and against Viëtor's principles was the result. The "reform," the "new," or the "phonetic method" was lauded and condemned in numberless articles and books, the crux of the controversy being a strictly oral procedure with ample use of *realia* in opposition to older methods, which professed to favor "intellectual and aesthetic interests." The debate ended in a compromise, and the "direct method" finally evolved out of the bitter struggle.[3]

Space does not allow us to discuss the interesting details of the quarrel. May it suffice to mention that Breymann and Steinmüller collected, summarized, and evaluated the large number of books and articles in *Die neusprachliche Reform-Literatur von 1876–1909: Eine bibliographisch-kritische Übersicht.*[4] A final sum-

---

[1] Bahlsen, *op. cit.*, pp. 35 ff.; Viëtor, *op. cit.*, pp. 34 ff.; Buchanan and MacPhee, *op. cit.*, p. 14.

[2] "How much longer?" the first words of Cicero's First Oration Against Catiline. Viëtor's pamphlet appeared later as the *Dritte durch Anmerkungen erweiterte Auflage* (Leipzig, 1905), 52 pp.

[3] Note the terms, "new," "reform," "phonetic," and "direct method"; the latter method has survived in name, and is still used in this country in a modified form.

[4] Leipzig: 1895–1909, Vols. 1–4. For a discussion of these, see Buchanan and MacPhee, *op. cit.*, pp. 73–79.

ming up of the controversy over the direct method appeared in 1909. It read:

"The Reform has fulfilled its mission. It has laid the ghosts of the grammatical method, which made a fetish of the study of grammar with excessive attention to translation from and into the foreign language. Reading formerly served chiefly as a handmaiden to grammar, and was too exclusively limited to historical-literary works. Speaking ability was kept in the background and correct pronunciation was neglected. Such an antiquated method of teaching is now once and for all impossible. But what the grammatical method neglected, practical and correct use of the spoken language, the reform method has pushed to extremes. In making mastery of the spoken language the chief objective, the nature and function of secondary schools was overlooked, because such an objective under normal conditions of mass instruction is only attainable in a modest degree. The reform method requires not only a teacher who possesses a perfect mastery of the foreign language, but makes such claims on his nervous and physical energy as to entail premature exhaustion. Average pupils, not to mention weaker ones, do not justify the demands made by the oral use of the language; they soon weary, are overburdened and revolt. Early adherents of the new method, after their enthusiasm has been dashed by stern realities, have gradually broken away." [1]

The most distinguished exponent of the direct method was MAX WALTER, for many years Director of the *Musterschule* at Frankfurt, who, through his extraordinary genius as a teacher and through his books, exerted a powerful and far-reaching influence.[2]

[1] Buchanan and MacPhee, *op. cit.*, pp. 19 f.

[2] Walter's books still repay close study. All were published by the Ewert'sche Buchhandlung in Marburg, Hessen:

> *Der Gebrauch der Fremdsprache bei der Lektüre in den Oberklassen*, 1914.
> *Aneignung und Verarbeitung des Wortschatzes im neusprachlichen Unterricht*, 1914.
> *Der französische Klassenunterricht auf der Unterstufe*, 1895.
> *Die Reform des neusprachlichen Unterrichts auf Schule und Universität*, 1912.
> *Zur Methodik des neusprachlichen Unterrichts* (vierte Auflage, bearbeitet von Paul Olbrich, 1931).

Compare also the "Walter" number of the *Monatshefte für deutsche Sprache und Pädagogik*, 1917; and Carl A. Krause, *The Direct Method in Modern Languages* (New York, 1916).

Bagster-Collins in his interesting monograph on *The History of Modern Language Teaching in the United States* tells us that scant reference was made to the direct method in journals and articles written before 1900, the year when the *Report of the Committee of Twelve*, of which we must speak presently, contained a brief summary of the "phonetic method," or the "direct method" in its earlier stages. The latter was an admirable combination of features or means taken from earlier methods, or, in Bagster-Collins' terms, "an eclectic method in which is utilized the method lore of centuries." [1] We may add that the German reformers greatly enriched our teaching devices by inventing many new ones quite unknown before them.

Between 1900 and 1916 there appeared a number of texts attempting to adapt the direct method to American conditions, the most notable being Professor Prokosch's *Introduction to German.*[2] During the World War, when passions ran amuck, instruction in German reached its lowest point, and no notable contributions were made until 1924, when a new era was to begin.

During the last decade of the nineteenth century there arose in this country a lively interest in the restudy and reshaping of secondary education, and in 1892 the National Education Association began a nation-wide survey in an attempt to revise the secondary-school curriculum. A number of committees were formed. Their task was to redefine the objectives and the content of the various subjects. One of the committees represented the Modern Language Association of America. It was appointed in 1898 and became known as *The Committee of Twelve*.

This committee was composed of experienced high-school and college instructors, many of them former teachers of the classics, who, according to tradition, did not differentiate between high-school and college teaching. Their findings were not based on research or experiments; they were, as the chairman, Calvin Thomas, stated in his Introduction to the report, the result of "practical counsel, embodying the best thought and experience of the day." Their final report was to be a tentative effort toward the creation of high national standards in language teaching, and

---

[1] Bagster-Collins, *op. cit.*, p. 90, in *Studies in Modern Language Teaching.* The Macmillan Company, 1930.   [2] Henry Holt and Company, 1911.

to have no more "value than that of a normative scheme" which might "serve provisionally the efforts of teachers and focus criticism." [1] Yet events were to run a different course. *The Report of the Committee of Twelve* "became a classic for the following generation of modern language teachers. In content and even in wording it was taken over into school syllabi and college announcements and the requirements of standardizing agencies . . . ; and it can still be read with interest and profit" [2] even today.

In the light of present trends in language teaching it is interesting to note that the Committee of Twelve stated that, in the general scheme of things then prevailing, it was quite possible to learn to read French and German easily, that the ability to speak should be regarded as of secondary importance, and that "it must be remembered that the process of learning to speak a foreign language has no educational value except as it is connected with, and grows out of, the improvement of the mind." [3] However, a vigorous protest was launched about thirty years later against the one-sided aim of reading at the expense of all other abilities. [4]

In the meantime certain changes in the conditions of our social life made necessary new inquiries and new changes in the curriculum. The time-honored contention that the secondary-school curriculum was a part of college instruction was challenged and undermined. The colleges were no longer to dictate to the secondary schools. In 1918, educators, forced by public opinion, began an ardent search for social objectives which were to justify the teaching of certain subjects in high school. As early as 1914 the National Education Association had appointed a committee to investigate the teaching of modern languages. The committee issued no official report, confining itself to a statement concerning *Methods of Teaching Modern Languages*. [5] In 1920 the National

[1] *Report of the Committee of Twelve* (D. C. Heath and Company, 1900), pp. iii ff.
[2] Robert Herndon Fife, *A Summary of Reports on the Modern Foreign Languages with an Index to the Reports, Issued by the Modern Foreign Language Study and the Canadian Committee on Modern Languages* (The Macmillan Company, 1931), p. 2.
[3] *Report of the Committee of Twelve*, p. 13.
[4] William R. Price, "Critique of the Teaching of Foreign Languages in the United States," *The German Quarterly*, II, 4 (Nov. 1929), pp. 117–21.
[5] Published by D. C. Heath and Company, 1915.

Education Association again appointed a committee who turned out a report on modern languages in the junior high school.[1]

The Classical Investigation [2] inquiring into the teaching of Latin struck a new note in policy. It sought to determine the validity of objectives and, with the help of educational psychologists, it produced a mass of valuable experimental data.

On December 31, 1923, Dr. F. P. Keppel, President of the Carnegie Corporation, invited a group of prominent language teachers to discuss with him the possibility of undertaking an investigation similar to that of the classical languages. This gathering marked the eventful beginning of the *Modern Foreign Language Study*,[3] the most significant inquiry in scope and nature ever undertaken.

The organization of the *Study* included a Committee on Direction and Control, three special investigators — one for each, French, Spanish, and German — and one educational psychologist. Eight geographical areas of the United States were the basis of a regional organization. The Committee on Direction and Control met four times, the last and final meeting being held in 1927 in Toronto, partly as a joint meeting with the Canadian Committee, which had been organized in 1924. At this meeting some reports were discussed and approved for publication.[4]

The findings of the *Study* are and will be for a long time to come of basic importance. They were recorded in seventeen volumes as the *Publications of the American and Canadian Committees on Modern Languages*. The contents of these volumes are analyzed and briefed with admirable clearness and precision by the chairman of the survey, Robert Herndon Fife. Professor Fife's book, which we have mentioned before, is indispensable for anyone anxious to gain a preliminary knowledge of the problems involved in the *Study*. In the space of 203 pages it gives us a concise analysis and résumé of the seventeen volumes, each of which presents a significant contribution of its own.

[1] Fife, *op. cit.*, p. 2.
[2] Princeton University Press, Part I, 1924; Part III, 1925. Part II has never been published.
[3] Hereafter referred to as the *Study* or the *Survey*.
[4] For a more detailed account of the organization of the *Study* (or *Survey*), see Robert Herndon Fife, *op. cit.*, pp. 4–16.

It is now our duty to give the reader at least a bowing acquaintance with each of the titles and possibly a glimpse into the contents of each of these seventeen volumes. Knowing, however, that no one could summarize the high points of these volumes better than Professor Fife himself, we shall follow the illustrious example of Mark Twain, who once remarked that he was in the habit of stealing only from the best authorities. In the following we shall quote from Fife's *A Brief Summary of the Publications* as given in Coleman's *Analytical Bibliography of Modern Language Teaching, 1927–1932.*[1] It is necessary to confine ourselves to those summaries which are of immediate interest for future teachers of German.[2]

Vol. I. Wood, Ben D. *New York Experiments with Modern Language Tests.* New York: Macmillan, 1927. xxii + 339 pp.

The work gives: (1) results of administration of new-type tests (A. C. Beta) in junior high schools of New York City in 1925 and 1926 to 20,000 students of French and about 5000 students of Spanish, with analyses showing dependability of tests used, overlapping of classes, general heterogeneity of groups, and lack of progress from year to year; (2) results of administration of old-type and new-type tests at Regents' examination to 31,000 students of French, German, and Spanish from New York State schools, showing superiority of new-type over old-type form in reliability, and demonstrating wide variations in school standards, overlapping of classes throughout schools, and general misclassification. Strong presentation of case for objective, standardized tests, supported by 52 tables and 52 charts.

Vol. II. Buswell, G. T. *A Laboratory Study of the Reading of Modern Foreign Languages.* New York: Macmillan, 1927. xii + 100 pp.

Report of an investigation by means of photographic apparatus at University of Chicago Laboratory of Educational Psychology of eye movements and eye fixations. Six groups of students contributed data showing behavior in learning to read foreign languages. Work

[1] Compiled for the Committee on Modern Language Teaching with the assistance of Agnes Jacques (The University of Chicago Press, 1933), pp. 1–10.

[2] For omitted résumés consult the Analytical Bibliography mentioned above.

shows: (1) behavior as registered by eye movements at different stages of progress in silent reading; (2) superiority of direct methods of instruction in promoting reading habits; (3) small deviations in behavior in learning to read French, German, and Spanish. Book includes 43 plates, showing text material as measured by eye movements, with 21 tables and 15 charts projecting results.

Vol. III.   Buchanan, M. A.   *A Graded Spanish Word Book*.   Toronto: The University of Toronto Press, 1927 (3d ed. 1932).   195 pp.

Vol. IV.   Wheeler, C. A., and Others.   *Enrollment in the Modern Foreign Languages in Secondary Schools and Colleges of the United States.   Compiled with the Co-operation of the Bureau* (now "Office") *of Education*.   With Introduction and Analysis by Robert Herndon Fife.   New York: Macmillan, 1928.   xxi + 453 pp.

Vol. V.   Henmon, V. A. C.   *Achievement Tests in the Modern Foreign Languages*.   New York: Macmillan, 1929.   xxvi + 363 pp.

A description of the American Council tests, Alpha and Beta, in French, German, and Spanish, with other tests sponsored by the Committees and an account of the results of the administration, mainly in 1926–27, in the United States, Canada, and England. Report explains and justifies techniques selected for testing vocabulary, grammar, reading, and free composition; analyzes the tests for reliability and validity; and discusses results of their administration, with deductions showing overlapping of classes, variations in school standards, and relationship of school and college achievement. Results are compared for the three countries. Included also are reports on achievement tests in French in the Quebec schools (compiled by H. E. Ford). Finally, conclusions are drawn concerning factors governing modern language achievement. Appendixes give a bibliography of modern language tests and a list of schools which administered the A. C. series. Statistical analysis is supported by 120 tables and 94 graphs.

Vol. VI.   (Canadian Committee)   *Modern Language Instruction in Canada*.   I. Toronto: The University of Toronto Press, 1928. xlviii + 547 pp.

Vol. VII.   (Canadian Committee)   *Modern Language Administration in Canada*.   II.   Toronto: The University of Toronto Press, 1928. 852 pp.

Vol. VIII. Buchanan, M. A., and MacPhee, E. D. *An Annotated Bibliography of Modern Language Methodology*. Toronto: The University of Toronto Press, 1928 (reprinted from Vol. VI above). 428 pp.

A bibliography for teachers and research students, with a critical analysis of works cited. The Introduction surveys extensively theories in regard to language teaching since the Renaissance, with a special examination of recent contributions by psychologists. It then discusses present problems, especially those relating to the influence of method on acquisition of various abilities, as well as questions of transfer and effect of practice. Four-fifths of the work is devoted to lists and analyses of books and articles appearing in Europe and America from 1880 to 1927, grouped as works of reference, histories, works on objectives and method, on language and the learning processes, and on tests and measurements, with a glimpse at recent development abroad. Within these categories works are cited in chronological order of appearance.

Vol. IX. Morgan, B. Q. *A German Frequency Word Book, Based on Kaeding's Häufigkeitswörterbuch der deutschen Sprache*. New York: Macmillan, 1928. xiii + 87 pp.

Work comprises: (1) a basic list of 2402 German words occurring 200 times or more in Kaeding's count, arranged in 85 groups, each with a designated frequency-range from the commonest to the least common; (2) an alphabetical list of 6000 words, including the basic list above and cognate or derived words related to these basic words in history or content. Here the basic word is italicized in its group and followed by its serial number in the basic list. The Preface describes Kaeding's count and the manner in which the present list has been made from it, with indications of the uses of the list for German teaching.

Vol. X. Hauch, Edward F. *A German Idiom List, Selected on the Basis of Frequency and Range of Occurrence*. New York: Macmillan, 1929. xi + 98 pp.

Results of a count of idioms occurring in 57 text units (totaling more than 1,000,000 running words), comprising prose fiction, nonfiction, and drama, from the eighteenth to the twentieth century. List of collaborators includes 46 school and college teachers. The Preface outlines the system of assembly of idioms and arrangement of results, and lists the texts used in count. There follow: (1) a sequential list of 959 idioms, arranged after their key words in a descending order of frequency of occurrence, with serial number, total number of occurrences (frequency), and total number of texts in which found (range); (2) an alphabetical list of key words, followed by the idioms which each indexes, with a translation of the idioms into English, and frequency, range, and serial numbers.

Vol. XI. Keniston, Hayward. *A Spanish Idiom List, Selected on Basis of Range and Frequency of Occurrence.* New York: Macmillan, 1929. xiii + 108 pp.

Vol. XII. Coleman, Algernon. *The Teaching of Modern Foreign Languages in the United States.* New York: Macmillan, 1929. xx + 299 pp.

The Introduction reviews the sources studied, including results contained in previous volumes of series as basis for findings. The discussion then covers four general topics: (1) Objectives of modern language instruction, with their experimental and social bases. Evidence of validity and degree of attainment is examined, and showings on the test administrations are analyzed, all leading to a revised list of objectives and concluding recommendations. (2) Content of the modern language course. This is surveyed by an examination of the attitude of teachers and by an analysis of present vocabulary and reading material. A discussion of practice in reading as training for reading follows, based on a study of length of present courses, and on experimental evidence concerning rapid methods of learning to read, with suggestions for revision of program respecting grammar and study of foreign civilization. Final conclusions cover curriculum content and organization. (3) Organization of classes, investigated on the basis of teacher opinion and experimental evidences of misclassification derived from test administrations. Suggestions are made for desirable changes in testing practice, with special reference to new-type forms and their construction; and final conclusions are drawn respecting reorganization of classes, based on length of the course, through help of adequate testing. (4) Considerations regarding method. A review of current tendencies, as indicated by teacher opinion and classroom procedure. An examination of method, as measured by achievement in certain selected schools, and of hypotheses regarding oral work, and a final section containing general considerations as to method. The work is illustrated by

34 tables and 44 graphs, and is supplemented by appendixes containing lists of problems for investigation and of projects undertaken under the sponsorship of the Committees, and by an index.

Vol. XIII. Purin, C. M. *The Training of Teachers of the Modern Foreign Languages.* New York: Macmillan, 1929. xiv + 112 pp. (See Chapter X.)

Vol. XIV. Henmon, V. A. C., and Others. *Prognosis Tests in Modern Foreign Languages.* New York: Macmillan, 1929. xviii + 182 pp. (See Chapter XI.)

Vol. XV. Cheydleur, Frederic D. *French Idiom List, Based on a Running Count of 1,183,000 Words.* New York: Macmillan, 1929. ix + 154 pp.

Vol. XVI. Vander Beke, George E. *French Word Book.* New York: Macmillan, 1929. xiii + 188 pp.

Vol. XVII. *Studies in Modern Language Teaching.* New York: Macmillan, 1930. xxxi + 491 pp.

Researches and experiments relating to teaching of modern languages by 15 scholars at various institutions. E. W. Bagster-Collins (work also published separately [Macmillan, 1931]) traces the history of modern language teaching in United States from colonial days to the present, including various types of schools and the colleges, with surveys of the development of modern language scholarship, training of teachers, and development of methods and of the new-type examination. O. H. Werner describes a testing experiment with Nebraska high school and college pupils to determine influence of modern language study on development of abilities in English. Clifford Woody reports on administration of the Hootkins English Vocabulary Test in Michigan schools to determine influence on English vocabulary of study of French and Latin in comparison with no foreign language study. Frederick S. Breed demonstrates superior reliability of Trabue French Composition Scale in scoring as compared with percentage method, and H. E. Ford examines reliability of this scale for longer (10-minute) compositions. B. Q. Morgan and Lydia M. Oberdeck show differences in acquisition of active and passive vocabulary by students of German at Wisconsin University. Gertrude M. Gilman measures cultural material in French curriculum of Illinois high schools by a scale devised for evaluation of this material, while Harry and Grace Kurz apply same scale to measure the informational and interpretative aspects of 10 French college readers, and Margaret and John Van Horne apply it to Spanish reading material (20 texts) at junior college level. James B. Tharp reports on experiments at University of Illinois in sectioning first-year French and Spanish students with use of Iowa aptitude tests and students in later semesters with use of achievement tests and previous grades, in comparison with sectioning without these selective criteria. George A. Rice studies achievement in French and Spanish in 30 California high schools to determine results of class procedure and of size of school and to find methodological and other factors that promote success in foreign language study. August Dvorak investigates present practices in 28 American universities with reference to foreign language requirements of Master's and Doctor's candidates and experience of individuals holding degrees with their foreign language equipment. Interpretations in the volume are assisted by 188 tables and 13 graphs.

Besides these seventeen volumes, we have already mentioned two others: Robert Herndon Fife's *Summary of the Reports* and Algernon Coleman's *Analytical Bibliography*.[1]

And now let us briefly review our all too short survey of the field of language instruction in the course of the centuries. We noted the ardent struggle for an adequate pedagogy of Latin during the Middle Ages and the doleful fact that progressive endeavors were thwarted by lethargy, reaction, or lack of insight. We heard the warnings of men like Melanchthon, Luther, and Ratichius, and we took cognizance of the essence of the natural method as exemplified by Michel de Montaigne. We paid our respects to Comenius and his thoroughly commendable ideas which were so completely forgotten that, as some writers inform us, no important progress was made for a century and a half after his death. We read John Locke's wise and sturdy counsel, and we were reminded of Montaigne and Comenius. Then, during the eighteenth century and throughout the nineteenth we witnessed the development of the grammar-translation method or methods, partly counteracted by Hamilton, Jacotot, Heness, Marcel, and Gouin. Briefly we mentioned important and basic contributions of English, French, and German scholars, to whose efforts we owe the science of phonetics.

[1] See p. 17, note 2 and p. 19, note 1.

Passing on to Viëtor and Walter we spoke of the "new," "reform," "phonetic," or "direct" method, giving, moreover, a summary of the final outcome of the reformers' struggle against a system of teaching languages which had remained stagnant for more than a hundred years. And yet, we must hasten to say that even the representatives of the grammar-translation method contributed their share to our present means and devices. Even now translation from and into the foreign language is considered by many, if not most, teachers a splendid means of checking, controlling, and overcoming certain difficulties.[1] Finally we came to the *Report of the Committee of Twelve* and the *Modern Foreign Language Study* with its seventeen volumes as summarized by Robert Herndon Fife.

Goethe once said: „Es ist gut, in den neuesten Büchern alte Gedanken zu sagen, weil man die alten Werke, worin sie stehen, nicht liest; von manchen Wahrheiten müssen, wie von fremden Musterwerken, in jedem Jahrfünfzig neue Übersetzungen gegeben werden." It was in this spirit that we offered a short survey of some important thoughts on language teaching, touching in the main on those contributors who have been instrumental in bringing about the various types of methods which are: the "grammar-translation," the "natural," the "psychological," the "direct," and finally, the "reading" method.[2]

We shall now turn to Volume Twelve of the *Survey* and to Coleman's summarizing conclusions, which are of particular importance at this point.

BIBLIOGRAPHY

BAGSTER-COLLINS, E. W. *The Teaching of Modern Languages in the United States*. Reprinted from *Studies in Modern Language Teaching*, Vol. XVII of the Publications of the American and Canadian Committees on Modern Languages. New York: The Macmillan Company, 1930.

[1] In spite of Viëtor's pronouncement: „Das Übersetzen in fremde Sprachen ist eine Kunst, welche die Schule nichts angeht." Compare B. Q. Morgan. "In Defense of Translation." *Modern Language Journal*, I, 7 (April, 1917), pp. 235–41.

[2] The methods are discussed in this sequence in the *Report of the Committee of Twelve*. The ambitious student of language methodology will want to supplement this sketch by supplementary reading; see Bibliography following.

BAHLSEN, LEOPOLD. *The Teaching of Modern Languages.* Boston: Ginn and Company, 1905, pp. 1–18.

BUCHANAN, M. A. and MacPHEE, E. D. *Modern Language Instruction in Canada*, Vol. I. (Toronto: The University of Toronto Press, 1928), pp. 1–25.

ESCHER, ERWIN. *The Direct Method of Studying Foreign Languages, A Contribution to the History of Its Sources and Development.* Part I: *Antecedents of the Direct Method to the End of the Eighteenth Century.* Unpublished Doctor's thesis. University of Chicago, 1928, xiii + 336 pp. Part II: *Essay on the Sources and the History of the Direct Method of Teaching Modern Languages, until Its Establishment in France and Germany.* Unpublished Master's thesis. University of Chicago, 1919, iv + 127 pp.

MÜNCH, WILHELM. *Didaktik und Methodik des französischen Unterrichts.* München, 1910, pp. 11–22, *Der tatsächliche Kampf um die Methode*, an attempt to mediate between extremists.

SCHWEITZER ET SIMONNOT. *Methodologie des langues vivantes.* Paris, 1917. Pages 1–44 are an *Esquisse du mouvement réformiste de l'enseignement des langues vivantes à l'étranger et en France;* perhaps somewhat unfair and, in places, irritated, since written during the World War.

VIËTOR, WILHELM. *Die Methodik des neusprachlichen Unterrichts.* Leipzig, 1902. *Die moderne Reform* is described on pp. 29–56.

For further articles on this topic, consult T. E. Oliver, *The Modern Language Teacher's Handbook* (Boston: D. C. Heath and Company, 1935), pp. 243 ff.

SUGGESTIONS FOR DISCUSSIONS AND REPORTS

1. Discuss the importance for the history of language teaching of each of the following personalities: Donatus, di Marinis, Montaigne, Comenius, Locke, Hamilton, Plötz, Heness, Marcel, Gouin, Viëtor, Walter.
2. Place each of the persons named above in the century in which they lived.
3. Consult Monroe's *Cyclopedia of Education* and report on Melanchthon, Luther, and Ratichius in relation to language teaching.
4. Name some of the founders of the science of phonetics and give their principal works.
5. Compare the natural method as described by Montaigne with the natural method as you know it from experience or descriptions.

6. Prepare a brief report on Bagster-Collins' book, mentioning only the most important points.
7. Read Marcel's book carefully and report on his theory of learning to read a foreign language.
8. Read carefully Fife's summary (pp. 19–24) and name the titles and volumes which bear particularly on the teaching of German.
9. Prepare a sketch on the history of language teaching, using the sources mentioned in this chapter.
10. Which volumes of the *Study* will you read as soon as possible in order to supplement your studies in this course?

CHAPTER TWO

COLEMAN'S SUMMARIZING CONCLUSIONS

IN VOLUME XII of the Publications of the American and Canadian Committees on Modern Languages Professor Coleman reviews and analyzes the material which the Committee had gathered. His work is a synthesis of all the findings of the Committee in regard to the problems of teaching languages. We shall state Coleman's summarizing conclusions, and attempt to add some brief comments which seem advisable at this point.[1]

1. "While the vocational need for a knowledge of modern languages is limited, the proportion of former students of these subjects who consider that their language study time in secondary school and in college was well spent, and who record that their language knowledge has been useful to them in after life, is sufficiently large to give encouragement to the advocates of modern language teaching in public secondary schools and in colleges. At the same time, however, the testimony of a number of these persons and of various professional groups in regard to the usableness of their knowledge of the languages they have studied makes it evident that modern language courses should yield a higher degree of ability to use the languages than is now generally the case." (Coleman, p. 109)

This point is largely based on *The Reading of Modern Foreign Languages*, by M. V. O'Shea,[2] whose rather pessimistic report has

---

[1] Coleman's 21 conclusions are stated in Vol. 12 of the *Study: The Teaching of Modern Foreign Languages in the United States* (The Macmillan Company, 1929), pp. 109 ff., 169 ff., 232 ff., and 276 ff. They are here reprinted by the special permission of the Macmillan Company. The 21 conclusions are numbered, and the page in Coleman's book is indicated at the end of each quotation.

[2] Published by the United States Government Printing Office, Bulletin No. 16, 1927.

caused the profession as a whole to search for more effective ways of teaching to read a foreign language. As for a higher degree of ability, we must try in the immediate future to determine, by carefully devised and controlled experiments, just how much more can be accomplished by a certain type of student under certain well-defined conditions within a given time.

2. "The existing variableness in the scholastic point and age at which a modern language is begun in junior high school, in almost any year of regular and senior high schools and in college, and the almost total lack of experimental data in regard to the attainment under these varying conditions, makes it practically impossible to formulate definite recommendations regarding the optimum point of the beginning and the minimum length of a useful course. Figures given elsewhere, however, make it clear that two years is at present the maximum period of study for a very large majority of secondary students in the United States, and that in schools enrolling about 20 per cent of modern language students instruction is limited to two years. Consequently, whatever results of modern language study are valuable for general educative purposes and for specific usefulness in after life, must, under present conditions, be attained by most students within this period of time." [1] (Coleman, pp. 109 f.)

There are no comparative studies concerning the optimum point of beginning language courses. According to the writer's experience the optimum point of beginning for American conditions lies, strangely enough, beyond high-school age. Experiments with adults at Columbia University in learning Esperanto seem to support this view. In *A Survey of Tendencies in Modern Language*

---

[1] The figure above, 20 per cent, is evidently an error. Compare in the same volume (p. 26) where Coleman states: "It is also clear that for about 83 per cent of those who begin modern language in the public and private secondary schools for which we have data, two years is the maximum period for study of the subject . . ."

Compare also Carlton A. Wheeler, *Enrollment in the Foreign Languages in the Secondary Schools and Colleges of the United States* (The Macmillan Company, 1928), pp. 352 ff., and Robert Herndon Fife in Coleman's *Experiments and Studies in Modern Language Teaching* (The University of Chicago Press, 1934), p. 4, who states that "the two-year maximum course for 80 per cent of the secondary-school pupils seems, at least for the present, a fixity."

Teaching, 1927–33: Retrospect and Prospect,[1] Fife states that very small differences were shown in ability between the ages of twenty-two and forty, and much more rapid progress in the subject by an adult group in comparison with students under eighteen.

These results with Esperanto have been confirmed with French students at the vocational school of the University of Wisconsin at Madison,[2] where adults were shown to have a higher rate of learning in vocabulary and reading with comprehension than younger groups. These findings are quite revolutionary in their implications. While the experiments dealt with special conditions and a limited number of cases, their results point at least to the probability that an early beginning with language study is, as regards certain linguistic abilities, without justification psychologically.

In regard to the two-year maximum of study which appears to be the maximum for not less than 83 per cent of high-school pupils, Fife says:

The results of the modern-language survey have impressed the need of grappling with the two-year course and the danger of a dissipation of energies in the effort to train the pupil in several abilities within the prescribed time. The tendency is to admit that the reading objective stands first, and the argument that it is the only generally attainable objective in a two-year course has plainly made an impression. That this situation must be accepted and made the basis of a program is not admitted, however, by all teachers, for there are some who hold that it would be better to concentrate on eliminating weaklings and extending the course for the selected group.[3] The elevation of a single objective to a paramount position has plainly caused misgivings to a great many, and one result of this has been to stimulate an effort to show that achievement can also be attained in a limited period of study in aural and oral fields; . . .[4]

[1] Robert Herndon Fife in Coleman's *Experiments and Studies in Modern Language Reading*, compiled for the Committee on Modern Language Teaching (The University of Chicago Press, 1934), p. 8.

[2] F. D. Cheydleur, "An Experiment in Adult Learning of French at Madison, Wisconsin, Vocation School," *Journal of Educational Research*, XXVI (1933), pp. 259–75.

[3] W. R. Price in the *French Review*, III (1929), pp. 17 ff.; also in *Modern Language Journal*, XVIII (1933), pp. 78 ff., 153 ff. Suggestions looking toward a synthesis of divergent ideas are given in L. J. A. Mercier, "Diverging Trends in Modern Foreign Language Teaching and Their Possible Reconciliation," *French Review*, VI, No. 5 (April, 1933), pp. 368–86. [4] Coleman, *Experiments, op. cit.*, p. 13.

3. "It is generally accepted as a fact that the desirable results of foreign language study are cumulative in character and, other things being equal, bear a close relationship in quality to continuance in the subject through a period of time. It is highly to be desired, therefore, (1) that the question of continuance in the subject be studied in schools and in school systems from various points of view; and (2) that more serious efforts be made to evaluate achievement under ordinary and under experimental conditions, particularly with regard to what usable and durable language abilities are developed and can be developed in a given period. This is all the more necessary (1) because only a minority of the selected teachers consulted were of the opinion that a two-year course is long enough to enable as many as 50 per cent of their pupils to develop the ability to read and to write the language — and a still smaller minority in the case of ability to speak; and (2) because the scores made on the American Council Tests in French, German, and Spanish indicate that at least 50 per cent of the two-year group and at least 30 per cent of the three-year group cannot use the foreign language for reading and for writing with even a moderate degree of ease." (Coleman, p. 110)

That the results of language study are cumulative in nature is a well-known fact. One-year high-school courses, for this reason, are practically worthless and should not be tolerated. In regard to continuance in the subject, Fife tells us that:

> four-fifths of French pupils in this country may study that language for three years if they desire, ... that there is no prevailing year of beginning for the modern languages, ... that nearly four-fifths of all French pupils and more than four-fifths of those in German and Spanish are found in the first two years of study. The crucial problem of this discontinuance is thus laid bare in all its starkness: a beginners' class in French of 100 will normally fall away to forty-three at the opening of the second year, to twenty in the third year, and less than three will continue the subject into the fourth year.[1]

The inevitable conclusion appears to be either that students are not sufficiently interested in language study in general, or that

---

[1] Robert Herndon Fife, "A Summary of Reports on the Modern Foreign Language Study with an Index to the Reports" (The Macmillan Company, 1931), p. 23.

they were advised not to continue, or possibly were prevented from doing so by other curriculum requirements, or that teachers are unable to create interest and love for the subject under prevailing conditions.

One of the invaluable results of the Modern Foreign Language Study is that we have become more critical concerning the character and the effect of our courses. In this spirit H. E. Ford and R. K. Hicks have made a study of the results of teaching French in England, Canada, and the United States. Their results involve 6000 pupils for England, 4000 for Canada, and 2500 for the United States. In summarizing this experiment Professor Coleman states:

> The authors explain the superiority of students in the United States by the more mature age at which they begin . . . This superiority is especially striking in regard to reading, where the American student in the middle of the second year has the capacity of a fourth-year English or Canadian student. English schools surpass only in free composition. The authors believe that this superiority is due to the greater emphasis on oral work, and indicate the need for oral tests to measure the effect of oral training. They also call attention to the fact that the Canadian schools tend to greater uniformity of quality than the English and United States schools.[1]

The experiment by Ford and Hicks does not indicate, to be sure, "what usable and durable language abilities are developed in a given period," but the experiment does have distinct merits. It points out, on the basis of a large number of cases, the positive value of experimentation by showing the relative teaching results under widely varying conditions; and, by implication, it suggests that we might try to determine experimentally what "usable and durable language abilities" could really be achieved if we were to concentrate our energies on one single aim, that of reading.

The second half of point 3, which deals with teachers' opinions regarding attainable ends, and the scores of the American Council Tests will be discussed in subsequent chapters.

4. "Teachers in general appear to have less confidence that their

[1] "French Tests in English and American Schools," *Modern Languages*, X, 6 (June, 1929), pp. 181–85, as summarized by Algernon Coleman in *An Analytical Bibliography of Modern Language Teaching, 1927–1932* (The University of Chicago Press, 1933), pp. 214 ff.

pupils realize the instrumental aims (reading, writing, speaking, understanding the spoken word) than that they attain other and less direct objectives, such as improvement in English, the development of literary and artistic appreciation, of habits of sustained effort and the like. There is evidence that the attainment of some of this group of objectives is favored in a superior degree by modern language study; in other cases either no evidence is available or what we have is difficult to interpret with confidence. While a similar uncertainty in regard to the attainment of many ultimate objectives prevails in all fields, it is the part of wisdom in modern languages to narrow the list of objectives to those items that may be directly connected with definite classroom activities, and to assume that few or no desirable results can usually be attained unless, deliberately or unwittingly, the teacher and the class engage in activities that contribute to their achievement.

"It is, furthermore, not unlikely that the prevalent complaint of teachers that they have an overlarge proportion of students who lack 'linguistic ability' is to be explained in part by their failure to limit their aims to the kind of abilities that can be generally developed and to the kind of knowledge that can be mastered in the time allotted to modern languages in the programs of most secondary school students." (Coleman, p. 110)

Some serious-minded scholars hold that the less direct objectives are the only ones which may be achieved in two-year high-school courses. Yet Coleman's recommendation, in my opinion, is fundamentally sound. We have been guilty of striving toward unattainable aims. We have wanted everything and have accomplished far too little. In brief courses our salvation lies in being much less ambitious concerning speaking and writing, and in being much more effective in concentrating our efforts on the passive phases of our subject, namely aural comprehension and reading. In language study, learning is specific. We do not learn to read by a useless over-emphasis on other phases of our work. In a brief course we learn to read by reading and by making all other activities strictly subservient to that one and only aim.[1]

---

[1] Cf. *Language Learning* (The University of Chicago Press, 1935); the chapter on Reading (pp. 113–35) presents a brief outline of the main problems involved.

We shall come back to "lack of linguistic ability" in our chapter on Testing (cf. Chapter XI).

5. "The choice of the basic vocabulary, of the idiomatic expressions and of the grammatical topics for study and drill in the elementary stages of the modern language course has hitherto been made largely on the basis of tradition, of chance or of individual judgment, and great diversity prevails, particularly with respect to the stock of words and idioms emphasized at this level. Wise use of word and of idiom counts will enable teachers to introduce their students from the outset to the stock of words and phrases that they will most need for reading. We may hope with considerable confidence that ways will be found to render possible the more difficult task of providing similar apparatus in the field of syntax." (Coleman, p. 169)

The scientific determination of the frequency of words, idioms, and usage of syntax is one of the most significant and far-reaching achievements of the *Study*. Formerly we were in the habit of facing the total sum of words, idioms, and syntax usages without regarding their frequency or their difficulty. We did not know which were frequent and, therefore, important, and which ones were rare and, therefore, comparatively insignificant. Our position is now much more favorable. If we avail ourselves of what has been accomplished, we can teach languages with much greater probability of success. In choosing a beginners' text, grammar, or reader, we should expect that the author give us a strict accounting: (1) of the number of words or word stems; (2) of the number of idioms; and (3) of the number of occurrences of each word and idiom.

The *German Frequency Word Book* by B. Q. Morgan,[1] and the *German Idiom List* compiled by Edward F. Hauch [2] are of basic importance for all authors and editors of texts. The same is true of the *Minimum Standard German Vocabulary* prepared in dictionary form by Walter Wadepuhl and B. Q. Morgan.[3] The German syntax count is in preparation.[4]

[1] Publications of the American and Canadian Committees on Modern Languages, Volume IX. The Macmillan Company, 1929.

[2] Publications of the American and Canadian Committees on Modern Languages, Volume X. The Macmillan Company, 1929.

[3] F. S. Crofts & Co., 1936.   [4] Only the *Spanish Syntax List, A Statistical*

6. "Investigations of the 'realia,' or 'cultural' elements, in the modern language course reveal, as might have been expected, that the amount of explicit material of this kind in the texts commonly read is small and unevenly distributed. It is, therefore, all the more necessary for teachers to keep in view the aim of acquainting their students with various aspects of the foreign civilization and to make definite provision therefor in order to supplement the material in the books chosen. In this connection, the teacher's responsibility for an adequate knowledge of the geography, the history, the literature, the customs of the foreign country, through study and reading and through personal contacts, is even more exacting than has commonly been assumed." (Coleman, pp. 169 f.)

The question of *realia* is, as far as 83 per cent of our students are concerned, in the same state of uncertainty and bewilderment as was the question of words and idioms before the *Study* began.

The demand for *Kulturkunde* came to us by way of the direct method. Its representatives required that the student be given an intimate acquaintance with the foreign civilization and, through a comparison of this civilization with the native culture, be enabled to enrich and deepen his own cultural experiences. This high aim is easy to understand if we consider the conditions under which German reformers worked: small classes, selected students, highly trained teachers, the guarded atmosphere of the *Gymnasium* or *Realschule*, and courses lasting from four to seven or eight years. Our classes are crowded, our students not selected, our teachers often poorly trained or incompetent, and our courses last two years for more than four-fifths of our students.

The problem mentioned may be reduced to three questions:

1. Should we, in brief courses, expect our pupils to learn to read a foreign language and, besides, study significant facts concerning the foreign civilization?

2. If so, should we impart such knowledge through English or German?

3. Precisely how much of the vast amount of such cultural in-

Study of Grammatical Usage in Contemporary Spanish Prose on the Basis of Range and Frequency by Hayward Keniston has been published (Henry Holt and Company, 1937). The French list, begun under the supervision of the late Algernon Coleman, will be continued by Hayward Keniston. The German syntax list is being prepared under the supervision of E. W. Bagster-Collins.

formation can reasonably be expected of our pupils at the end of the second high-school year?

There is more to be considered. Cultural material offered in the foreign language requires the knowledge of about 2000 word stems. This means, if we count what must be counted, namely derivations, compounds, and idioms, a passive knowledge of approximately 6000 words and more than 300 idioms.[1] Are we prepared to teach nearly that much to high-school students in two years or even to college students in one? Definitely no!

The demand for *realia* and cultural material, moreover, is an unconscious contradiction in itself. On the one hand we try to teach, if possible, only the first 1000 most frequent words; on the other hand we find that these most frequent 1000 words are, at least to some extent, not the ones required in a discussion of cultural material. In other words, we are trying to reconcile two aims which are mutually exclusive. The extent of this mutual exclusion cannot be established until we decide just which topics we ought to discuss in our beginners' texts, and which ones ought to be excluded as too difficult. Too difficult may mean too mature in thought content, or requiring too many words and idioms outside of the limits of a definite vocabulary agreed upon.

We propose that this problem be submitted to a Committee duly appointed by the American Association of Teachers of German. The Committee should then report its findings and recommendations in one of our language journals, so that we might, in the end, arrive at some compromise acceptable to all concerned. The Committee's accepted report would conceivably: (1) reject the requirement that cultural material be presented in the foreign language; (2) name the topics and outline the extent of information expected of a student at the end of two years in high school or one year in college; (3) recommend certain topics which, according to actual experience, can be presented in the foreign language without seriously exceeding the vocabulary limit set for these brief courses (but see Chapter IX).

---

[1] These figures are based on my experience with the series of *Graded German Readers*. (The Heath-Chicago Series. D. C. Heath and Company, 1933–1938) The first thirteen readers use 1815 words and 301 idioms. Words are counted according to their stems (see *Allerlei*, p. vi).

It is of interest to note that at the University of Chicago no attempt is made to offer cultural material written in the foreign language during the first and most of the second quarter. At the end of the second quarter and during the third our students read the last four *Graded German Readers*, which contain an abundance of *realia* and cultural material.[1] In addition our students are encouraged to read as many books on Germany as they have time to read. Such books, all written in English, are available in a special collection.

The trend away from unattainable aims seems clearly indicated through an excellent book which gives an abundance of cultural material in English.[2]

7. "Experience and statistical evidence in teaching the vernacular indicate that the amount of reading that pupils do is directly related to achievement both in rate of silent reading and in comprehension. Furthermore, experiments show conclusively that increasing the amount of reading that is required results in rapid progress in rate and in comprehension. Experimental data in the modern language field warrant the hypothesis that there is a close correspondence between limited reading experience and the poor attainment in reading by large numbers of second- and third-year students as attainment is evaluated by the American Council Reading Tests and by teacher opinion. It is fair to assume that if, as the result of a shift of emphasis, the amount of reading were considerably increased in modern language classes, there would result more rapid growth in rate and in comprehension, as has been demonstrated in the case of classes in the vernacular.

"Since reading ability is the one objective on which all agree, classroom efforts during the first two years should center primarily on developing the ability to understand the foreign language readily through the eye and through the ear. The goal must be to read the foreign language directly with a degree of understanding comparable to that possessed in reading the vernacular.

---

[1] The titles of books 10–13 are: 10. *Ein Sommer in Deutschland*, 11. *Land und Leute*, 12. *Aus deutscher Vergangenheit*, 13. *Von deutscher Sprache und Dichtung*. (The Heath-Chicago Series. D. C. Heath and Company, 1934–1938)

[2] Charles H. Handschin, *Introduction to German Civilization*. Prentice-Hall, Inc., 1937.

In order that students may attain this goal, reading experience must be adequate and the results of all other types of class exercise must converge toward the same end.

"In order that more abundant and more attractive reading material may be provided, modern language departments and committees on modern language courses should draw up considerable lists of reading texts in the foreign languages that are attractive to the varying tastes and interests of adolescents and of older students — fiction, drama, books of travel, history, science, biography and the like — and should make the texts available in school collections for free reading and for reading on assigned topics. Local, state, and regional modern language associations can contribute very definitely to the realization of such a plan." (Coleman, p. 170)

The Coleman Report, as Volume XII of the *Survey* is usually called, was published in 1929. Long before its appearance we had, at the University of Chicago, made a special inquiry into the problems involved in the reading of foreign languages, and had carried out experiments on which we reported from time to time in various journals.[1] Our findings coincided in general with the

---

[1] The following articles appeared between 1924 and 1929.

Otto F. Bond:

(1) *The Organization and Administration of a First-Year French Course at the College Level*, "Studies in Secondary Education," Supplementary Educational Monograph, No. 26 (Chicago: University of Chicago School of Education, 1925), II, pp. 177–200.

(2) "The Organization and Use of a Departmental Reading Collection," *Modern Language Journal* (May, 1925), pp. 483–88.

(3) "Reading for Language Power," *Modern Language Journal*, X, 7 (April, 1926), pp. 411–26.

(4) "The Reading Objective," *Proceedings of the High School Conference*, Illinois Bulletin XXIV, 17 (Urbana: University of Illinois), pp. 270–74.

(5) "Junior College Work in Modern Foreign Languages," Chapter XIV in Gray's *The Junior College Curriculum* (Chicago: The University of Chicago Press, 1929), pp. 181–200.

Peter Hagboldt:

(6) "Reading and Its Influence upon Other Language Objectives," Jahrbuch 1924 of *Monatshefte für deutschen Unterricht*, pp. 1–11.

(7) "Experimenting with First Year College German," *Modern Language Journal* (Feb. 1925), pp. 293–305.

(8) "An Experiment on Reading Known Material in Beginners' Classes," *Modern Language Journal* (March, 1925), pp. 345–52.

contents of point 7 mentioned on pp. 37–38, and this same point raised an issue, on which a lively, stimulating controversy arose. Professor Hohlfeld, strongly on one side of the question, stated:

> I cannot but believe that the unsatisfactory results which obtain are generally due to causes but little, if at all, remediable by increasing the ground that is to be covered. In cases where even a limited amount of work is inadequately done — and they are the ones that bring down the general average — a considerable increase in reading requirements, even though this be offset by lessening the time spent on other exercises and by devoting more time to actual practice in reading, is likely to do more harm than good, and may even prove a step backward in the direction of reading by translation.[1]

We must not dwell, at this point, on the interesting controversy that followed, and which is listed in Oliver's *The Modern Language Teacher's Handbook* [2] with complete references to all the participants in this often heated debate. May it suffice to remark that Professor Hohlfeld's point is well taken in a state where a large part of the students are of German parentage, where it is natural and inevitable to consider the spoken word as the basic principle of language instruction, and where a time-honored tradition points to a direct approach as a possible solution. What prompted Professor Hohlfeld to express himself as he did was the fact that

(9) "On Inference in Reading," *Modern Language Journal*, XI, 2 (Nov. 1926), pp. 73–78.

(10) "Making the Reading Lesson Effective," *Modern Language Journal*, XI, 3 (Dec. 1926), pp. 129–32.

(11) "Presenting Grammar Inductively," *Modern Language Journal*, XII, 6 (March, 1928), pp. 440–45.

(12) "Elements of Art and Science in Modern Language Teaching," *Modern Language Journal*, XIII, 3 (Dec. 1928), pp. 192–96.

(13) "The Relative Importance of Grammar in a German Reading Course," *The German Quarterly*, I, 1 (Jan. 1928), pp. 18–21.

(14) "Achievement at the End of the Second Quarter Measured by the American Council Test," *The German Quarterly*, I, 4 (Nov. 1928), pp. 160–69.

(15) "Achievement after Three Quarters of College German as Measured by the American Council Alpha Test, Form B," *The German Quarterly*, II, 2 (March, 1929), pp. 33–43.

[1] Coleman, *The Teaching of Modern Languages*, p. 170.

[2] D. C. Heath and Company (1935), pp. 105 ff., an indispensable book for language teachers. See also Coleman, *Analytical Bibliography* (1927–1932), pp. 12–16.

very satisfactory results, according to the statistics gathered, were attained with widely differing methods. This he interpreted as proof that a good teacher teaching under favorable circumstances will achieve good results with any of them, whereas from inadequately prepared teachers half-way acceptable results can be expected only when a limited amount of reading is fairly thoroughly done. Professor Hohlfeld has no quarrel whatever with "direct reading"; what he wishes to emphasize is that to him adequate training of teachers is more important than prescriptions as to method.

One of our main tasks is to unriddle the extremely difficult problems arising out of brief courses, for which we must find a solution soon.[1]

A consoling thought is that healthy discontent makes for progress. The wider we are apart in our convictions, the greater is the probability that we shall, in the end, find the comfort of a satisfactory compromise, or even the blessings of a happy solution.[2]

8. "The attainment in one year in modern languages in secondary schools is in general so small when measured in terms of knowledge of the language that only under exceptional circumstances may the study of the subject for one year only be considered educationally advisable." (Coleman, p. 232)

We have discussed this recommendation briefly under point 3; let me add our experiences at the University of Chicago. At the beginning of the Fall Quarter we usually give for adequate placing the American Council Test. Students with one year of high-school training score so low on this test in all abilities that they voluntarily ask for a new start in a beginners' class.

9. "Because of the complexity of the task of learning a modern language, particularly when laying substantial foundations for speaking is among the objectives, and because of the apparent need for a somewhat prolonged period of contact with a new language in order to profit fully by the cumulative effect of this type of learning, interested and successful students should not

[1] For a critical analysis of the "direct method," see *Language Learning*, "The Best Method," pp. 100–10. These pages were published previously in the *Modern Language Journal*, XVI, 8 (May, 1932), pp. 625–31.

[2] A potential solution is suggested on pp. 39–41 of *Language Learning*, pages dealing with passive and active phases of language study.

only be enabled to pursue the subject during a minimum period of three years, but should be definitely encouraged to do so by school authorities. To this end, existing two-year courses in secondary schools should be lengthened and college authorities should exercise some control over the too frequent practice under which entering freshmen elect a new language, instead of continuing one in which they have had a two-year course or less in secondary school. The extent to which this latter situation prevails indicates a definite lack of correlation between the work done in secondary school and what the college expects. A more sympathetic study of the question by both types of institutions should bring about greater harmony in the choice of objectives and in attainment by students." (Coleman, p. 232)

We do not dare to hope that school authorities will, in the near future, advise pupils to continue with a subject the usefulness of which they themselves ordinarily belittle. The findings of the *Survey* naturally have not changed their attitudes for the better. Neither is it advisable to hope for a lengthening of two-year courses to three, except, perhaps, in a few privately endowed institutions. A more effective control regarding continuation, to be sure, should be furthered, as should also a better correlation of high-school and college subjects regarding definite standards of attainment.

10. "If, for local reasons, only a two-year course is feasible, or if, in any instance, a considerable percentage of students discontinue the modern language at the end of the fourth semester, it is particularly recommended that the course be organized with ability to read the modern language directly as the central aim, with an acceptable standard of reading ability as the minimum requisite for passing." (Coleman, p. 232)

This issue seems to be sufficiently discussed for the time being under point 4. We cannot help asking: Are we far from the truth in saying that within a not far distant time, reading ability will be the only true and generally recognized aim in short courses, and, for this reason, the only legitimate standard of achievement?

11. "The lack of homogeneity in knowledge of the subject by modern language students grouped in the same classes is lamentable. Equally distressing is the wide diversity in standards of

achievement in different schools and even in the same schools at different semester levels. Students may be placed more discriminatingly by the use of scores on uniform, comprehensive, and objectively scored tests administered to all who are enrolled in modern languages, and supplemented by scholastic records, teachers' judgments and other pertinent data. It would also be highly advantageous both to the pupils and to effective teaching in modern languages if school authorities would co-operate in grouping students on the basis of their previous scholastic record and of scores on intelligence tests, and if they would make it possible to reclassify or to drop from the subject those who do not keep up with their classes, whether from incapacity or from other causes." (Coleman, pp. 232 f.)

The lack of homogeneity in knowledge is closely related to the "fallacy of the time-serving basis" in the classification of students. Professor Ben D. Wood aptly states:

> Teachers who have not struggled with such heterogeneity in large classes, or who have never experienced the delight of working with reasonably homogeneous classes, can scarcely apprehend the full extent of the evils — in terms of the sacrifice of bright students on the altar of mediocrity, in terms of the cruel and more than useless brow-beating of dull students, and in terms of wasted energies and frayed nerves of teachers, — which are inevitable concomitants of such misplacement and misguiding of students as this survey has uncovered in the junior high schools of New York City.[1]

Professor Wood finds, moreover, that one-third of students in French classes were misplaced by one year or more, and that sixty per cent were misplaced by one semester or more.[2] Unfortunately his findings have not influenced schools in general. Wood tested two years in succession. In the second year the misplacement was no better, in spite of the fact that the situation was made clear to the principals.

The other recommendations of Professor Coleman we find sound and significant, particularly the dropping of ungifted students

---

[1] "New York Experiments with New Type of Modern Language Tests," *Publications of the American and Canadian Committees on Modern Languages,* Vol. I (The Macmillan Company, 1927), p. 26.

[2] Wood, *op. cit.,* pp. 157 ff.

who, to my mind, are far more harmful to the cause of effective language teaching than we have cared to admit.

12. "Students who fail have in many schools the opportunity to repeat the subject twice or oftener or to begin another modern language. Such records of repeaters as are accessible suggest that this is not often profitable to the student, and that each individual case should be examined for the purpose of ascertaining whether it would be better for the student to continue in the language work or to take another subject." (Coleman, p. 233)

A thorough and fair final test after examining the sum total of the facts of the case should be decisive. My colleague, Otto F. Bond, who once made an interesting study of the possible causes for failure in college French classes, found not less than forty-five potential reasons, all attributable to some natural conditioning factor.[1]

13. "Teachers would find it profitable to study the technique of constructing objective tests, based on the material of their course, to standardize them roughly for local or departmental purposes, to keep records of student performance from semester to semester based on such tests, on others more fully standardized and on intelligence scores, and thus to establish local standards of attainment and of progress." (Coleman, p. 233)

Nothing should be done without establishing certain definite standards of achievement. Only through them is it possible (1) to measure individual progress or deficiency in the various phases of the work; (2) to know the weak and strong points of our courses and practices; (3) to determine how our pupils rank in comparison with students in other schools. In short, without them we do not know whether or not our work is poor, good, or superior.

14. "The percentage of continuation in modern language, both in high school and in junior high school, should be studied in every school and school system over a period of several years. In cases where it is low, it should be determined whether this is due to individual or to administrative conditions, or to weaknesses in the instruction. Careful analysis of a number of local situations would furnish a basis for the general inferences which can not now be drawn for lack of sufficient data." (Coleman, p. 233)

[1] "Causes of Failure in Elementary French and Spanish Classes," *School Review*, XXXII (April, 1924), pp. 276–87.

It would be interesting to have definite data on this problem. To my knowledge at this writing no such investigations have been undertaken.

15. "Objective, uniform, and comprehensive tests, properly constructed and standardized, and supplemented by information concerning the students' secondary school record, would be of great value to colleges for the placement of incoming students, and are recommended to such accrediting agencies as the College Entrance Examination Board for the testing of achievement and for placement." (Coleman, p. 233)

A great deal has been accomplished since the publication of the American Council Tests.[1] A Cooperative Test Service was organized by the American Council on Education through its Committee on Tests and Measurements. Its offices for public contact are located at 15 Amsterdam Ave., New York City. Its director is Ben D. Wood. Through the Cooperative Test Service we are enabled to keep informed on the newest methods of placing students at their proper level, and of evaluating their achievement correctly.[2]

16. "In all departments of two or more teachers in the same modern language, great profit would result from cooperation in the establishment of objectives, of course-content, of method, and of standards of attainment by uniform testing. In large schools a more centralized departmental direction is an advantage, and in school systems much is to be gained by placing all the modern language work under the same supervision of competent specialists, who will work in collaboration with the city organization for educational research." (Coleman, p. 233)

Cooperation is indispensable. Wherever it is weak or unharmonious, the student suffers and with him the teacher, the school, and, particularly, the subject of instruction. The aim, the content of the course, the devices by which a particular objective is to be reached, and also the specific standard of achievement, all these important factors depend largely on the friendly joining of forces toward one single end. Pleasant relations in any given department rest entirely on a certain degree of respect for the professional experiences and convictions of our colleagues. To be unyielding

[1] World Book Company, 1926.   [2] See pp. 245–73 and 290–92.

and stubborn leads to disappointment and failure; to meet one's fellow teacher half way, and to discuss with him points of disagreement frankly, is always the better part of wisdom, and often leads to unexpected, far-reaching and pleasant results. Collaboration always wins.

A centralized department of direction is greatly advantageous in the hands of an experienced, strong, yet kind person, who should, if circumstances allow, secure the cooperation of an accredited organization for educational research.

17. "The fundamental consideration in determining the choice of a teaching technique in modern languages is that the activities in which teacher and students engage must be such as to give the students the maximum amount of practice during the period of study in doing the kinds of things that are included in the objectives approved for a given teaching situation. A method can be considered appropriate only when this principle is observed and when other important factors are kept in mind, such as the linguistic equipment of teachers, their capacity to organize the material and to conform intelligently and eagerly to the guiding principles of a given procedure, and the other general conditions prevailing in any given teaching situation." (Coleman, p. 276)

In any teaching situation the aim is the key to the means to be employed. Expressed more briefly: the objective determines the method, or in terms of an old maxim, trite but true, we learn by doing. If speaking be the aim, not the instructor but the student must do the speaking, and so it is in regard to every other language skill. As for the rest, the teacher's competence will win the day (see Chapter X).

18. "Despite a certain amount of experimentation that has been done, there is little concrete and wholly trustworthy evidence to show to what extent a given classroom method is, in itself, productive of superior or of inferior results. At the same time, the distinct trend of secondary school teachers away from translation as a means and as an end, and toward some form of 'direct' approach to the thought contained in a foreign text, is marked, and has apparently been beneficial in arousing more interest in students and in causing teachers themselves to learn the foreign language more effectively." (Coleman, p. 276)

It is extremely difficult to measure the results of any method. The main obstacle is that no two instructors proceed exactly in the same way. Their personality and their preparation are not alike, and, therefore, their ways of teaching cannot be alike. Each one tends to emphasize an ability in which he excels, especially in college teaching. One excels in conversation, the other in historical grammar, still another in phonetics or literary history. The problem is not to digress and to keep one's knowledge in check until the student is ready to absorb it in classes devoted to that specific topic.

As soon as we decide to bend our energies toward a more direct approach in whatever ability we wish to achieve, we are on the road to success. At the University of Chicago we have encouraged and cultivated "direct reading" in early courses ever since 1923 (see Chapter VI).

19. "There is a widespread belief among secondary school and college teachers that inability on the part of members of the profession to speak the languages they teach is the most important single cause of poor results in developing oral ability in the classroom. The fact that a very large majority of the modern language teachers in the United States have neither traveled nor studied in countries where the languages are spoken is a factor of importance in this connection. While this situation has a very direct bearing on the extent to which American schools in general may safely adopt the direct method as commonly conceived, it also lays on college departments a heavy obligation to train prospective teachers more effectively to pronounce, to understand, and to speak the foreign language, and upon the prospective and practicing teachers the responsibility of developing themselves in this direction by study here and abroad." (Coleman, pp. 276 f.)

An old German saying is: „Wer einen Teil lehren will, muß das Ganze wissen." The saying is correct. The teacher "should know his business." Even in a reading course it is highly advantageous to use the foreign language freely, though cautiously, and always speaking strictly within the words, idioms, and grammatical forms previously taught. This is a difficult task, but well worth while in the end.

If study abroad [1] is impossible we advise attendance at the German School in Bristol, Vermont,[2] membership in a German club or church, a private tutor, a course in conversation at a school or college under competent guidance, gramophone records, radio programs, lectures, sound films, etc., etc.

The "direct method" is not to be recommended in brief courses, but it can and should be thoroughly revised so as to retain all those features which do not hinder progress in a reading course.

20. "So many factors are involved in every teaching situation that none of the various efforts made by the *Study* to secure unequivocal testimony in regard to the comparative results from different teaching methods were wholly successful. In most classes in which the best results were observed the foreign language was largely used, but good oral attainment was not always accompanied by success in reading and in writing. In all the superior schools the organization of the work, the kind of supervision in the departments, the quality of the teaching, and the administrations in the better schools warrant no entirely clear-cut conclusions in regard to method when considered apart from other factors. They do, however, give definite support to the view that there is a direct ratio between teaching emphasis and the results obtained in terms of grammar or of composition or of reading." (Coleman, p. 277)

We have mentioned under point 18 the difficulty of measuring the effectiveness of any method. However, taking it for granted that a given school is superior in the quality of teaching, in organization and supervision, it is safe to assume that emphasis determines the result. For "the manner of teaching corresponds point for point to the desired result of learning. We learn to hear by hearing, to read by reading, to speak by speaking, to write by writing; we get only what we give, we reap only what we sow." [3]

---

[1] See Oliver, *op. cit.*, pp. 202–05. Fellowships for graduate study in Germany under the American German Student Exchange are administered by the Institute of International Education, 2 West 45th Street, New York.

[2] Its director is Professor Ernst Feise, Johns Hopkins University, Baltimore, Maryland.

The department of Germanic Languages and Literatures of Columbia University offered in the Summer Session of 1939 opportunity for intensive study of the German language during six weeks of living in a German residence, and may continue to do so in the future.   [3] *Language Learning*, p. 156.

21. "There is great need of careful experimentation to determine more definitely the effect upon learning a foreign language of the various procedures as applied under typical American school conditions. Especially is this true with respect to the relative effect upon reading power during the elementary stage of 'intensive' study of a small amount of reading material, as now generally practiced, as compared with more abundant 'direct' reading experience, accompanied by less detailed study of grammar and less written practice in translation from English and in reproduction in the foreign tongue. With the aid of carefully controlled experimentation it should be possible to test more thoroughly the theory that a procedure of the latter kind aids the student to develop more quickly the fluency in immediate understanding of the printed page that is essential for reading with ease and enjoyment." (Coleman, p. 277)

The recommendation to carry out experiments on a large scale is sound. It should not be too difficult to secure competent persons to plan and devise experiments wisely, to find experienced teachers, and to finance such undertakings. To make success reasonably certain, it would be best to enlist for each experiment the services and the full sympathy of a psychologist, an educationist, and a practical specialist in linguistic pedagogy. The latter would be in charge of a select group of teachers, friendly in their attitude, and quite capable of carrying out the practical side of the experiment in all its carefully worked out details. Valuable information might be gathered by such a project.[1]

These twenty-one points constitute the findings of the Modern Foreign Language Study as stated in Coleman's summarizing conclusions. Besides these points Coleman reports that the Committee on Investigation arrived at certain other judgments of a general nature, which need not delay us here.[2] They will be discussed in the course of subsequent chapters.

We shall now attempt to reduce these facts and recommendations to a few outstanding points which may be called, perhaps, those of the most basic importance:

[1] Compare Coleman, *Experiments*, pp. 100–90, for experiments of similar nature.

[2] Coleman, *The Teaching of Modern Foreign Languages*, pp. 277 f.

1. We must achieve better results, particularly in courses of one or two years' duration.
2. Since one-half to two-thirds of our pupils waste their time in trying to achieve the impossible, it is imperative to bend our efforts toward one well-defined, clear-cut, and attainable aim: that of reading ability within certain limits.
3. Our texts should utilize the noteworthy results of word, idiom, and syntax counts, and the problem of *realia* should receive special attention in this respect.
4. Placement tests must effect a more homogeneous grouping of students, and objective measurements must establish definite standards.
5. Cooperation of teachers with administrative officers, collaboration within the department — high school or college — possibly under a person of acknowledged competence, must better conditions for all concerned, particularly in regard to aims, to methods, and to definite standards of achievement.

The net result of the *Survey* is admirably epitomized by Professor Fife:

> New ideas seem to germinate and take root with exasperating slowness. An outworn methodology and threadbare dogmas continue to hold the center of the stage, with no support except constant iteration, and the same old songs are sung in tones of special propaganda and *a priori* conviction that long ago ceased to thrill the audience.[1]

These words will sadden those who have long and vainly awaited beneficial changes after an inquiry so extensive and imposing; yet we like to believe that they will encourage all those who are eager to carry on regardless of some of the *Study's* disheartening findings. We have no right to be discouraged. There is no reason to be. For every truth of whatever nature gained in the history of progress is no more, and never will be more, than a mere step toward deeper and more significant knowledge.

BIBLIOGRAPHY

BAGSTER-COLLINS, E. W. "Observations on Extensive Reading." *German Quarterly*, III, 1 (Jan. 1930), pp. 18–27.

[1] Coleman, *Experiments*, p. 48.

BOND, OTTO F. "Causes of Failure in Elementary French and Spanish Classes." *School Review* (April, 1924), pp. 268–86.

COLE, ROBERT D. "The Old and the New in Modern Language Teaching." *High School*, IX, 5 (Jan. 1932), pp. 286–91.

COLEMAN, ALGERNON. *The Teaching of Modern Foreign Languages in the United States.* A Report prepared for The Modern Foreign Language Study. New York: The Macmillan Company, 1929.

—— *Experiments and Studies in Modern Language Teaching.* Chicago: The University of Chicago Press, 1934.

HAUCH, EDWARD F. "The Reading Objective." *German Quarterly*, IV, 2 (March, 1931), pp. 96–110.

HENMON, V. A. C. "Some Significant Results of the Modern Foreign Language Study." *Journal of Educational Research*, XIX, 2 (Feb. 1929), pp. 79–91.

MERCIER, LOUIS J. A. "Is the Coleman Report Justified in Its Restatement of Objectives for Modern Language Study?" *French Review*, III, 6 (May, 1930), pp. 397–415.

MORGAN, B. Q. "The Coleman Report." *Modern Language Journal*, XIV, 8 (May, 1930), pp. 618–23.

O'SHEA, M. V. *The Reading of Modern Foreign Languages.* Department of the Interior, Bull. XVI. Washington, D. C.: U. S. Printing Office, 1927. 78 pp.

SUGGESTIONS FOR DISCUSSIONS AND REPORTS

1. Discuss Bagster-Collins' and Hauch's articles and their specific recommendations in regard to reading.
2. Report on Bond's article.
3. Report on the articles by Cole and by Henmon. Emphasize the most important results of the *Study*.
4. Read Morgan's and Mercier's articles. Sum up their objections to the Coleman Report.
5. Read Coleman's replies to the various articles directed against his report. See Oliver, p. 106. Prepare for a class discussion.
6. Study carefully Coleman's 21 summarizing conclusions and try to give a résumé in not more than 10 points.
7. A class discussion of point 7 of the Coleman Report.
8. Read and report on Mercier's article: "Diverging Trends in Modern Foreign Language Teaching and Their Possible Reconciliation." *French Review* (April, 1933), pp. 368–86.

CHAPTER THREE

THE LEARNING PROCESS AND THE METHOD

IN THE course of the centuries innumerable books, monographs, and articles have been written on the difficult and delicate task of learning a new language. So large and bewildering is the mass of these publications that we must first clear the way for new progress. But new progress is possible only if we state concisely what is known at present about language learning, and if we apply this knowledge to that which we are anxious to achieve. In other words, we must first define our present knowledge, and then use this knowledge toward specific and definite objectives.

We shall therefore attempt to: (I) name the processes by which we learn a new language; (II) analyze and describe the five types of methods, observing at the same time whether and how these processes are used in them; (III) point out some fallacies in current practices and suggest one single principle for an optimum procedure under our widely varying conditions.

To begin with, let me name the most important principle or laws which underlie the processes of language learning.

I. FUNDAMENTAL PRINCIPLES

1. *Interest.* The importance of the student's interest in learning cannot be overestimated. William James speaks of "the law of interest." According to this law, the most interesting part of a given subject resists longest the tendency to be forgotten. If interest is keen, laziness vanishes, discipline is self-inflicted. There arises that quiet zeal so favorable to all learning. The student no longer yearns for an empty grade, but follows an inner impulse, the satisfaction of which is the learner's ample reward. Interest

carries him to successful achievement, and achievement sometimes changes interest into a lifelong and ardent love.[1]

2. *Will.* We learn best when we will to learn. Mere frequency of repetition is not effective. Repetition must be supported by a firm will to retain, for when the will to retain is lacking, recall is a matter of sheer accident. The more deliberately we will to obtain not merely a transient but a lasting effect, the more certainly is the desired effect produced.[2]

3. *Attention and association.* Learning depends largely on two types of mental action; on imprinting by concentrated attention, and on rendering permanent by a wealth of associations that which has been imprinted. Without attention we cannot associate new impressions with older ones. Attention is in a certain sense the father of association; it weighs, compares, and scrutinizes the parts of a whole, linking each impression so gained to an older one from the past. In any case a definite bond is established; a new association has come to life.

Goethe once called attention the greatest of all virtues. Association may perhaps be called the greatest preserver of knowledge gained by attention. Yet neither attention nor association can entirely disregard the significance of repetition; for even clear impressions and strong associations are likely to fade if they occur in consciousness but once.[3]

4. *Repetition.* Forgetting begins the very moment we turn our attention away from one impression or thought to another. The older impression falls to a lower degree of awareness, is no longer made secure by attention, and is suppressed or dislodged by new impressions or ideas. Physiologically speaking, one may conceive of forgetting as a very definite force attacking and destroying the paths in our neural system which imprinting and exercise have formed. To fall into disuse means to be forgotten. Forgetting and disuse are synonymous. Repetition is as necessary for learning as breathing is for life. New habits of speech can be formed only by many repetitions willed to bring about lasting results.[4]

5. *Presentation.* It has not yet been established whether it is

---

[1] Peter Hagboldt, *Language Learning* (The University of Chicago Press, 1935), pp. 56–60.

[2] *Ibid.*, pp. 60–66.   [3] *Ibid.*, pp. 66–78.   [4] *Ibid.*, pp. 78–88.

more effective to present materials to the visual, the auditory, or the motor memory. The importance of this moot question has probably been much exaggerated. Effectiveness of presentation does not depend so much on the appeal to one sense or another as it depends on the intensity and vividness of impressions, on the frequency with which impressions are repeated, on the wealth of associations, and, last but not least, on the interest, eagerness, and will to mastery which each individual learner brings to the subject.[1]

6. *Order* has been praised throughout the ages as basic to all things. Homer: "The best in all things is order"; Shakespeare: "Order gives each thing view"; a German proverb: „Ordnung ift das halbe Leben." Orderliness, method, and systematic presentation have been found an important aid in language learning.[2]

7. *Practice.* The "law of distributed practice" has established that it is not profitable to attempt to master a given amount of material by one continued effort. Distributed practice has been found best, but each type of learning and each type of material has its own optimum number of repetitions distributed in a definite way, and this optimum distribution again may vary with individuals.[3]

8. *Recall and recognition.* In learning a foreign language it is more favorable to memorize and recall words, idioms, and constructions than to try merely to recognize them.[4]

9. *"Rhyme, rhythm, assonance, and meter* are memory aids.

---

[1] Peter Hagboldt, *Language Learning* (The University of Chicago Press, 1935), pp. 95 ff. For a discussion of students with extreme types of memory, see pp. 88–99.

[2] Compare H. R. Huse, *The Psychology of Foreign Language Study* (The University of North Carolina Press, 1931), p. 77, point 10.

[3] Peter Hagboldt, *op. cit.*, p. 83.

[4] Compare my article, "The Relative Importance of Grammar in a German Reading Course," *The German Quarterly*, I (Jan. 1928), p. 20: "If we require a student to be able to recognize a certain set of forms he will usually not be able to recognize them. If we tell him, however, that he should commit these forms to memory, he will, to be sure, not commit them to memory, but he will at least know them passively, that is, understand them when found in reading." See also H. R. Huse, *op. cit.*, pp. 60 ff. and 76, point 6.

We may be able to modify somewhat our attitude toward this important point after experimenting with two distinct types of grammars, one intended for recognition, the other for recall, and both presenting the same limited vocabulary (see Chapter VII, pp. 141–44).

Articulation, besides other advantages, may, in some cases, facilitate learning." [1]

10. "*Typographical devices* which lend variety to a page, up to a certain point, are an aid in increasing the total retention, apart from their value in distinguishing the important from the unimportant." [2]

11. *The law of use.* According to William James we remember best what we have learned last and, therefore, the most important principle has been left to the last: the law of facilitation by exercise or the law of use.[3] This, indeed, is a common-sense law. We all know that language becomes easier with practice, exercise, or use; but we are not at all sufficiently aware of the rigid specificness of the law of practice, exercise, or use. All functions of language are developed in a specific manner, and this specific manner determines the result. We learn only that which we specifically practice. For all but the most gifted and exceptional student, learning is decidedly specific, and no reliance should be placed on the vain hope of transfer.[4]

To sum up, I may say that while the findings yielded by experiments with various methods and devices in language teaching seem to be slight, I am nevertheless greatly impressed by their importance. If we look closely we find that these laws, principles, or rules are nothing but a restatement of ancient principles used throughout the centuries by superior teachers. They merely justify the best teachers' time-honored practices; they are the crystallization of effective practices.

Let us give a brief summary:

1. Interest is the basic principle of all learning, for interest determines the will to master, and the will to master, in turn, clinches attention, favors association, and impels repetition.
2. Presentation, to be effective, must be vital and vivid.
3. Orderliness is the foundation of all learning.

---

[1] Huse, *op. cit.*, p. 77, point 11.   [2] *Ibid.*, p. 76, point 4.
[3] Robert D. Cole in *Modern Foreign Languages and Their Teaching*, revised by James Burton Tharp (Appleton-Century Company, 1937), p. 161, speaks of two laws which really are one. Compare Horace B. English, *A Student's Dictionary of Psychological Terms.* The Antioch Press, Yellow Springs, Ohio, 1928.   [4] But see *Language Learning*, pp. 47–55.

4. Distributed practice is best.
5. Recall is more advantageous for learning than recognition.
6. Rhythm and rhyme, assonance, and meter aid memory.
7. Typographical devices may be effectively utilized.
8. We learn what we specifically practice.

II. TYPES OF METHODS

We have stated briefly a few basic principles of language learning, and now we shall describe the various types of methods, and inquire whether and to what extent these basic principles were utilized in them. Let us be careful, however, not to take these descriptions too rigidly. Probably no two instructors would entirely agree on any given analysis of any given method. Each instructor has his own experiences; experiences differ and, therefore, interpretations differ. Yet it is important that we come to a rather clear understanding in regard to our terms, for loose terms are dangerous.

In the discussion of methods it suffices to form clear-cut concepts. The basic idea of any method is the core. The fringes surrounding the core are less important. All that really matters is the basic idea or the core of the method. We shall try to get at the core.

We are fortunate in having adequate definitions of the various types of methods. They were formulated by the Committee of Twelve. We have, besides, several lucid diagnoses by Professor Eduard Prokosch, who describes the grammar-translation method as follows:

THE GRAMMAR AND TRANSLATION METHOD

As the name implies, the grammar and translation method lays the principal stress on the acquisition of a clear feeling for grammatical analysis, through training in the grammatical structure of the foreign language, and readiness in fluent and good translation from the foreign language into the mother tongue and vice versa. This method, which has been in use for centuries in the teaching of classical languages, possesses distinct values as regards mental discipline and formal development, but it never produces anything like a command of the language studied, within the time at disposal in our secondary schools. For this reason, if for no other, this method should not occupy the first place in the teaching of modern foreign languages.[1]

The *Report of the Committee of Twelve* supplements this statement by describing what seem to have been earlier practices, which, we hope, are no longer in vogue:

> According to this method the pupil is first put through a volume of paradigms, rules, exceptions, and examples which he learns by heart. Only when he has thoroughly mastered this book he is allowed to read; and even then his reading is usually regarded as a means of illustrating and emphasizing grammatical principles, rather than as a source of inspiration or of literary education. The amount of foreign literature studied by the class is, moreover, very small; but it is all carefully analyzed and translated, every lesson being, in general, repeated several times. Composition is used as an instrument for increasing still more the student's familiarity with inflections and rules. The foreign language is never spoken, and pronunciation is considered unimportant.[2]

As we see, both the Committee of Twelve and Prokosch admit certain advantages, such as "mental discipline," "formal development," and "training in mnemonic faculty," of which we no longer speak. Both reject the method as a whole.

The laws of interest, will, attention, and association were, presumably, applied as far as such a method permitted. Systematic and orderly presentation was as poor or as excellent as the instructor. Practice and repetition were probably enforced *ad nauseam*. We do not know whether or not typographical devices were used. The law of use or exercise, no doubt, made the superior student proficient in translation from and into the foreign language, while the average pupil accomplished as much as his natural gifts permitted. In brief, emphasis determined the result.

Translation from (Serüberſetzung) and into the foreign language (Sinüberſetzung) is the specific contribution of this method.

---

[1] E. Prokosch, *The Teaching of German in Secondary Schools* (Bulletin No. 41 of the University of Texas, 1915), pp. 6 f.

[2] *Report of the Committee of Twelve* (D. C. Heath and Company, 1900), pp. 14 f.

THE NATURAL METHOD

There are a number of so-called methods, sometimes grouped under the vague name "natural," and sometimes even incorrectly referred to as "direct," which aim primarily at the achievement of a speaking knowledge, or, rather, at acquiring facility in the use of words and phrases for definite conversational purposes. To this aim these colloquial methods subordinate, and often sacrifice, both . . . accuracy and system.

It may be granted that, by concentration on a limited vocabulary and constant practice of well selected phrases, some of them seem to attain brilliant results within a comparatively short time. However, experience has shown conclusively that the unmodified and exclusive use of purely colloquial methods tends to hinder, rather than to help the later formation of a thorough, extensive, and intelligent reading knowledge. This fact limits their legitimate use to conditions where the first elements of a colloquial knowledge of the foreign language constitute the one purpose for its study.[1]

To this lucid interpretation of Prokosch we may add a few interesting words from the *Report of the Committee of Twelve:*

It is a principle, an impulse, rather than a plan; and its products depend, to a greater extent than those of any other school, on the personality of the instructor . . . The mother tongue is strictly banished . . . Not until a considerable familiarity with the spoken idiom has been attained is the scholar permitted to see the foreign language in print; the study of grammar is reserved for a still later period. Composition consists of the written reproduction of the phrases orally acquired.[2]

These analyses are nearly complete. Little more need be said. The method, as we have stated, is ancient. Viëtor wittily called it the *Bonnen* or *Papageien Methode.* The instructor, usually a native, as a rule is quite innocent of any training that would equip him to use any other method.[3] Strictly speaking, no training is necessary. The spoken word is all that matters. The foreign language is simply "talked into" the pupil. The gifted child may acquire the foreign language easily and fluently in about six

---

[1] E. Prokosch, *op. cit.,* p. 7.   [2] *Report of the Committee of Twelve,* pp. 16 f.
[3] Heness and his followers were laudable exceptions to this rather rigid rule, as their success fully indicates.

years, just as Montaigne acquired Latin, and just as many American children today learn French, German, or Spanish.

Brilliant results may be achieved by the gifted adult, determined in his efforts, and knowing just what he wants to learn. Yet even the superior mature student cannot succeed unless he himself puts order into the natural chaos by systematizing his studies, and by using a brief grammar to supplement his work in class. For it is a matter of everyday experience that the forms of words, sentences, and phrases remain, as it were, crystallized and rigid unless they are by exercise made pliable and applicable to widely different and quickly changing situations.

The "natural method" is still in vogue in many countries at various language schools, such as the Berlitz School, where travelers prepare for their stay abroad, or ladies interested in language "pick up" some French, Spanish, or German, or teachers lacking other opportunities "brush up" their foreign language.

The one outstanding feature is the specificness of the procedure. Of the principles of language learning, the law of use or practice, besides the law of interest, plays the most important part. Again we see that it is emphasis which decides what the learner will know in the end.

The Psychological Method

Invented and developed, as we know, by François Gouin, and later taken over and adapted by Bétis and Swan,[1] this method is adequately described as follows:

The psychological method rests on the principle of the association of ideas and the habit of "mental visualization." The whole current vocabulary of a language, in the form of short, idiomatic sentences, is divided up into groups . . . On presenting each new word to the beginner the instructor exhorts him to close his eyes and form a distinct mental picture of the thing or act represented . . . Sometimes real objects or drawings are used, and pantomime is frequently resorted to; . . . It is never considered a sin to put in a word or two in English, and at the outset that language is very freely employed. Although most of the talking is done by the teacher, the pupils are constantly called upon to repeat his sentences and to answer questions. After

[1] *The Facts of Life* (New York, 1896) was their text.

the first lessons, written compositions may be prepared, made up of phrases already acquired. Grammatical instruction is begun early, concurrently with other exercises, but the reading of consecutive texts is postponed until the bulk of the ordinary vocabulary has been learned . . .

The Bétis method has . . . obvious advantages: It trains the memory; it fascinates the student, and holds his attention more closely than any other mode of teaching now in vogue; . . . it affords, through some of its conversational groups, an insight into the life of a foreign country . . . It affords but little opportunity for the exercise of judgment; it entirely neglects, in the first years, the cultivation of the aesthetic sense, and assigns literary study to a stage which high-school pupils will scarcely reach. Moreover, its treatment of pronunciation is decidedly unsatisfactory [1] . . .

We have referred to Kron's book on Gouin, and now must point out certain factors which finally proved responsible for abandoning the *Seriensystem* as a whole:

(1) The arrangement of sentences in series, though orderly and logical, is often made unnatural and forced by too much detail. (2) Ordinary language consists of questions and answers rather than of meticulously arranged sentences giving descriptions of actions. (3) The careful detail of descriptions does not correspond to the tempo of our thoughts. (4) Fascinating in the beginning, the *Seriensystem* grows progressively monotonous because its approach to language is altogether too one-sided; and the magnitude of its aim is very discouraging.[2]

The psychological method has, in part, been utilized in the "direct method." As we plainly see from the analysis of the Committee of Twelve, the adaptation of Gouin's method was a decided advance over procedures previously in vogue. The principles of language learning were effectively used. Interest was keen, presentation vital and vivid, and orderliness a basic feature. Practice occupied an important place, and recall of memorized materials simultaneously dramatized formed a solid basis for excellent achievements. We have no reason to doubt that here, too, the pronounced emphasis on speaking determined the result.

[1] *Report of the Committee of Twelve*, pp. 20 f. [2] Compare Chapter I, pp. 12–13.

THE DIRECT METHOD

This method is clearly described by Professor Prokosch:

> The direct method, in Germany usually called *Reformmethode*, aims primarily at a reading knowledge, but incidentally supplies the most satisfactory foundation for a speaking knowledge. It recognizes the necessity of a thorough training in grammar, and emphasizes the fact that any degree of mastery of a foreign language must start from the mastery of its sounds; therefore, its work is based on a perfect pronunciation. It avoids the use of the mother tongue, teaches grammar inductively and systematically, and builds a vocabulary on the basis of connected texts instead of isolated words or sentences. This method is the outcome of decades of patient work on the part of European educators, especially Germans, and represents the mature and thoroughly tested results of ripe experience and psychological investigation. The *Frankfurter Reformplan* may be considered the standard of the direct method, but it appears necessary to modify it in order to adapt it to the needs of American schools and teachers.[1]

This definition, written in 1915, gives us a clear description of the "direct method" as a pleasant and effective approach to reading. No one could have foreseen at the time that this method was to be pitifully misused. For instead of applying it as an introduction to reading, teachers made a fetish of grammar, of oral exercises, of speaking, and of composition, forgetting entirely what they were trying to achieve. Instead of coming at once to the core of their problem in a simple and direct way, they unwittingly cultivated more indirect objectives of an intangible nature,[2] and when the time came to show what could be accomplished in a given time, no satisfactory report was available.[3]

And yet the Committee of Twelve had pointed out in unmistakable terms that reading should not be postponed to a stage beyond the secondary period. It had urged to bear in mind that the vast majority of pupils — those for whom the course was planned — would not continue their education beyond high-school age.[4] This recommendation, by no means intended to fit our present state of affairs, frequently needs to be taken to heart even now.

---

[1] Prokosch, *op. cit.*, p. 7.   [2] Cf. Chapter II, p. 31, point 3.   [3] Cf. Chapter I, p. 17.   [4] *Report of the Committee of Twelve*, p. 27.

Errors are good errors if they teach a lesson. The lesson is: If, in a brief course, your aim be to teach reading ability, do not act as though your students were going to enter a contest in public speaking or debating in the foreign language. Stick to your aim!

The "direct method" satisfies the main principles of language study. But even though adapted to typical American conditions, it often fails in one point, unfortunately the most important one. It fails in emphasis. It is too ambitious in its aims. It imparts a vague and limited knowledge in all the phases of the foreign language instead of developing one single phase to a definite and well-defined degree. We shall have to discuss this basic problem in more detail in several of the subsequent chapters. May it suffice here to say that the "direct method" must be, can be, and will be some day modified to fit the most typical of our American language courses, the brief one. When finally changed to meet the requirements of the brief course, it will use the principle of directness, fusing with its best features into that much praised, more maligned, and most ill-used of all methods, the "reading method."

THE READING METHOD

This method is described by the Committee of Twelve as follows:

The study of texts from the very beginning of the course, abundant practice in translation at sight, leading ultimately to the ability to read the foreign language with ease and without interposition of English, are the principal features of this programme. Grammar and composition are regarded merely as a help to reading, and are reduced to essentials; sometimes accidence and syntax are first learned inductively, but oftener a small text-book is used concurrently with translation. Great importance is attached to the use of good English in the renderings. Pronunciation receives scant attention; there is little or no oral exercise . . .

The great advantage of the process is that it quickly enables the student to read French and German literature — not with the complete appreciation that only an all-around command of the language can give, but with the same kind of intelligence and enjoyment with which good classical scholars read Latin. Indirectly, it helps the pupil to form a good style, and to increase the volume and the precision of his English vocabulary; it cultivates the taste by dwelling upon delicacies of expression; it exercises the memory through the enforced retention of words and idioms; it trains the linguistic sense by calling attention to the points of resemblance and difference in various tongues; and the exact fitting of phrase to thought forms an excellent discipline for the judgment.[1]

The Committee of Twelve adds that on the other hand it deals only with one phase of language study, that it lacks in vivacity and in stimulus to attention, and interests only the more serious student. Moreover, the Committee expresses its concern that "the continued use, year after year, of an easy way of teaching . . . requires but little training" and "may prove demoralizing to the instructor, dull his appetite for self-improvement, and make him indolent and easily satisfied with his qualifications." [2]

These objections must not be taken too seriously. In part they are no longer valid. One-sidedness is inevitable in brief courses. Consistent concentration on one single objective is better than an unwise pursuit of unattainable aims. Lack of vivacity and lack of stimulus to attention are bedfellows of poor texts. "The easy way of teaching, requiring but little training" as well as the "demoralizing effect on the instructor" we may safely leave to the future when the "reading method" will be more fully developed, and when teachers realize, as they may even now, that a reading course, ably given, is anything but an "easy way of teaching." Proof of this is seen in the fact that the teacher must, if possible, always speak within his students' vocabulary in order to illustrate adequate pronunciation and develop aural comprehension together with reading ability.

Even at the first glance we notice a decided difference between the "direct method" as described by Professor Prokosch and the "reading method" as analyzed by the Committee of Twelve. And yet both methods profess to pursue the same aim. Is this difference real or imaginary, is it in theory or practice, in principle or application? Let us look closely and, for easier comparison, give their main features in opposite columns.

---

[1] *Report of the Committee of Twelve*, pp. 29 f.   [2] *Ibid.*, p. 30.

DIRECT AND READING METHODS COMPARED

Direct Method	*Reading Method*
	Common aim: reading ability
1. Satisfactory foundation is laid for speaking knowledge. Native language is avoided.	There is little or no oral exercise.
2. Mastery of sounds is sought.	Pronunciation receives little attention.
3. Thorough training in grammar which is presented inductively.	Grammar and composition are used as a help to reading, and reduced to essentials. A brief grammar is mostly used.
4. Vocabulary is taught through connected texts.	The same procedure, but with abundant practice in translation at sight and with direct reading as the final aim. Stress on good English.
5. The aim of an all-around command is not stated but implied.	The method quickly prepares for reading ability, not with complete appreciation that only an all-around command can give, but with the same kind of enjoyment with which good classical scholars read Latin. Various other advantages are mentioned.

From points (1) and (2) we see at once that there is a sharp difference in aim as well as in practice. The direct method in avoiding the vernacular and in aiming at mastery of sounds is inevitably forced to practice the formation of correct sounds in abundant oral exercises. In the reading method there is little or no attention paid to either pronunciation or oral practice. In point (3) we note that the direct method aims at thoroughness in grammar, while the reading method contents itself with a recognition knowledge of basic essentials. Point (4) in the direct method permits different interpretations, as does also the same point in the reading method, at least as far as the nature and the extent of translation is concerned. Point (5) in the direct method alludes by implication to a comprehensive aim; the reading method comes closer to reality in being more specific and also more modest in its aims.

And the result of our analysis? As stated the two methods are identical in aim. They differ in their means rather than in their fundamental theory. Their fundamental theory is directness of approach. But this directness differs within the two methods. The "direct method" devotes much time to pronunciation and oral practice; the "reading method" reduces such exercises to a minimum, using the time as far as possible for reading. In beeline fashion it comes directly to the core of the problem and, therefore, seems even more direct than the direct method; and, indeed, it *is* more direct if we find just the proper amount of training in pronunciation and oral practice.[1]

We summarize the result of our discussion. There is one common element which is basic and governs the final result of any and all methods. This basic element is emphasis or stress. The "grammar-translation method" stresses translation; the student may or may not learn to translate. The "natural and the psychological methods" stress speaking; the student may achieve facility in oral expression. The direct method professes to teach primarily reading, but is anxious to impart other abilities as a means to an end. The reading method stresses reading and seems to be our only hope for creditable results in short courses.

THE MOST IMPORTANT LAW among our principles of language learning is the law of use or practice. This law, if applied, results in emphasis or stress. Emphasis or stress rules with an iron hand the result of all methods.

III. FALLACIES IN CURRENT PRACTICES

There seem to be two clear and distinct reasons why our progress is lagging. Both have been expressed at various times by Professor Fife:

> Grammar still occupies a leading place in the minds of the majority of modern-language teachers in this country ... the American

[1] For direct and indirect associations, see *Language Learning*, pp. 19–22; for interdependence of phases of language see *ibid.*, pp. 41–43.

teacher continues to devote much of the classroom time and effort to drill in the French irregular verbs and the German adjective inflections, and to an ingenious invention of practice sentences, often as fantastic as those satirized by Henry Sweet a generation ago, with the object of enticing his pupils into the use of elusive flexions and idioms. The subjunctive of indirect discourse still invites to classroom analysis and discussion; the distinction between past descriptive and the preterite in Spanish still lies on the conscience of the teacher and becomes an active concern of the pupils.[1]

The other reason, too, has been repeatedly stated by the same writer. The main point in his criticism is that the majority of teachers profess to the reading aim in theory, not in practice; that they render lip service, while the attainment of their goal demands immediate and continuing experiment; that we "have not yet learned to define the objectives of our language teaching in terms of our national needs and to adapt our practice toward a fulfillment of these needs."[2]

The single and simple principle for the best procedure under our widely varying conditions seems to be a clear-cut realization of our aims and the directness of our approach. For "whatever the future may yield for modern language learning, this fundamental law holds fast: The manner of learning corresponds point for point to the desired result of learning. We learn to hear by hearing, to read by reading, to speak by speaking, to write by writing; we get only what we give, we reap only what we sow."[3]

BIBLIOGRAPHY

COLE, ROBERT D. *Modern Foreign Languages and Their Teaching*. Revised by James Burton Tharp (New York: Appleton-Century Company, 1937), pp. 1–70.

COLEMAN, ALGERNON. *An Analytical Bibliography of Modern Language Teaching, 1927–1932* (Chicago: The University of Chicago Press, 1933). Articles on objectives, pp. 69–73.

[1] Robert Herndon Fife in Coleman's *Experiments and Studies in Modern Language Teaching* (The University of Chicago Press, 1934), p. 30.
[2] Robert Herndon Fife, "The Reading Objective," *The German Quarterly* (May, 1929), p. 87.   [3] *Language Learning*, p. 156.

FIFE, ROBERT HERNDON. "A Survey of Tendencies in Modern Language Teaching, 1927–33: Retrospect and Prospect" in Coleman's *Experiments and Studies in Modern Language Teaching* (Chicago: The University of Chicago Press, 1934), pp. 1–50.

—— "Some New Paths in Teaching German." *The German Quarterly* (Jan. 1928), pp. 7–17.

—— "The Reading Objective." *The German Quarterly* (May, 1929), pp. 73–87.

HAGBOLDT, PETER. *Language Learning.* Chicago: The University of Chicago Press, 1935.

HANDSCHIN, CHARLES H. *Methods of Teaching Modern Languages* (Yonkers-on-Hudson, N. Y.: World Book Company, 1923), pp. 20–46.

HUSE, H. R. *The Psychology of Foreign Language Study* (Chapel Hill, N. C.: The University of North Carolina Press, 1931), pp. 3–77.

OLIVER, THOMAS EDWARD. *The Modern Language Teacher's Handbook* (Boston: D. C. Heath and Company, 1935). Articles on aims, pp. 4–7.

PROKOSCH, E. *The Teaching of German in Secondary Schools* (Bulletin No. 41 of the University of Texas, 1915), pp. 6–18. The pamphlet, written by a great teacher, is out of print. It contains lucid instructions to teachers.

Report of the Committee of Twelve (Boston: D. C. Heath and Company, 1900), pp. 14–30.

SUPPLEMENTARY READINGS

GOEDSCHE, C. R. "The First German Lesson for College Students." *German Quarterly*, V, 4 (Nov. 1932), pp. 153–60.

HUEBENER, THEODORE. *Forty Helpful Hints in Teaching Foreign Languages.* Foreign Language Monographs, No. 5. Board of Education, City of New York.

KOCH, ERNST. "Intermediate College German." *German Quarterly*, X, 4 (Nov. 1937), pp. 194–97.

POPE, PAUL R. "The First Vital Week of Beginning German." *German Quarterly*, X, 2 (March, 1937), pp. 54–59.

SUGGESTIONS FOR DISCUSSIONS AND REPORTS

1. Name at least eight fundamental principles which have been found important in language learning.
2. Discuss these principles.
3. Discuss the most important law.

4. Prepare a brief report on those principles which you personally have found most helpful in learning a foreign language.
5. Name the five methods mentioned in this chapter.
6. Characterize each of them.
7. Read carefully and then report on Fife's two articles.
8. Read and report on Fife's "Survey of Tendencies in Modern Language Teaching" in Coleman's *Experiments and Studies*.
9. Read and report on Hagboldt's *Language Learning*, Chap. I, pp. 1–55.

CHAPTER FOUR

PRONUNCIATION: PRACTICAL PHONETICS AS A BASIS

BEFORE Viëtor's memorable pamphlet, *Der Sprachunterricht muß umkehren*,[1] the study of grammar had been the central point in the teaching of modern languages. Through the discovery and the development of the science of phonetics, there came about a radical change in attitude toward grammar. Emphasis was laid on speaking, and stress on pronunciation thus became the inevitable result.

A GOOD PRONUNCIATION is now generally recognized as the basic and first requirement in all language courses. There are two ways of acquiring an adequate pronunciation: (1) by imitating a person who has lost all traces of dialect or provincialism; (2) by a course in practical phonetics where imitation is supplemented by science, that is, by a careful physiological explanation of each sound. Imitation is best for children and natural-born linguists. But even children and highly gifted linguists often listen to speakers whose pronunciation is quite unworthy of imitation. For the schoolroom, imitation alone will not do; imitation carefully corrected by practical phonetics is the safest way.

NEGLECT OF PRONUNCIATION inevitably leads to grief. The student cannot understand when spoken to. He cannot pronounce and therefore cannot converse. Even falsely uttered sounds have a tendency to become permanently engraved in the student's memory if not corrected at once. Thus, if he reads widely, which he must to satisfy his most urgent needs, he will perpetuate his faulty pronunciation. His loss will be great and irreparable. Rhyme and rhythm, color of tone, beauty of diction, and splendor

---

[1] Leipzig, 1905; first and second edition 1882 and 1886 respectively.

of cadence — all the highly significant elements — remain empty concepts to him, things heard about but never experienced.

In short, our student will never be able to enjoy the feeling of genuine accomplishment. He will never feel competent to read aloud even the simplest sentence in German. Since pronunciation is the very basis of language study, reasonable correctness is the first aim to strive for. This is the absolute minimum requirement.[1]

THE MODEL GIVEN BY THE TEACHER is all important. No one should risk serving as an example to his students who has not examined and overcome his own shortcomings in pronunciation. Nobody can teach what he cannot exemplify in a flawless manner. If the teacher's pronunciation is faulty, that of his students will be more so. No stream can rise higher than its source. There can and will be no gain in our students' achievement unless thoroughly competent teachers lead the way.

Professor Bagster-Collins writing in 1904 states that as a rule native teachers are apt to be even more handicapped by provincialisms and dialects than their American colleagues who have studied abroad.[2] Indeed, study abroad cannot and does not prevent a future teacher from imitating that which he hears. However, during the last decades conditions have changed. The phonograph and the radio have probably had a normalizing effect on the situation as a whole. A course in practical phonetics is now required as a basic preparation of all teaching candidates, and it is to be hoped that fewer and fewer students will be misled by faulty models.

Incidentally, American broadcasting might be improved in the interest of students as well as the general public if some radio announcers were given a modicum of training in the pronunciation of common French, German, Italian, and Spanish words, which they mispronounce with complete confidence.

THE BEST GERMAN is spoken by cultured natives who, through their surroundings, education, or travels have lost every trace of dialect or provincialism. Their speech is called Deutſche Hoch=ſprache. Deutſche Hochſprache has been determined through a care-

---

[1] See *Language Learning* (The University of Chicago Press, 1925), pp. 3–7.
[2] *The Teaching of German in Secondary Schools* (Columbia University Press, 1916), pp. 41 ff.

ful study of the differences in the languages of the stage. In 1898 a committee of German scholars, among them Professors Sievers and Siebs, met in an effort to normalize the Bühnenaus=sprache. Supplementary meetings in 1908 and 1922 with persons vitally interested in this problem finally led to the publication of an important work: *Deutsche Bühnenaussprache-Hochsprache, auf Veranlassung des Deutschen Bühnenvereins und der Genossenschaft Deutscher Bühnenangehöriger bearbeitet von Theodor Siebs.*[1]

In the preface the author states: „Während nirgends im deutschen Sprachgebiete eine mustergültig zu nennende Aussprache herrscht, bietet uns die deutsche Bühnenaussprache ... eine Richtschnur, die in der Wissen=schaft und der Kunst anerkannt und auch für andere Gebiete deutscher Sprachpflege, namentlich durch die Schule, nutzbar zu machen ist. — Die deutsche Bühnenaussprache kann in diesem Sinne als deutsche Hochsprache bezeichnet werden."[2] It is Hochsprache, then, which we should teach in our schools, colleges, and universities, that is, a German free from all traces of dialects and, if possible, free from all "foreign" variations from good German.

For your convenience we give below the titles of various books to supplement your studies in the course on phonetics.[3]

NATURAL LIMITATIONS. An adequate pronunciation must be our aim, but moderation should guide us in our effort to reach it. Nature sets definite limitations for each individual. Beyond these limitations all efforts are futile.

---

[1] Verlag von Albert Ahn, Köln, 1927. Vierzehnte Auflage. [2] Cf. *op. cit.*, p. 1.

[3] George Oliver Curme, "Best German Pronunciation," *Journal of English and Germanic Philology,* IX (1910), pp. 1–19.

C. H. Grandgent, *German and English Sounds.* Ginn and Company, 1892.

Eduard Prokosch, *Sounds and History of the German Language* (Henry Holt and Company, 1916), particularly Chapters II and III; the same author's *The Teaching of German in Secondary Schools* (University of Texas, Bulletin No. 41), pp. 12–15.

Wilhelm Viëtor, *Wie ist die Aussprache des Deutschen zu lehren?* Marburg, 1928. 25 cents.

Viëtor's *Deutsches Aussprachewörterbuch* (Vierte und fünfte Auflage. Leipzig, 1931) is an important reference book for all instructors of German.

W. Kuhlmann, *Deutsche Aussprache: Lehr- und Lesebuch für Ausländer.* Heidelberg, 1933.

Erich Drach, *Deutsche Aussprachelehre für den Gebrauch im Ausland.* Frankfurt am Main, 1931.

Erwin Meyenburg, *Kleine Phonetik für Ausländer aus der Praxis für die Praxis.* Berlin: Verlag des akademischen Auskunftsamts, 1928.

Experiments seem to indicate that accuracy in pitch discrimination can probably not be improved by practice or by teaching. Moreover, about 5 to 10 per cent of all students suffer from defective hearing.[1] If these statements be correct, we must be prepared to find, in a class of thirty-three, two or three students with an extremely defective pronunciation. Actual experience verifies this finding. Roughly speaking, approximately 5 to 10 per cent of the students in a given class may be called excellent in pronunciation, 10 to 20 per cent good, the large majority not more than fair, and 5 to 10 per cent decidedly poor. Therefore, it remains the part of wisdom not to expect greater accuracy in pronunciation than the students' and the instructor's own natural limitations allow. Patience, endurance, and sympathetic understanding are the practical phonetician's greatest virtues. Above all, be patient. Nicht Kunst und Wissenschaft allein, Gedulb will bei dem Werke sein.[2] "Patience is genius," Buffon once wrote.

Naturally, the first lessons must be devoted largely to the problems of the German sound system. We may proceed in different ways. I shall describe four of them fully because I know them by experimentation.

Tested Ways of Teaching German Sounds

A first way seems particularly advantageous for brief courses. Phonetic symbols may be omitted or supplied according to the age and the needs of the student.[3]

(1) We explain the nature of the sound physiologically. Beginning with the vowel *i* we state: German i, like English *i*, may be short or long. If short, it is like *i* in English *sin*. (2) The spelling of short *i* is i. (3) Examples are: in, bin, bist, ist, sind, finden, Wind, Winter, Finger, Ring.

[1] Daniel Starch, *Educational Psychology* (The Macmillan Company, 1927), pp. 141 ff.   [2] Goethe, *Faust*, I. 6.

[3] Some teachers feel that neither phonetic symbols nor phonetic transcriptions are needed in elementary German classes. This opinion is no doubt strongly influenced by our exceedingly short courses. As for my own experience, I have found that phonetic symbols, if their deeper meaning is carefully explained, have a strong tendency to remind the student of the organic basis of German sounds. Phonetic transcriptions are, naturally, imperative in a course on practical phonetics.

We proceed to long i, stating: (1) Long i is pronounced nearly like *ee* in English *free* but articulated somewhat higher in the mouth. (2) The spelling varies and is either *i, ie, ih,* or *ieh.* (3) Examples are: die, sie, wir, ihr, hier, Bier, Tier, Bieh, sieh.

In short, we first explain the sound physiologically and compare it with the nearest English sound, provided there is one. Then we explain that the same sound is not always expressed by the same letters. Finally, we give examples carefully illustrating our explanations. And so we continue systematically through the vowels and the consonants.

This method of presenting the German sound system will, if properly handled, result in several distinct advantages. The number of illustrative words can be limited to the most frequent ones and contain, moreover, many cognates. The words used as examples may be repeated again and again in illustration of different sounds. For instance, Wind can be used three times: once for w, once for i, and once for final d; Finger may be repeated four times: once for f, once for short i, once for liquid ng, and once for final er. Almost any word may be repeated in like manner. The obvious advantages are: repetition of frequent words; concentration on the problems implied in each word; actual occurrence of these words in subsequent short sentences, which must always follow words used in isolation.[1]

A second way is more difficult for the instructor, but far more interesting for the student. We take a coherent text from the first lesson of our grammar. We address the class, saying: "I am going to read to you two German words which mean *first lesson.* I shall pronounce these words several times, first slowly, then as in natural speech." The instructor pronounces Erste Aufgabe. The class repeats several times. "Gut! Fein! — Pardon me. I did not intend to speak German as yet. But do you know what I said?" The class gives the obvious meanings. Result: a pleasant atmosphere.

The teacher continues and states that he will explain physiologically each sound of these first two words. He explains, more-

---

[1] This presentation of the German sound system is attempted in Hagboldt-Kaufmann, *A Brief Course in German* (The Heath-Chicago Series. D. C. Heath and Company, 1937), pp. 3–10.

over, that all the sounds of German are contained in the first text of the first lesson with the exception of a few sounds to follow soon. He takes up each sound in turn, first the e, then the two possible ways of pronouncing the r as lingual r or uvular r,[1] then the ß and the t, neither of which offers any difficulty in erſte, and at last the final e. Now he goes on to the word Aufgabe, briefly describing au, f, g, a, b, and final e, which latter has occurred before in the word erſte.

All these explanations must be given concisely and clearly. The sounds which present no difficulty in the words in question may be ignored for the time being. Having explained and described each sound of the first two words, the teacher goes on to the title of the text, Das Schulzimmer, and to the first sentence, Hier iſt das Schulzimmer. Then he continues through the text of the first lesson, proceeding exactly as before. He explains carefully each individual sound and has the class and individual students repeat the sound and the word several times.

The first ten lines of text contain nearly all the sounds of the German language; and since the teacher has carefully marked down each word under its proper phonetic symbol, he finds the following words on the blackboard by the time he has finished the text of the first lesson:

[a] (*long*): da, ja, Tafel; (*short*): das, Wand, Papier
[e] (*long*): er, wer, Lehrer
[ɛ] (*short*): Decke, Fenſter, Heft, gelb, Herr
[ə] (*unaccented as in* the book): Boden, Zimmer, Decke, eine, feine, oben
[i] (*long*): wir, ihr; die, ſie, hier, Papier
[i] (*short*): iſt, bin, ich, Tiſch
[o] (*long*): wo, Boden, rot, oben
[ɔ] (*short*): dort
[u] (*long*): Stuhl, Schulzimmer, du

---

[1] Theodor Siebs, *op. cit.*, p. 60, says: „Es iſt in allen Fällen durchaus Zungenſpitzen-r zu fordern . . ." See, however, George O. Curme, *A Grammar of the German Language* (The Macmillan Company, 1922), p. 34, where he refers to the lingual r stating: "It is disappearing despite its adoption by the stage and certain enthusiasts. The more common r is uvular."
Compare also M. W. Quadt, "Zur Aussprache des Deutschen im Unterricht," *Monatshefte für deutschen Unterricht* (Feb. 1928), pp. 39–42. My opinion is that we should try to achieve Hochſprache by all means. Natural limitations will prevent us from becoming "too correct."

[y] (*long*): Tür, grün, Schüler
[au] (*as* ow *in* now): grau, braun, blau, auch
[ai] (*as* i *in* wine): ein, kein, nein, fein, weiß, Bleiſtift
[b] blau, Buch, bin, biſt
[p] gelb
[d] da, das, Decke, Boden, oder
[t] Tiſch, Tür, Heft, dort; Wand, und, ſind, ſeid
[z] (*as* z *in* zeal): ſein, ſie, ſind, ſeid
[s] (*as* s *in* sad): das, was, es, iſt, Hans
[st] (*as* st *in* still): iſt, biſt, erſte
[ʃt] (= sht): Stuhl, Bleiſtift
[ts] (*as* ts *in* rats): Schulzimmer, ſchwarz
[r] or [R] rot, wer, Herr, Papier, grün, grau, braun, Lehrer
[v] (*as* v *in* van): wo, wie, was, wer, weiß, Wand, wir, ſchwarz
[ç] [x] ich; auch, Buch

The net result is that nearly all the sounds of the German language have occurred and have been explained in twenty-four lines of coherent, meaningful text. The student sees them carefully arranged in their proper places. The vowels are preceded by the word *long* or *short*. They are, moreover, underlined on the board or printed in bold-faced type in the book. Sounds offering special difficulties — i, ie, ei, ü, (ö occurs later); final b, d, g; ſ and ſt in initial position; r, v, w, ch, etc. — have been lifted from their context and are ready to be repeated and reviewed.[1]

The advantages are the following: (1) The student learns the sound when he needs it, and not before; (2) he has the feeling of something definitely accomplished even after the first recitation; (3) he has studied a coherent text, has uttered words of great frequency in meaningful sentences, and has been encouraged by the instructor's example to imitate proper intonation, so important in the early phases of language study.[2]

The only disadvantage is that this manner of introduction into the sound system of German is extremely strenuous for the instructor. Not more than 12 to 14 lines of text can be taken up in one class hour, two sessions being needed for a text of about 24

---

[1] This presentation is attempted in *Deutsch für Anfänger* (The Heath-Chicago Series. D. C. Heath and Company); see Lessons 1 to 5; for brief physiological explanations of the sounds see pp. 2–8.

[2] Cf. Daniel Jones, "The Importance of Intonation in the Pronunciation of Foreign Languages," *Modern Language Teaching* (1914), pp. 201–05.

H. Klinghardt, *Sprechmelodie und Sprechtakt*. Marburg, 1925.

lines. Yet after one lesson has been given in this fashion, the following can be done easily and quickly. After the second lesson all the problems of German pronunciation are likely to have occurred frequently.

A *third way*, now rapidly going into discard, is the habit of spending several weeks exclusively on the sounds of German. The *Introduction* to the grammar usually served as a basis. Words used as illustrations were rarely given with their meanings, and had no direct relation to the texts of the grammar. Rare words were often given as illustrations. They occurred but once, and were promptly forgotten together with the sound they were to exemplify. There was no attempt to link the first step to the second: the sound system to the text and the exercises of the lesson. In brief, there was no organic connection between two steps which ought to follow each other at once with logical necessity.

The sooner we remedy this faulty practice, the better it will be for the teaching of German in particular and languages in general.

A *fourth way*, depending entirely on simple imitation, is often pursued by teachers untrained in phonetics. Sometimes it is defended even by capable phoneticians, who believe German pronunciation so simple that pure imitation will suffice and no practical phonetics are needed. No doubt we might come nearer to the truth by saying: Some capable phoneticians defend the presentation of sounds without the aid of practical phonetics not because they believe teachers do not need phonetics, but because they themselves know all "the tricks of the trade" gained by phonetics, and have become impatient with a lengthy introduction to the sounds of German.

However this may be, it is true that the task of the teacher of German is far easier than that of his colleague in French or Spanish; and that able and experienced teachers can reduce phonetics to a minimum.[1] Nevertheless, as a general rule, the

---

[1] See for instance Charles M. Purin, "German Pronunciation," *Monatshefte für deutschen Unterricht* (Nov. 1930), pp. 214–15, and Lydia M. Schmidt, "A Practical Course in Phonetics," *School Review* (Oct. 1915), pp. 555–58.

more conscientious way of practical phonetics will be found not only more interesting for the serious student, but also far more reliable and lasting in its results. And these results are all-important.[1]

Of the several ways above described I personally find the second one best, for it begins with life, with living language, with language in function. It proceeds from the single sound to the syllable and the word, from the word to the phrase, then to the sentence, and finally to the combination of sentences forming the paragraphs of a coherent text. Not only sound but also intonation is easily taught in this manner. Yet there are many ways to heaven. Each experienced teacher is bound to find his own best way, which is always the result of a compromise between an ideal and stern reality. The main thing is practice, not theory. To be precise: an ounce of theory and a ton of practice.

It should be mentioned that the second way can be easily adapted by an experienced teacher to any text whatsoever.

A PRONUNCIATION TEST to measure progress after the sounds of German have been taught is desirable and, according to my personal experience, highly effective. If we scrutinize the sounds to be taught, and include those sounds which students often find bothersome, we shall find approximately 62 different points. Supposing now that we attempt to prepare a pronunciation test, then we may place horizontally in the first line long i with the various ways of expressing this sound orthographically, for instance: wir, mir, hier, ihn, sieht. In the second line we give short i: in, bin, ist, Tisch, immer. In the third line we continue with long e: er, wer, her, See, Lehrer; then comes short e: Nest, Herr, Kälte, Heft, lernen, and finally unaccented e. In the sixth and seventh line we continue with a, long and short, and so on through Viëtor's triangle, and through the consonants, paying due regard to the glottal stop and the problems of stress and quantity. Thus we would finally have something like the following:

[1] In this belief I recommend Lilian L. Stroebe, *Practical Exercises in German Pronunciation* (Henry Holt and Company, 1929), 23 pp.; John Whyte, "On the Teaching of German Pronunciation," *The German Quarterly* (Nov. 1929), pp. 137–50; and other articles and books listed in Oliver's *The Modern Language Teacher's Handbook* (D. C. Heath and Company, 1935) under "Phonetics," "Pronunciation," etc.

	A	B	C	D	E	
1.	wir	mir	hier	ihn	sieht	long i
2.	in	bin	ist	Tisch	immer	short i
3.	er	wer	her	See	Lehrer	long e
4.	Nest	Herr	Kälte	Heft	lernen	short e
5.	{ genau	Schule	alle	haben	Garten }	unstressed e
	{ Mutter	Vater	Schwester	Bruder	Bücher }	
6.	ja	Aal	Vater	Haar	Jahr	long a
7.	dann	Stadt	naß	fallen	hatte	short a
8.	wo	oben	Boot	wohnen	Ohr	long o
9.	kommen	Sonne	dort	morgen	Gott	short o
10.	du	gut	Kuh	Schule	Uhr	long u
11.	um	und	Butter	Mutter	Nuß	short u
12.	für	über	Tür	Schüler	führen	long ü
13.	Hütte	füllen	küssen	müssen	wünschen	short ü
14.	typisch	lyrisch	Syrien	symmetrisch	Synonym	y = ü long or short
15.	schön	König	Öfen	Höhle	Söhne	long ö
16.	öffnen	zwölf	Körper	können	Hölle	short ö
17.	sägen	prägen	Nähe	Ähre	mähen	long ä
18.	Bälle	Bäcker	Männer	Gäste	älter	short ä
19.	Fräulein	läuft	heute	Freund	neu	äu, eu
20.	ein	kein	Seite	Main	Kaiser	ei, ai
21.	auf	Haus	laut	grau	braun	au
22.	Melodie	Poesie	Manie	Partie	Rhapsodie	stressed final ie
23.	Familie	Linie	Spanien	Lilie	Arabien	−ie
24.	Bibel	leben	beben	Biene	Ebbe	b
25.	Park	Lippe	Preis	gelb	herab	p (final b)
26.	Pfennig	Pferd	Apfel	pflegen	Pflicht	pf
27.	dumm	denken	leider	decken	denn	d
28.	Tasche	Tasse	Wand	Wind	rund	t (final d)
29.	Thron	These	Theater	Katheder	Theologie	th = t
30.	gehen	gegen	gegangen	Gegend	geglückt	g
31.	können	kosten	Tag	Krieg	Weg	k (final g)
32.	Christus	Chor	Chaos	Charakter	Chloroform	ch as k
33.	laufen	fallen	bald	Ball	leicht	l
34.	man	manchmal	muß	immer	im	m
35.	nah	Name	nennen	nein	niemand	n
36.	fangen	singen	Ring	Finger	hängen	ng
37.	Knabe	Knie	Knochen	Knopf	Knecht	kn
38.	quer	Quelle	Quadrat	Quartier	Quantität	qu = kw
39.	für	hoffen	Vater	Vetter	von	f
40.	Philosoph	Prophet	Philipp	Sophie	Phantasie	ph = f
41.	was	wissen	weiß	fleißig	wessen	voiceless s

	A	B	C	D	E	
42.	ſo	ſagen	ſie	Roſe	reiſen	voiced ſ
43.	zu	zeigen	Fritz	Hitze	jetzt	z, tz = ts
44.	wahr	Wand	Löwe	zwei	zwar	w = v
45.	November	Klavier	Vaſe	Violine	Villa	v voiced in some words
46.	ſcharf	ſcheinen	ſchlafen	Kirſche	Buſch	ſch = sh
47.	{ ich, Chemie, König	nicht, China, wenig	recht, Chineſe, richtig	ſchlecht, chemiſch, wichtig	rechnen, Chirurg, nichtig }	ich-sound
48.	ach	Tochter	auch	noch	Buch	ach-sound
49.	Fuchs	Ochs	Dachs	Hexe	Axt	–chs and x as ks
50.	ja	jeder	Johanna	Jubel	Jahr	j
51.	ſpät	ſpielen	ſpringen	ſprechen	geſponnen	ſp in initial stem syllable
52.	Stadt	ſtark	anſtatt	Stein	ſterben	ſt in initial stem syllable
53.	Hammer	Held	gehorſam	Faulheit	dahin	h
54.	gehen	ſehen	ſtehlen	Mühe	nahe	silent h
55.	ach	oh	beachten	erinnern	Verein	glottal stop
56.	Raum	Bart	Narr	irren	rühren	r
57.	Nation	Revolution	Aktie	Patient	rationell	ti in foreign words = tsi
58.	{ Antwort, Unſinn, ausgehen	Erzfeind, untreu, ankommen	uralt, unzufrieden, wiederkommen	anmutig, unſchön, aufmachen	angenehm, unartig, zuſchließen }	stressed prefix
59.	Schmeichelei	Heuchelei	Bäckerei	Fiſcherei	Schreiberei	stressed suffix
60.	marſchieren	telefonieren	ſtudieren	telegraphieren	abſorbieren	–ieren
61.	begreifen	empfangen	entgehen	erfahren	zerreißen	unstressed prefix
62.	Student	Muſik	Botanik	Grammatik	Charakter	changing stress

The foregoing is the corrected form of a pronunciation test which I prepared many years ago, to be given at the University of Chicago toward the end of the first quarter to each member of the class in private conference. This pronunciation test has a number of commendable points. The individual student's knowledge of German sounds is quickly established. The 62 lines may be read in full or in part; in full by students not blessed with a sensitive ear; in part by students who pronounce well. The latter will read any one of the five columns and now and then a line straight across. The former, having read the larger part of the test to the instructor, will be told to which points they must pay special attention. They may also be given corrective exercises of a specific nature.

The marginal notes, of course, are merely for the convenience of the instructor.

The test as a whole, however, may be improved. From item 24 on, the arrangement might be more systematic. Not all problems are included, and several columns contain items of unequal validity.

For younger students the test may be reduced to fewer items. For them systematic arrangement is of minor importance. In high school the main point is that the test be confined to words of high frequency or to words which pupils have actually found in their class texts. The test needs a number of coherent sentences or paragraphs so as to check the student's intonation.

TEACHING DEVICES FOR PRONUNCIATION

1. Describe the German sound physiologically. Compare and contrast it with its nearest English sound. Have the students watch your lips. Then pronounce the sound again and again, and have the class repeat after you. Listen closely for mispronunciation. Explain as often as necessary.

2. Proceed from the sound to the syllable, from the syllable to the word, from the word to the word group, the clause, the sentence, and the paragraph.

3. Explain carefully the difference in the organic basis, that is, the way in which persons of different nationalities use their vocal organs.[1] Typical mispronunciations arising naturally from the fixed behavior of the vocal organs of English-speaking students are the following:

Short vowels and consonants are lengthened where they should be pronounced short: Maann for Mann; uund for und.

Unaccented e is pronounced as a long e in final position: Knabee

[1] See the lucid analysis of Prokosch in his *Sounds and History of the German Language* (Henry Holt and Company), pp. 48–50.

for Knabe; Schulee for Schule. A good way of explaining unaccented e is e as in *the book.*

Umlaut vowels are often mispronounced: Schieler for Schüler; scheen for schön; effnen for öffnen. To correct these common errors explain as follows: ü is produced by the lip position for u plus the tongue position for i. Say: Round your lips energetically and pronounce u; now move the tongue forward for the position of i and pronounce ü.

Do likewise for ö. Explain that ö is produced by the lip position for o plus the tongue position for e. Say: Round your lips energetically and pronounce o; move your tongue forward for the position of e and pronounce ö.

ie as a j-sound [iə] causes trouble in such words as Familie, Spanien, Lilie, ie [iə] being often mistaken for long ie in Melodie, Poesie, Offizier, etc.

ie and ei are best taught by saying to the student: "Pronounce the last letter in English."

b, d, and g in final position are often voiced instead of unvoiced: gelb, halb; — Geld, Land; — mag, Tag.

w is mispronounced like English *w* instead of like *v* in *van.* Corrective example: Wir Waschweiber wollen wollene Wäsche waschen.

z or tz is mispronounced like English *z* in *zoo* instead of *ts* in *rats:* Fritz sitzt jetzt zu Hause im Zimmer.

Students often fail to voice s in initial or intervocalic position: So sagen sie Rose, Riese, Rasen.

ch is a troublesome sound for many students. Have the class pronounce *year* with strong emphasis on the *j*-sound. Explain that the unvoiced *j*-sound is equal to the German ch-sound. Then illustrate how the point of articulation of ch varies automatically with the preceding vowel: ich, recht, acht, auch, noch, Buch. Ich habe das Buch noch nicht recht gelesen. Ach, ich auch noch nicht recht.

Another approach to the ch-sound is to say to the student: "Pronounce i, whisper it, raise your tongue and pronounce ich, nicht, recht; pronounce u, whisper it, raise your tongue and pronounce ach, doch, Buch.

The middle Western *r* (often called "inverted *r*" because the tip of the tongue is turned back or inverted) is usually substituted for the lingual or the uvular *r.*

The lingual *r* is produced by two or three taps of the tongue against the ridge of the upper gums directly behind the teeth. Have the students pronounce slowly English *bring.* Have them emphasize the *r*-sound which, when pronounced as in London English, gives an excellent basis for the lingual *r*.

The uvular *r* can be taught in an amusing way by satirizing a German who carries his Zäpfchen r into English words: *roast beef and brown gravy; cream and crackers; our dear brother Rudi.*

The glottal stop [?] is often omitted, and words are run together: der Vereiniſtinamerika instead of Der Ver ?ein ?iſt ?in ?Amerika.

The l-sound causes difficulty in certain positions for English-speaking students. In German the tip of the tongue touches the front edge of the upper gums; the blade of the tongue remains flat and does not arch as in the English *l*; I in initial position usually causes no difficulty; in final position and before consonants it is found difficult not to arch the tongue backward: lang, liegen, leben, bald, hell, Ball, Knall.

4. Before asking your student to repeat, first pronounce slowly several times. Have the class repeat. Then pronounce in natural tempo, asking the class to do likewise. Remember that the teacher's ear must be very attentive.

5. Concert work in the beginning should be planned and prepared. In preparing it, mark your text, divide it into word groups, clauses, and sentences, always visualizing the class confronting you.

6. Make use of the best speakers in the class. They will relieve you of the strain of constant corrections. Assign one problem to each, permitting them to correct a mistake in pronunciation as soon as it has been made. Students so honored are grateful and lighten your task considerably.

7. In the beginning it is very important that every text assigned for oral reading should be previously gone through or even practiced in class, at least in high school, during the first semester.

8. Prepare exercises to practice difficult sounds which are often mispronounced: Knie, Knabe; Familie, Symphonie; ich, echt, acht, auch, Woche, Tuch; schon, schön; Buch, Bücher; Beine, Biene, Bühne; zeige, Ziege, Züge; etc.

9. Have the students read aloud for a short period every day. At first correct each mispronunciation. Later do not interrupt, but listen carefully, mark down errors, and comment only after the reading is finished, or have the best speakers in the class do so.

10. Encourage reading in a low tone at home. Students whose pronunciation has been neglected ordinarily show a decided improvement after a short time.

11. Have poems memorized. As soon as possible procure phonograph records which will recite the poem as often as the students wish to hear it. There are several firms specializing in records. The persons recording are for the most part well-known phoneticians, actors, or artists. The phonograph is of the utmost importance. No instructor, however strong, can hope to equal the endurance, patience, and precision of the machine.[1]

12. When you have finished a class text, assign to each student one page for fluent reading. In this manner a given text can be reread in class within a short time. In a good college class 15 to 20 pages can be read in a 50-minute period. This is an excellent exercise. It reviews pronunciation, vocabulary, idioms, and sentence structure. Students usually find it highly enjoyable and encouraging.

13. Give individual assignments to individual students to overcome their specific difficulties. Say for instance: "Mr. Jones, will you try to make a special effort with your favorite sounds, the ie and the ei, the ü and ö, the final b and the initial s?"

14. Use German as much as possible in class. The more training you give your student in hearing, the better his own pronunciation is likely to become. The learner's ability to understand and pronounce correctly depends entirely on the amount of correct German he listens to with serious intent to learn.

15. Correct untiringly. Do not hope for perfection. The task will never end, neither for you, nor for the student. Yet faith, energy, and endurance will bring certain reward.

DICTATION is a teaching device of great effectiveness. It is perhaps the most economical exercise in all language teaching and learning. Nevertheless we often hear that dictation is quite unimportant in reading courses. In very brief courses of six to twelve weeks' duration this argument carries weight. In courses

---

[1] Cf. H. M. Schulze, "Sprechmaschine und Schule," *Die neueren Sprachen* (Sept. 1926), pp. 625–28. Also John Whyte, "On the Use of Phonograph Records in the Teaching of German Pronunciation," *German Quarterly* (Nov. 1931), pp. 170–74. Also see Oliver, *op. cit.*, pp. 495 ff.

of two years in high school or college, however, we should devote as much time to this effective exercise as circumstances allow. To be fully convinced of this we need only consider the following:

When we dictate, the student hears, writes, speaks, and reads. More precisely: he listens carefully to what is dictated; he writes down what he hears or believes he hears; while he writes he involuntarily pronounces silently the words he is writing; and when he has finished he reads and rereads his sentences and paragraphs for correction.

In other words, the student is forced to devote his undivided attention to the sounds uttered. He shows whether or not he can express orthographically the sounds he has heard, that is, he learns to spell. By the fourfold simultaneous activity of hearing, writing, silent speaking, and silent reading he exercises all the functions of language.

It is said that some students can write dictation without understanding what they are writing. This objection need not be taken too seriously. No experienced teacher fails to discover a Faulpelz. A clever bluffer with keen ears can probably write a Latin dictation, if masterfully given, fairly well without grasping its sense. In the case of French or Spanish this is far more unlikely because of frequent linkings and elisions, and an occasional progressive or regressive assimilation. In German it might under rare conditions be possible, but is hardly probable. The effectiveness of dictation, even though it may vary with different languages, with the student's attitude, and the instructor's experience, remains nevertheless fundamentally unimpaired, important, and far-reaching.

THE TECHNIQUE OF DICTATION

1. Prepare the material to be dictated carefully. Mark the difficult sounds; mark stress groups and word groups. The grouping of speech units is particularly important. Prepare for a dictation exercise by dictating the passage to an imaginary class.

2. The next day say to your students: „Wir ſchreiben ein Diktat. Nehmen Sie Feder und Papier. Ich leſe zuerſt den ganzen Satz, dann kurze Wortgruppen. Jeden Satz und jede Wortgruppe leſe ich zuerſt zweimal langſam, dann zweimal in natürlichem Tempo. Sehen Sie auf

meine Lippen. Schreiben Sie nicht, bevor ich es sage. Fertig?" Then begin. Take care that the words in your directions are clearly understood. Do not forget your promise. Dictate slowly. Repeat each word group several times.

3. Start with the next word groups when most of the students look up. Be patient. Students with defective hearing need sympathy, not rebuke. Consult with slow students after class.

4. Give dictations regularly, especially during the first quarter or semester. A short sentence a day is far better than a long paragraph given rarely. What counts is frequent practice. Students who are given dictation regularly show, as a rule, more interest, zest, and progress.

5. Do not become alarmed about the time problem. Give short assignments — two or three short sentences for thorough preparation at home in the beginning, a short paragraph later. The dictation itself may take 5 to 15 minutes, including corrections. Each student exchanges his paper with a neighbor at the left or the right, in front of, or behind him. The books are opened, and the student's paper is compared with the original version in the text. Errors are corrected and the number of errors is marked in large figures on each paper. Under the figure the correcting student writes: *Corrected by* and his name. After class, ten minutes, as a rule, are sufficient to examine the papers rapidly, and to get a fairly accurate idea of the results. On the whole, dictation can be called economical. It promotes faster learning with less drain on the teacher's time than any other exercise.

6. All dictations must be based on materials strictly corresponding to the level of the class. As the course progresses and the materials gradually become more advanced, the technique of dictation may be slightly modified. While in the beginning every dictation is first assigned for preparation at home, the teacher soon finds that many words and idioms can safely be taken for granted. Some instructors may find it advisable to dictate in longer word groups, pronounce each word group only once, and keep the class on the *qui vive* by reading faster.

7. A record of each student's errors should be kept in a special notebook showing other data of each pupil's performance. A glance at the record will indicate, through the numbers of errors

in each dictation, the student's ability to grasp sounds and to write them down correctly. By implication this is at the same time a fairly reliable indication of the learner's aural comprehension.

WHAT MIGHT BE DICTATED

1. Single words previously studied containing certain elusive sounds which frequently cause difficulty. Cognates are useful in driving home the specific points of difficulty they imply.

2. Short sentences and simple idioms of great frequency.

3. Verb forms which the class has previously studied.

4. Nouns for which the student has to supply the article, definite or indefinite.

5. Days of the week, names of the month, and numerals. The latter can serve two purposes, dictation and aural comprehension. For aural comprehension the numerals are read, and the student writes down the numbers.

6. Type sentences embodying specific grammatical problems.

7. An interesting short anecdote written entirely in words familiar to the class.

8. Directions which have often been given to the class.

9. Sentences differing slightly from the original through a change in person, tense, or number.

10. Sentences in which one vital form is omitted. The English translation is supplied first. Example: *He said he was ill.* Er sagte, er —— krank. *Supply the missing form.*

11. A short paragraph representing the instructor's summary of a text read in class.

12. Questions based on a book previously read. The student's answers which must be very brief and may be in English will show how well he has read the book.

13. A dictation given by the best speaker in the class.

14. Idioms lending themselves easily to manipulation. Example: Schreiben Sie im Perfektum: Es tut mir leid. Es gelingt mir nicht. Ich stelle eine Frage, etc., etc.

15. The assignment for the next class period, which may be written on the blackboard in the rear of the class so that weak students can copy later what has been dictated.

16. A dictation which is written by a superior student on the

blackboard in the rear. Later, students exchange papers and correct.

17. Double dictation. After the dictation the instructor asks his class to translate the passage into English.

These are but a few of the endless possibilities. A number of books and articles deal with the subject more fully.[1]

In conclusion we must point out that three things are certain to determine the result of instruction in pronunciation. The first is the model furnished by the instructor and based on a thorough knowledge of practical phonetics and all its aids. The second is patience tempered by sympathetic understanding. The third is endurance, which, according to Carlyle, is nothing more than patience concentrated.

BIBLIOGRAPHY

DRACH, ERICH. *Deutsche Aussprachelehre für den Gebrauch im Ausland.* Frankfurt am Main, 1931.

JONES, DANIEL. "The Importance of Intonation in the Pronunciation of Foreign Languages." *Modern Language Teaching* (1914), pp. 201–05.

KLINGHARDT, H. *Sprechmelodie und Sprechtakt.* Marburg, 1925.

KUHLMANN, W. *Deutsche Aussprache: Lehr- und Lesebuch für Ausländer.* Heidelberg, 1933.

PROKOSCH, EDUARD. *Sounds and History of the German Language* (New York: Henry Holt and Company, 1916), Chapters II and III.

PURIN, CHARLES M. "German Pronunciation." *Monatshefte für deutschen Unterricht* (Nov. 1930), pp. 214–15.

SCHMIDT, LYDIA M. "A Practical Course in Phonetics." *School Review* (Oct. 1915), pp. 555–58.

SCHULZE, H. M. "Sprechmaschine und Schule." *Die neueren Sprachen* (Sept. 1926), pp. 625–28.

SIEBS, THEODOR. *Deutsche Bühnenaussprache-Hochsprache.* Köln, 1927.

STROEBE, LILIAN L. *Practical Exercises in German Pronunciation.* New York: Henry Holt and Company, 1929. 23 pp.

VIËTOR, WILHELM. *Wie ist die Aussprache des Deutschen zu lehren?* Marburg, 1928.

—— *Deutsches Aussprachewörterbuch.* Vierte und fünfte Auflage. Leipzig, 1931.

---

[1] See Oliver, *op. cit.*, pp. 148 f.

WHYTE, JOHN. "On the Teaching of German Pronunciation." *The German Quarterly* (Nov. 1929), pp. 137-50.

—— "On the Use of Phonograph Records in the Teaching of German Pronunciation." *German Quarterly* (Nov. 1931), pp. 170-74.

SUGGESTIONS FOR DISCUSSIONS AND EXERCISES

1. Discuss briefly the importance of sound in all language learning.
2. Discuss phonetic or organic basis (Prokosch, §§ 51-52).
3. Read the articles of Purin and Schmidt; compare them as to their most important points, and write a summary combining the best features of both.
4. Explain each sound physiologically: ü, ö, ch, lingual r, uvular r, the glottal stop.
5. Name: (a) about five teaching devices for pronunciation enumerated above which you prefer to all others; (b) some important points in the technique of dictation; (c) the factors which make dictation important.
6. Dictate to the teachers' class (a) a number of sentences for beginners in high school; (b) a paragraph for second-year high-school pupils; (c) a paragraph for an advanced college class.
7. Prepare a pronunciation test: (a) for high-school pupils at the end of the first semester; (b) for college students at the end of this time; (c) for the teaching candidates in this course.
8. Prepare a pronunciation test using as a basis Morgan's 1018 starred words. See *Minimum Standard German Vocabulary* by Walter Wadepuhl and B. Q. Morgan (F. S. Crofts & Co., 1936).
9. Do likewise, confining yourself to the 500 words marked by a double asterisk in C. M. Purin's *Standard German Vocabulary* (The Heath-Chicago Series. D. C. Heath and Company, 1937).
10. Report on the following books and articles: (a) John Whyte, (b) Stroebe, (c) Daniel Jones, (d) Klinghardt, (e) Schulze, (f) Kuhlmann, (g) Drach, (h) Viëtor, (i) Siebs.

CHAPTER FIVE

WORDS AND IDIOMS

THE IMPORTANCE OF VOCABULARY. Professor Ben D. Wood in his thorough study of modern language tests observes that "deriding the value of mere vocabulary is not an infrequent indoor sport at some teachers' meetings." [1] Then he points out the close correlation which actually exists between vocabulary on the one hand and the various language skills on the other. In fact, the disregard for "mere knowledge of words" is completely unfounded. We are immediately convinced of this when students try to comprehend spoken or written discourse in the foreign language, or if they try to express themselves in it. The smaller their vocabulary, the more inefficient is their command of language for any purpose whatever. Words, after all, are the very substance from which language was developed in the course of the ages.

WORD COUNTS. Not long ago nothing was known about the relative frequency of a given word, an idiom, or a syntactical usage except in a rough approximation. Students were made to memorize words and idioms of rare frequency, and sentences typifying constructions of very infrequent occurrence. In 1898 there appeared Kaeding's *Häufigkeitswörterbuch der deutschen Sprache.*[2] About ten years later Professor E. W. Bagster-Collins suggested the use of frequency counts as a basis for the standardization of curriculum material in modern languages.[3] Then there followed

[1] Ben D. Wood, *New York Experiments with New-Type Modern Language Tests* (The Macmillan Company, 1927), p. 127.

[2] "Festgestellt durch einen Arbeitsausschuß der deutschen Stenographiesysteme" (Berlin, 1898).

[3] See "Beobachtungen auf dem Gebiete des fremdsprachlichen Unterrichts," *Monatshefte für deutsche Sprache und Pädagogik* (Oktober, 1909), pp. 216–25.

a number of important studies which proved that the idea of frequency as a basis for the construction of teaching materials had borne fruit.[1]

The significance of word counts has now been generally recognized. For those who object to them as a matter of principle, it is necessary to point out that it is quite impossible to make a judicious selection of words for beginners without first determining which words are of great utility and which ones are not. Wood, in an analysis of twelve grammars and four composition books, all in common use in French classes, found that approximately 6000 word stems occurred in all, and that only 134 word stems were common to all the sixteen books.[2] The same pitiful state of affairs had been shown for German by Wadepuhl in his excellent pioneer study as early as 1923.[3] Inquiries into the vocabularies used in Spanish textbooks failed to show more favorable results.[4] The implications are obvious:

Word counts and an exact knowledge of the frequency of words are advantageous to everyone concerned. The teacher knows what to teach, the student what to learn, the author of textbooks what words are of greatest utility. Administrative officers, through the use of tests which are confined to a definite vocabulary, are enabled to place students more easily and adequately. Moreover, the transfer of students from one institution to the other is greatly facilitated.

Nor are these the only potential benefits of determining the most frequent word stems. Supposing we know 2000 of them. Through the study of prefixes, suffixes, and word combinations, through

---

[1] E. W. Bagster-Collins, "A Brief Study Showing the Relation between the Vocabulary and Treatment of the Annotated Reading Text," *Modern Language Journal*, II (May, 1918), pp. 341–51. Robert Herndon Fife, "Frequency Word Lists," *Modern Language Forum* (Oct. 1930), pp. 125–28. V. A. C. Henmon, "The Vocabulary Problem in the Modern Foreign Languages," *Monatshefte für deutschen Unterricht* (Feb. 1930), pp. 33–39.

[2] "A Comparative Study of the Vocabularies of Sixteen Textbooks," *Modern Language Journal* (Feb. 1927), pp. 263–89.

[3] Walter Wadepuhl, "A Standardized Vocabulary for Elementary German," *Modern Language Journal* (Oct. 1923), pp. 23–30.

[4] C. W. Cartwright, "A Study of the Vocabularies of Eleven Spanish Grammars and Fifteen Reading Texts," *Modern Language Journal* (Oct. 1925), pp. 1–14.

cognates, synonyms, and antonyms, we can build up a vocabulary of, say, 7000 words or more. Or if we look into the future optimistically we may some day take about 1500 frequent words and construct a dictionary containing 24,000 words as Michael West and James Garret Endicott have so ably done for English.[1]

THE GERMAN FREQUENCY WORD BOOK by Bayard Q. Morgan appeared in 1929 as Volume IX of the *Study*.[2] Morgan gives us two word lists based on Kaeding's nearly 11,000,000 running words drawn from popular, literary, political, scientific, and technical material. List A contains 2402 in order of frequency. Each word is provided with a serial number from 1 (ber) to 2403 (Schwelle). List B is arranged in alphabetical order, each "basic" word being followed by a serial number indicating the frequency series established in the first list. After each basic word there follow its derivatives. List B as a whole contains 6000 words within the "threshold of frequency." [3]

In 1931 the American Association of Teachers of German appointed a committee to study the question of a minimum standard vocabulary. Two years later the committee submitted its final word list, which was adopted by the Association and published in two forms, as a mere word list,[4] and as a dictionary with English equivalents.[5] As Morgan states in the Preface, the dictionary was published by the Association "with the explicit object of helping to promote research into the problems of German pedagogy." In this spirit Professor C. M. Purin followed up his *Standard German Vocabulary of 2000 Words and Idioms* by a revised edition in which he avoided some inevitable shortcomings of the first.[6] The distinctive feature of his little book is that nearly every item

---

[1] *The New Method English Dictionary* explaining meanings of 24,000 items within a vocabulary of 1490 words. London: Longmans, Green & Co., 1935.

[2] Based on Kaeding's *Häufigkeitswörterbuch der deutschen Sprache* (The Macmillan Company, 1929), xiii + 87 pp.

[3] For further detail see Robert Herndon Fife, *A Summary of Reports on the Modern Foreign Languages* (The Macmillan Company, 1931), pp. 194–99.

[4] Cf. *German Quarterly* (May, 1934), pp. 87–119.

[5] Cf. Walter Wadepuhl and Bayard Quincy Morgan, *Minimum Standard German Vocabulary* (F. S. Crofts & Co., 1936).

[6] The University of Chicago Press, 1931; revised 1937 for the Heath-Chicago Series under the title *A Standard German Vocabulary of 2932 Words and 1500 Idioms*.

is used in an illustrative sentence, so that the learner is able to study words and idioms with immediate profit.

Professor Curtis C. D. Vail has done important work in facilitating the comparison of national and local standards in the choice of words. He subjected the existing word lists and certain books applying them to a searching criticism, and finally succeeded in reducing them to lists for the first, second, and third year respectively.[1] The total and final list was adopted by the committee of which he was chairman. It is known as the *New York State Basic German Word List*, and is used as a basis of instruction in many Eastern schools.[2]

THE STUDY OF WORDS AND IDIOMS lends itself readily to discussion under all phases of language learning: aural comprehension and reading; speaking and writing. But first we shall speak briefly of the word in isolation.

We may consider a word from three different aspects: (1) The word as a sequence of sounds represented by written or printed symbols or letters; (2) the word as a unit of speech containing a definite concept or idea; (3) the word as a component part of a sentence, within which it may vary in form and function, its meaning being determined by the sentence as a whole.

If we scrutinize these three aspects, we notice immediately that one is totally incomplete without the other, namely: (1) sound is empty without meaning; (2) meaning is established only after the sequence of sounds has been identified with its meaning many, many times; (3) word meanings often vary, depending entirely on the form and the function of a given word within a given sentence. Therefore the three aspects are inseparable in regard to language in function; and since they are inseparable in living language, word study should be functional rather than static, should proceed from the sentence rather than from the isolated word.[3]

---

[1] "Basic Vocabulary Studies," *German Quarterly* (May, 1932), pp. 123–30. "A Word List Correlation," *ibid.* (Jan. 1936), pp. 10–16. "Basic Word and Idiom Lists" (Albany: University of the State of New York Press, 1933), 22 pp.

[2] See also Vail's article in the *German Quarterly* for March, 1933: "Frequency List Problems," pp. 53–62.

[3] See *Language Learning* (The University of Chicago Press, 1935), pp. 7–16 and 33–43 for problems implicated in this chapter.

Of the laws of learning previously set forth,[1] two seem of particular importance in vocabulary and idiom study — the law of use or practice and the law of frequency or repetition. The former is adequately summarized in the sentence: Vocabulary is learned by being used; the latter, epitomized in the ancient saying: *Repetitio mater studiorum est,* leads us to the question of active and passive vocabulary.

ACTIVE AND PASSIVE VOCABULARY are closely related. Passive vocabulary is merely recognized in hearing and reading; active vocabulary can be used in speaking and writing. All vocabulary is passive in the beginning; through often repeated exercise in all language skills it gradually becomes active. Our passive vocabulary, native or foreign, surpasses the active one at all times. People who read widely are familiar with innumerable words which they cannot use in spoken or written discourse.

Unfortunately we do not know and cannot know at what stage the foreign passive vocabulary turns into an active one. All depends on elements, to a great extent, beyond observation and control. The basic deciding factors seem to be interest, will, application, and above all, native gifts. Nevertheless it is safe to state that the total amount of successful application, that is, mainly practice in speaking and writing, unfailingly determines the turning point of passive into active vocabulary.

All in all, repetition and practice decide.

B. Q. Morgan and Lydia M. Oberdeck have made a helpful study of active and passive vocabulary.[2] Their purpose was to throw further light on this question by measuring and determining, through a battery of tests, the rate of progress in acquiring active and passive vocabulary. About one hundred seventy students representing various stages of learning in the first to the fifth semester were tested. The authors conclude:

> The tendencies observed in this study may be summed up as follows:
>
> (1) There is considerable variation in the span of active and passive vocabulary among students of the same graded class.

[1] Cf. Chapter III, pp. 51–54.
[2] "Active and Passive Vocabulary," in *Studies in Modern Language Teaching, Publications of the American and Canadian Committees on Modern Languages,* Vol. XVII (The Macmillan Company, 1930), pp. 213–21.

(2) From the very start the passive vocabulary exceeds the active.

(3) As development in the language proceeds, the passive vocabulary develops faster than the active.

(4) When that stage of proficiency is approached in which there is considerable attention paid to the active use of the language, there is a compensating development of the active vocabulary.

(5) Despite this, progress in the mastery of the active vocabulary never equals that of the passive.[1]

In a personal letter Morgan confirms point 5 by stating: "Our study indicated that active vocabulary rarely equals half of the passive," a most interesting finding which is fully borne out by my personal experience both as student and as teacher.

HELPS AND DEVICES FOR BUILDING THE GERMAN VOCABULARY. The following table suggests twenty devices for acquiring a passive vocabulary and, in the opposite column, twenty more by which a passive vocabulary knowledge may gradually be converted into a more active one. First read the statements under *Passive* and *Active;* then read each item in opposite columns (1 and 15–20) separately, and items set off by brackets (2–4 and 5–14), the items at the left straight down, then the statement in the opposite column.

Passive: The general principle is recognition in aural comprehension and reading.	*Active:* The general principle is reconstruction in speaking and writing.
1. Listening attentively to words, phrases and sentences and vocalizing them according to the teacher's model.	1. Not merely listening and vocalizing, but committing them to memory.
2. Reading aloud. 3. Reading silently. 4. Rereading.	2–4. Not only reading aloud, silently, and rereading, but attempts at reproduction of what has been read.

[1] Otto P. Schinnerer and H. G. Wendt give in the March number of 1933 of *The German Quarterly,* pp. 77–90, "A Suggested List of 1,000 Active German Words." See also Michael West's important article, "The Present Position in Vocabulary Selection for Foreign Language Teaching," *Modern Language Journal* (March, 1937), pp. 433–37.

5. Judicious use of word lists.
6. Cognates.
7. Antonyms.
8. Synonyms.
9. Topical arrangement of words.
10. Prefixes and suffixes.
11. Word families.
12. Paraphrases and definitions.
13. Word combination.
14. Notebooks.

5–14. The devices listed in 5 to 14 are also applicable for the acquisition of an active vocabulary. The nature of the exercises and the degree of intensity with which they are executed repeatedly determine the result.

15. Exercises aiming at recognition of grammatical forms.

15. Exercises aiming at recall and application of grammatical forms.

16. Recognition of words, word forms, idioms, and sentences.

16. Reconstruction of these.

17. Any exercise involving the recognition of meanings.

17. Any exercise involving the reproduction of living language.

18. Constant repetition of words for passive use (hearing and reading).

18. Constant repetition of words for active use (oral exercises and writing).

19. Time for object lessons and dramatizing is usually lacking.

19. Object lessons and dramatizing are in vogue in some institutions.

20. Speaking and writing are used to facilitate recognition in reading.

20. Speaking and writing are constantly used to develop these skills for their own sake.

On reading the above table a second time, you will see clearly that the difference in passive and active vocabulary is mainly one of degree. In passive vocabulary one recalls the meaning; when the passive vocabulary, through repetition and practice, has become active, one recalls the meaning together with its application.

I shall now discuss in turn: (1) word lists; (2) cognates; (3) synonyms; (4) antonyms; (5) prefixes and suffixes; (6) word combinations; (7) word families; (8) topical arrangement; (9) paraphrases and definitions; (10) notebooks.

1. WORD LISTS are nothing but raw material. Memorizing such

lists mechanically is nothing short of medieval torture. Yet a resourceful teacher can treat a small word list so judiciously that it becomes interesting. Words of great frequency may be used with their most usual meaning in brief, preferably felicitous sentences, and be given to the class as a daily assignment. Five words a day equal five hundred words a semester.

Things to remember are these: Words without context are unnatural. *"Sentence words"* are rare. Most words have several or many meanings, and we generally learn one meaning at a time. Words in context are more easily retained than isolated words.

2. COGNATES are most important in the beginning. Cognates may (*a*) be full; (*b*) be partial; (*c*) be misleading; (*d*) show vowel change; (*e*) show consonant change; (*f*) show vowel and consonant change.

(*a*) Full cognates: Arm, Ball, Finger, Frost, Hunger, Name, Park, Ring, Sack, Sand, Wind, Winter, Wolf, Butter, Form, Hand, etc.

(*b*) Partial cognates: Appetit, Bär, Busch, Eisberg, Fisch, Garten, Mann, Marsch, Westen, Prinz, Puls, Schuh, Storch, etc.[1]

(*c*) Misleading cognates or cognates differing in meaning: Bein, Blume, Feind, Hose, Knabe, blank, eitel, glatt, handeln, krank, etc.[2]

(*d*) Cognates with vowel change:
German a to English *e:* Rast, Stamm, Wrack
German a to English *ea:* Jahr, Mahl, klar, mager
German ie to English *ee:* Bier, Knie, Kiel, Stier, fliehen, etc.

(*e*) Cognates with consonant change:
German t or tt to English *d:* Bett, Gott, Wort, Garten, Karte, Sattel, hart, unter
German d to English *th:* Dorn, Distel, Ding, dick, nord, danken
German b to English *v* or *f:* Salbe, Grab, Sieb, Silber, Stab, Kalb, etc.

(*f*) Cognates with vowel and consonant change:
alt, kalt, halten, Falte
Leber, Weib, leben, geben, streben
Buch, Deich, Grieche, brechen, etc.

[1] Examples are taken from *Allerlei* (The Heath-Chicago Series. D. C. Heath and Company, 1933), Graded German Reader, I, pp. 2 ff.

[2] Cf. *Building the German Vocabulary.* (The Heath-Chicago Series. D. C. Heath and Company, 1928), pp. 4 ff. For cognates with vowel or consonant change, or both, see *ibid.*, pp. 2–5.

Full and partial cognates are extremely helpful in a number of ways: in teaching sounds by contrasting German with English sounds; in introducing self-explanatory words; in presenting simple sentences understandable at once, making them excellent for practice in pronunciation and intonation.

3. Synonyms. Exact synonyms hardly exist, and all synonyms must be used with great caution. Only in rare cases is it possible to find for the carefully chosen word of the author a word or expression equally fitting. Yet synonyms can be used advantageously to explain words and phrases of a coherent text, and even then they merely serve as a potential help to the meaning. Or to state the same idea in other words:

The danger of synonyms lies: (1) in replacing das treffende Wort by one less fitting and proper; (2) in explaining an unknown word or expression by one equally unknown; (3) in using a rare word in explanation of a frequent one. Besides there is the danger of misjudging the usefulness of synonyms as a teaching device; for, like antonyms, they are merely a possible way of avoiding translation and keeping the learner steeped in the foreign language.

Let me give a few common words with their possible synonyms: haben — besitzen;   auch — ebenfalls;   selber — selbst;   schließen — zu= machen. The fitness of these explaining words depends entirely on the context to be explained and, even more, on the student's knowledge of words.

4. Antonyms. An antonym is ordinarily defined as a word which in meaning is directly opposed to another word in the same language. Antonyms are of much greater usefulness than synonyms, particularly if their use is limited to frequent words and if their meaning is a clear-cut opposite of the word to be explained. Are the following unmistakable antonyms? der Abend — der Morgen;   achten — mißachten;   ähnlich — unähnlich;   alles — nichts; alt — jung;   anfangen — enden;   angenehm — unangenehm;   die Angst — der Mut;   antworten — fragen;   arm — reich;   auf — unter;   auf= machen — zumachen;   aufpassen — schlafen;   außen — innen;   außer= ordentlich — gewöhnlich.

Not all of them are; achten may require verachten, ähnlich may need verschieden; alt may demand neu, and anfangen, aufhören. All depends on the context to be interpreted.

Unmistakable antonyms seem to be: geben — nehmen; stehen — liegen; stellen — legen; herrschen — dienen; kommen — gehen; leben — sterben; öffnen — schließen; lieben — hassen; sprechen — schweigen; Recht — Unrecht; Tag — Nacht; dieser — jener; unter — über; groß — klein; weit — nah; voll — leer; schwarz — weiß; viel — wenig; mehr — weniger; erst — letzt; hier — dort, and many others.

Unless the explaining antonym is known to the student and is, moreover, in unmistakably opposite meaning to the word to be explained, the latter must be translated.

5. PREFIXES AND SUFFIXES. The nature of the German language requires a more or less intensive study of the meanings and connotations of prefixes and suffixes, which are best introduced early in the grammar or the reader. These important particles should be practiced systematically as soon as a sufficient number of actual occurrences have been gathered from the text used. The most important suffixes for first-year high school are: -er, -in, -chen, -lein, -e, -heit, -keit, -ung, -ei, -ig, -isch, -lich. In the second year the use of certain verbal forms and additional suffixes might be taken up: infinitives, infinitive stems and past stems as nouns; -ling, -los, -nis, -sal, -schaft, -tum, -artig, -bar, -erlei, -fach, -haft. The most important connotations of inseparable prefixes: be-, ent-, er-, ge-, ver-, zer- (easiest are ent-, er-, and zer-) should be explained,[1] and some practice of word combination belongs in all elementary classes. However, nothing more definite can be said. All depends on conditions so varied in nature as to defy analysis as well as specific counsel.

In college classes of one-year duration these problems should, of course, receive as much attention as circumstances will allow.

6. THE STUDY OF WORD COMBINATIONS is of importance especially in intermediate and advanced classes. The most common types of word combinations are the following:

Noun and noun:

    der Sommerregen, die Abendsonne, der Augenblick, der Handschuh, der Sonntagmorgen, etc.

[1] Compare the exercises in the Graded German Readers 1–12, and *Building the German Vocabulary*, pp. 6–39.

Adjective and noun:

    der Dummkopf, der Edelmann, der Schnellzug, die Jungfrau, der Schwarzseher, etc.

Verb and noun:

    der Schreibfehler, das Badehaus, das Kaufhaus, das Lehrbuch, das Rauchzimmer, etc.

Adverb, preposition, or particle and noun:

    die Jetztzeit, das Fürwort, der Mißerfolg, das Übergewicht, der Oberarm, etc.

Noun and adjective:

    armlang, berghoch, bildschön, blutrot, charakterfest, ehrenvoll, eisenstark, fehlerfrei, etc.

Adjective (or adverb) and adjective:

    weitberühmt, dunkelblau, tiefernst, hochheilig, schwarzhaarig, überfein, immerfertig, bitterwenig, etc.

Word combinations are an excellent means for reviewing those words which have occurred singly before.[1]

7. WORD FAMILIES are groups of words built around the same stem: arbeiten, die Arbeit, der Arbeiter, die Arbeiterin, arbeitslos, bearbeiten, der Mitarbeiter.[2] The distinctive merit of a word family is that each member of the family supports each other member, that each is apt, through the stem common to all, to suggest or even to recall other members of the group. Review is effective to the extent to which members of the same word family have actually occurred before.

8. TOPICAL GROUPING of vocabulary serves a most desirable purpose. After a number of selections have been read and reread, or made the basis of oral exercises, a key word suggests a series of other words logically or psychologically connected; for instance:

die Familie: der Vater, die Mutter, der Großvater, die Großmutter; der Sohn, die Tochter, der Vetter, die Kusine, der Onkel, die Tante, etc., or

der Tag: die Nacht, der Abend, der Morgen, der Vormittag, der Nachmittag, der Sonntag, der Montag, etc., der Feiertag, der Schultag, der Regentag, der Schneetag, etc.

---

[1] Cf. *Building the German Vocabulary*, pp. 40–44.   [2] Cf. Wadepuhl and Morgan, *op. cit.*, for approximately 2150 word stems, many of which are developed through derivatives into word families.

The advantages of topical grouping of words become significant if the student has a notebook into which from time to time
he enters new words under their proper key word; or also if they
are used in advanced composition classes.

9. PARAPHRASES AND DEFINITIONS belong to a later stage of
language study. A paraphrase is a restatement or a rewording of
a given phrase or passage; a definition is a short description or a
detailed explanation of a word or a thing by its attributes, proper-
ties, or relations.

Paraphrases:

er ſetzte das Holzfeuer in Brand = er legte Feuer an das Holz;
ſich entkleiden = die Kleider abnehmen = ſich ausziehen;
er war unverwundbar = man konnte ihn nicht verwunden.

Definitions:

unterliegen = beſiegt werden; flüſtern = leiſe ſprechen;
ſchweigen = nichts ſagen, ſtill ſein, nicht ſprechen;
ein Imbiß = ein kleines Eſſen oder Mahl.

Definitions may require many sentences, sometimes even an
entire lecture, as for instance in a course on literature. Each of
the following definitions may be followed by a lengthy talk:

die Nibelungen = ein ſagenhaftes Volk von Helden, etc., etc.
Heinrich I. = deutſcher Kaiſer von 919 bis 936, etc., etc.
Melanchthon = ein berühmter Humaniſt des 16. Jahrhunderts, etc.

Both paraphrases and definitions are destined to play a much
greater role, even in our brief reading courses, than heretofore.
The more we develop the reading method, the nearer we are bound
to come to a more direct approach to the meanings of words.
Both devices are extremely effective in making reading direct.
They avoid translation and keep the student steeped in the foreign
tongue.

The danger of these helps lies, as in certain others discussed
above, in explaining that which is unknown by that which is more
unknown, or as Latin has it: *ignotus per ignotius*. In all paraphrases and definitions, unfamiliar words must be avoided or
given with their translations whenever the learner is not likely
to remember the explaining words.

NOTEBOOKS have often been recommended as a sure means to

all sorts of knowledge and skills. I am convinced that the effectiveness of the notebook depends entirely on the teacher. If the teacher has satisfied himself by previous experience that notebooks are effective under his specific conditions, they should be used. If he has found them a hindrance, they should be abandoned. In the former case he will never fail to give brief, concise, and effective directions to his students; in the latter he and his students are wasting precious time by not dropping a means which he has found ineffective. Common sense, precise guidance, and corrections at regular intervals by the instructor may turn the use of notebooks into a complete success.[1]

Finally we come to idioms — in French *idiotismes* — those elusive and bothersome Redewendungen which so eloquently express the specific and peculiar genius of the foreign tongue.

IDIOMS. What is an idiom? A precise definition is indispensable; first, because of the elusiveness of the term; second, because many instructors fail to recognize an idiom when they see one. Idioms are important. Unless we pay due attention to them, we fail to give instruction in one of the most difficult features of the German language.

In his *Spanish Idiom List*, Professor Hayward Keniston, for the purposes of his study, defines an idiom as "(1) an expression peculiar to Spanish, or (2) an expression which differs in form from its English equivalent."[2] Similarly Professor Frederic D. Cheydleur in the *French Idiom List* states: an idiom is defined as being "(1) an expression peculiar to French in thought, or (2) as differing from its English equivalent in grammatical form or in vocabulary."[3] Professor Edward F. Hauch calls an idiom "an expression

[1] Helpful suggestions may be found in J. D. Deihl, "Individual Differences and Notebook Work in Modern Foreign Languages," *The Modern Language Journal* (Nov. 1916), pp. 52–58. See also I. H. B. Spiers, *Notebook of Modern Languages* to facilitate and encourage the systematic taking of notes by the pupil (D. C. Heath and Company). 80 cents.

Concerning the use of pictures in learning vocabulary, see Chapter I, pp. 7 f., note 2. Object lessons as a help to acquiring vocabulary are discussed in Chapter VIII, pp. 177 f.

[2] The Macmillan Company (1929), p. 2. In his lectures, Hayward Keniston gives an explanation of an idiom from the standpoint of any language: "An expression is idiomatic when the meaning of the whole expression cannot be derived from (or is different from) the sum of the meaning of its parts."

[3] The Macmillan Company (1929), p. 7.

that cannot be brought under any recognized syntactical category, and when literally translated into English conveys no adequate meaning or one essentially different from the actual one." [1] In short, an idiom is a trouble-making expression which, when literally translated, often turns into nonsense in English.

THE LISTING OF IDIOMS. Under which key word a given idiom should be listed is a bothersome problem. Unless we determine in advance how and in what order to list the idioms of a text, we are compelled to give it under several possible entries. Hauch in his *German Idiom List* gives his items in the following order: noun, adjective, adverb, verb, preposition, conjunction, interjection, pronoun. Hayward Keniston lists his idioms thus: verb, noun, adjective, adverb, conjunction, pronoun, preposition. Cheydleur lists his items in essentially the same way, but he arranges his key words alphabetically.

No single system of listing can be wholly satisfactory. The safest way to facilitate for the student the finding of idioms in a given vocabulary is to enter each idiom under two or, if necessary, three different key words, as most editors are in the habit of doing.[2]

DEVICES FOR THE TEACHING OF IDIOMS have not been developed to any appreciable extent. In addition to some well-known techniques, I shall, therefore, suggest a number of others which, according to my experience, "get idioms across."

1. All idioms of a rigid nature must be memorized with their best free rendering: noch nicht = *not yet;* immer noch = *still;* gar nicht = *not at all.*

2. Whenever an idiom can be manipulated, it must be taken through effective mutation exercises: er hält ihn für dumm = *he considers him stupid;* er hielt ihn für dumm, er hat ihn für dumm gehalten, er hatte ihn für dumm gehalten, er wird ihn für dumm halten, er wird ihn für dumm gehalten haben. This exercise may be improved by a so-called sliding synopsis: ich halte ihn für dumm, du hieltest ihn für dumm, er hat ihn für dumm gehalten, etc.

3. Literal translation into English is certain to drive home the

---

[1] *German Idiom List*, selected on the basis of frequency and range of occurrence. The Macmillan Company (1929), p. 1.

[2] Ernst Rose in "Vocabularies in German Textbooks," *Modern Language Journal* (Feb. 1933), pp. 334–41, regrets the absence of standard procedures in the listing of German vocabularies.

idea that "transverbalizing" is foolish and grotesque, and that an idiom must be learned by heart with its best free translation: es gibt (literally: 'it gives') = *there is, there are;* er hat sie lieb (literally: 'he has her dear') = *he is fond of her;* es geht mir gut (literally: 'it goes to me good') = *I am well.*

4. Attempted translation from English into German quickly reveals the inadequacy of any literal rendering of idioms. The student is forced to take the only correct attitude by rendering the spirit of the idiom as a whole. He does not translate words; he translates the thought: *I am well,* es geht mir gut.

5. Some idioms vary in meaning with the situation in which they are used. For instance, bitte schön may mean *certainly* or *please* or *don't mention it:* Darf ich eintreten? Bitte schön (*Certainly*). Darf ich einschenken? Bitte schön (*Please*). Ich danke Ihnen sehr. Bitte schön (*Don't mention it*).

6. Many idioms can be paraphrased easily: er wird immer schlimmer = er wird schlimmer und schlimmer; hin und her = auf und ab; ich lernte ihn kennen = ich wurde mit ihm bekannt, ich machte seine Bekanntschaft; es handelt sich um Leben und Tod = es ist eine Frage von Leben und Tod.

7. Some idioms may be explained by others, already familiar, of the same general meaning: er macht große Sprünge = er lebt auf großem Fuße; er läßt sich empfehlen = er läßt Grüße bestellen; sie zürnt ihm = sie ist böse auf ihn; auf Ihr Wohl = Prosit.

8. In rather advanced courses idioms may be arranged under definite key words:

der Tag: acht Tage = *a week;* alle Tage = *every day;* am Tage = *in the daytime;* es liegt am Tage = *it is clear;* den ganzen lieben Tag = *the whole livelong day.*

das Spiel: er setzt alles aufs Spiel = *he risks everything;* er treibt sein Spiel mit ihm = *he trifles with him;* es ist Böses im Spiel = *evil is brewing.*

9. A clever artist can illustrate idioms humorously and effectively: große Sprünge machen (*to spend money lavishly*) can be illustrated by the drawing of a man with long arms and legs who takes both feet into his hands and leaps; jemanden am Halse haben (*to have someone on one's neck, be burdened by someone*) may be pic-

tured by a man on whose shoulders sits a second man, his arms firmly around the neck of the first; mit dem Kopf durch die Wand wollen (*to be stubborn or obstinate, insist on the impossible*) can be made clear by a strong man, crashing his head with great force against a solid wall.[1]

We are hardly far from the truth in saying that among the most frequent causes for the chronic lack of vocabulary are the following: Homework is taboo in many schools, study halls and even libraries are often noisy, and students are frequently not held responsible for their tasks. Far too rarely do instructors take the trouble of speaking within the limits of the vocabulary defined for the specific level of the class. In brief courses, emphatically professing to foster a reading aim which gives basic importance to words and idioms, students read little. Besides, in many schools and colleges the conscientious and systematic reviewing of vocabulary at regular intervals is unknown. Words and idioms are studied once; nature takes its inevitable course, and all is completely forgotten.

The possibilities of teaching words and idioms effectively are numerous, and yet the one basic principle remains the same. Words and idioms are not assimilated by theories; they are learned by being used in many ways, but mainly in that specific way in which the learner wants to excel.

BIBLIOGRAPHY

ENGEL, E. F. "The Use of a Standardized Vocabulary in Beginning German." *Modern Language Journal* (Jan. 1931), pp. 281–91.

FINDLAY, J. J. "A Note on the Acquirement of Vocabulary." *Modern Languages* (Oct. 1927), pp. 4–7.

HAGBOLDT, PETER. "The Association of the Central West and South Adopts a New Standard Word List." *German Quarterly* (May, 1931), pp. 118–23.

—— *Building the German Vocabulary.* The Heath-Chicago Series. Boston: D. C. Heath and Company, 1928. xiii + 71 pp.

[1] These and many other illustrations for idiomatic expressions appeared in various issues of *Das deutsche Echo* for 1936. Representatives for American schools and colleges, F. S. Crofts & Co., 41 Union Square West, New York City.

HANDSCHIN, C. H. "The Question of Most Economical Learning of the German Vocabulary." *Modern Language Journal* (Dec. 1932), pp. 195–99.

MEIER, HERMANN. *The 1000 Most Frequent German Words, with a Brief Synopsis of Grammar.* Oxford Library of German Texts. New York: Oxford University Press, 1931. 24 pp.

MORGAN, B. Q. "Minimum Standard Vocabulary for German." *German Quarterly* (May, 1934), pp. 87–119.

ORTMANN, ARNOLD A. "A Study in First-Year German Vocabulary." *German Quarterly* (May, 1935), pp. 119–28.

PRICE, WILLIAM R. "What Price Vocabulary Frequencies?" *German Quarterly* (Jan. 1929), pp. 1–5.

PURIN, C. M. *A Standard German Vocabulary of 2932 Words and 1500 Idioms.* The Heath-Chicago Series. Boston: D. C. Heath and Company, 1937. 186 pp.

SIMMONS, L. V. T. "A Vocabulary Count Based on Three German Dramas." *Modern Language Journal* (Oct. 1929), pp. 33–36.

VAIL, CURTIS C. D. "Basic Vocabulary Studies." *German Quarterly* (May, 1932), pp. 123–30.

—— "Frequency List Problems." *Ibid.* (March, 1933), pp. 53–62.

—— "A Word List Correlation." *Ibid.* (Jan. 1936), pp. 10–16.

—— *Basic Word and Idiom Lists.* Albany: University of the State of New York Press, 1933. 22 pp.

WADEPUHL, WALTER. "German Idioms." *German Quarterly* (March, 1928), pp. 68–73.

—— AND MORGAN, B. Q. *Minimum Standard German Vocabulary.* Prepared in Dictionary Form. New York: F. S. Crofts & Co., 1936. v–vii + 90 pp.

WALPOLE, H. "The Theory of Definition and Its Application to Vocabulary Limitation." *Modern Language Journal* (March, 1937), pp. 398–402.

WALTER, MAX. *Aneignung und Verarbeitung des Wortschatzes im neusprachlichen Unterricht.* Marburg, 1914. 69 pp.

WEST, MICHAEL. "Speaking Vocabulary in a Foreign Language (1000 Words)." *Modern Language Journal* (April, 1930), pp. 509–21.

SUPPLEMENTARY READINGS

GIESEKE, ERNST. "Cognates, Stem-Meanings and the Vocabulary Problem." *Monatshefte,* XXIX, 2 (Feb. 1937), pp. 73–76.

KAULFERS, WALTER V. "Exercises in Paraphrase for Beginners in German." *German Quarterly,* X, 4 (Nov. 1937), pp. 161–68.

TATE, HARRY L. "Two Experiments in Reading Vocabulary Building." *Modern Language Journal*, XXIII, 3 (Dec. 1938), pp. 214–18.

THIELE, FRIEDRICH. "Deutscher und englischer Sprachgebrauch in gegenseitiger Erhellung." *German Quarterly*, XI, 1 (Jan. 1938), pp. 42–50; *Ibid.*, XI, 2 (March, 1938), pp. 87–94; *Ibid.*, XI, 4 (Nov. 1938), pp. 185–90.

—— "Er weiß, wo Barthel den Most holt." *Ibid.*, XII, 1, (Jan. 1939), pp. 11–15.

SUGGESTIONS FOR DISCUSSIONS AND REPORTS

1. What can you say in defense of frequency word counts after reading Price's article?
2. How does Ortmann arrive at his 400 frequent words?
3. Compare the articles of Findlay and Handschin and discuss their difference of approach. Write a synthesis of both.
4. Which exercises in Hagboldt's *Building the German Vocabulary* have you found most useful and effective?
5. If Wadepuhl and Morgan's *Minimum Standard German Vocabulary* were to be used by high-school and college students, what improvements would you suggest?
6. What (if any) are the disadvantages of specifying a definite vocabulary for each high-school year? (See Vail's *Basic Word and Idiom List*.)
7. Discuss Walpole's "Theory of Definition and Its Application to Vocabulary Limitation" (*a*) affirmatively, (*b*) negatively, (*c*) critically, *i.e.*, in part both.
8. Report on L. V. T. Simmons' article.
9. Prepare a list of 100 frequent idioms for first-year high-school pupils. Consult Oliver's *Modern Language Teacher's Handbook* and Coleman's two *Analytical Bibliographies*, 1927–1937 (The University of Chicago Press, 1936 and 1938 respectively). Use as a basis the articles by Wadepuhl, Hauch, Vail and the Wordbook of the *Graded German Readers*, 1–10.
10. Give a report on Walter's book, evaluating the fitness of his devices in a two-year high-school course.

CHAPTER SIX

PASSIVE PHASES: AURAL COMPREHENSION
AND READING [1]

AURAL COMPREHENSION is the ability to interpret by ear meaningful sequences of sound which form words, word groups, and sentences. In principle, aural comprehension should, perhaps, be taught to a well-defined degree even in brief courses; in practice, all depends on the teacher's ability and health. Important reasons argue for the teaching of at least some aural comprehension together with reading.

Sound is the basis in all functions of normal speech. To acquire reading ability, we first perfect our pronunciation by practical phonetics. Through sound and sequences of sound which we frequently associate with their meanings, reading finally becomes direct. Sound is the basis of oral reading; sound is the basis of silent reading. Hence, aural comprehension when acquired in a reading course depends largely on correct oral and silent reading.

Or, the same thought expressed differently: In oral reading we listen to sound sequences we pronounce aloud; in silent reading we listen to sound sequences we pronounce silently. The degree to which the learner pronounces correctly sequences of sound in oral and silent reading largely determines his ability to understand by ear.

The extent of aural comprehension, if it should be made a secondary aim in reading courses, must be definitely limited to those words and forms which have actually been taught through a variety of means. As the technique of reading courses becomes more and more developed and refined, we shall, perhaps, find ways

[1] Cf. *Language Learning* (The University of Chicago Press, 1935), pp. 111–13, and pp. 113–35.

of integrating aural comprehension with reading without serious loss of time.

READING. *The Committee of Twelve* urged in 1898 that reading be made the first and major aim in all modern language courses.[1] Six years later Bagster-Collins stated with equal emphasis, as innumerable scholars and teachers have done since:

> It is now widely recognized that reading shall form the center of instruction in a modern language course, and that all other elements shall serve to further the ends of reading. The successful practical outcome of a secondary school course is that pupils shall be able to read German readily. This presupposes that the pupils shall have read a great deal, and carefully, and that the major part of their time has been spent in reading the foreign language.[2]

Save for a few laudable exceptions, this sound advice was destined to remain quite unheeded for more than twenty-five years. After 1900 there came from Germany a number of highly competent teachers who expounded the superior results achieved by the "direct method." This method was, and in its modified form [3] still is, a superior way of teaching, its distinguishing feature being the direct oral approach. Max Walter explains:

> Das Wesentliche an unserer Methode ist die Mündlichkeit des Verfahrens. Die Sprache ist da, um gesprochen zu werden. Das ist für uns ein durchgreifender Grundsatz.[4]

> Grundsätzlich wird bei geschlossenem Buche gearbeitet, da der Schüler erst die fremde Sprache durch das Ohr aufnehmen und auf diesem Wege den neuen Sprach- stoff, unabhängig vom Auge, erfassen soll.[5]

The direct method, intended and constructed for specific conditions entirely different from our own, cannot be a success except

---

[1] *Report of the Committee of Twelve* (D. C. Heath and Company, 1900), pp. 7–14.

[2] *The Teaching of German in Secondary Schools* (Columbia University Press, 1916), p. 162. First printing, 1904.

[3] Ernst Otto, *Methodik und Didaktik des neusprachlichen Unterrichts*, Bielefeld und Leipzig, 1925. Walter Hübner, *Didaktik der neueren Sprachen*, Frankfurt am Main, 1929. Hans Strohmeier, *Methodik des neusprachlichen Unterrichts*, Braunschweig, Berlin und Hamburg, 1928.

[4] *Der Gebrauch der Fremdsprache bei der Lektüre in den Oberklassen.* Mit Ergänzungen und Anmerkungen. 43 pp. (Marburg, Elwert, 1914), p. 29.

[5] *Zur Methodik des neusprachlichen Unterrichts*, vierte Auflage, bearbeitet von Paul Olbrich (Marburg, Elwert, 1931), p. 33.

where our teaching situations resemble closely those in Germany, which is rarely if ever the case. Transplanted into a class of American students, this superb method becomes ineffective and in certain ways ludicrous. All the factors which determined its features at the time when it was conceived are radically changed. The course does not last six to nine years, but only one or two.[1] The aim cannot be the acquisition of a well-rounded knowledge of the foreign language and culture; it must be reading ability. The instructor rarely has a mastery of the foreign tongue. Moreover, when he teaches in college he is likely, if not forced by the system in which he works, to be more interested in scholarly research than in teaching. The college student is older, more mature, and sophisticated, and yet he frequently has none of the fundamental notions of language which European students have ordinarily mastered. The spirit of the school and the community is as a rule amazingly practical, the foreign language being usually tolerated as a "tool subject" without independent value. As a result the whole finely constructed method unless greatly modified loses its foundation.[2]

READING AND SPEAKING CONTRASTED. The great difference in difficulty between the various language phases becomes evident when we scrutinize what sort of knowledge each skill requires. In order to speak a foreign tongue which we have not acquired as children, we must know the most important forms of grammar and the principles of syntax not as abstract rules but as word groups and set idiomatic expressions ready for immediate and spontaneous recall. When we read, on the other hand, our preparation need not be nearly so intensive. We find all the words used correctly in properly constructed sentences. We do not need to supply the gender, number, and case of articles and nouns. We need not supply the tense, mood, and position of the verb; nor are we compelled to puzzle over the origin of the elements in idiomatic expressions in their difficult, elusive aspect. The author has taken care of all these problems. He leaves us only the task of understanding and interpreting what he has written.[3]

---

[1] Cf. Chapter II, p. 29, note 1.   [2] See *Language Learning* (The University of Chicago Press, 1935), "The Best Method," pp. 100–10.
[3] *Ibid.*, p. 40.

We now realize the difficulty of speaking when compared to reading ability. But what exactly is reading ability?

READING ABILITY DEFINED in general terms is the skill to interpret correctly, quickly, and with ease the written or printed symbols of a given document or book.[1] For our purposes this definition is incomplete; it takes into consideration only the vernacular, and even there it ignores the reading of non-technical material. For as soon as we find a totally unfamiliar term which is needed for full comprehension, we pause, reflect, guess, and, at length, consult a dictionary. Since this occurs continually in reading a foreign language, we must formulate a more concise definition to fit our purposes.

We need a definition in terms of words and their forms, of phrases, idioms, and sentence patterns, in short, of units of speech.[2] Only a limited number of such units can we learn to recognize and interpret in a given time. Therefore, reading ability in a foreign language is always limited to those units of speech which we can read. We may define, then, reading ability in a foreign language as follows:

Reading ability is the skill to recognize and interpret accurately, quickly, and in a direct way those units of speech which students have been taught and can remember. If the learner's reading is as it should be — direct — his eye movements are characterized by long and accurate sweeps, which never overreach the span of their recognition.[3]

READING IN OTHER METHODS was never given the place which it deserves under American conditions (cf. Chapter III). The grammar translation method until recent times used reading in homeopathic doses only to indulge in more grammar and more translation. Adherents of the natural method did not permit the learner to see the foreign language in print before he had

---

[1] Henry C. Morrison defines reading adaptation as "the ability to see through the symbolic complex of the printed page to the thought or scene of action which is the subject of the discourse without constant focal consciousness of the discourse itself"; cf. *The Practice of Teaching in the Secondary School* (The University of Chicago Press, 1926), p. 8.

[2] *Language Learning*, pp. 13–16.

[3] *Ibid.*, pp. 114–16. For a careful treatise on eye movements see G. T. Buswell, *Fundamental Reading Habits: A Study of Their Development.* Supplementary Educational Monographs, No. 21, 1922.

acquired a considerable familiarity with the spoken language. The psychological method, like the natural, was strictly oral. A supposedly direct method used by a group of selected teachers did not enable students to read more than 260 pages of German in two years.[1] The reading method roughly described by the Committee of Twelve is the subject of our discussion. Encouraging results have been reported from time to time in various journals.[2] In spite of results far better than those attained by other methods, some critics are quite dissatisfied.

OBJECTIONS TO THE READING METHOD occupied considerable space in journal articles immediately following the Coleman Report. Some of the standard objections, which I shall try to answer briefly, are:

1. "Oral work helps to a better understanding of word meanings, idioms as well as grammar, both of which are indispensable in reading."

We all believe this, yet in a reading course we cannot make a fetish of oral work. Time compels us to distinguish sharply between two types of oral work; oral work of an imitative nature and such of a more advanced, more reproductive nature, which approaches free speaking. Oral work in a reading course should consist in (a) vocalizing; (b) reading aloud; and (c) controlled speaking, that is, text-reproducing questions. Exercises to supplement this type of oral work should be (d) daily written exercises of a simple nature; (e) aural practice effected by the instructor, who always speaks within the range of familiar vocabulary; and (f) progressive reading, to the success of which all other activities should be strictly subservient.

2. "One or two years are not sufficient to give enough background either in vocabulary or in grammar."

---

[1] Algernon Coleman, *The Teaching of Modern Languages in the United States* (The Macmillan Company, 1929), pp. 121–23.

[2] See for instance O. F. Bond, "Junior College Work in Modern Languages," in W. S. Gray's *The Junior College Curriculum* (The University of Chicago Press, 1929), pp. 190–94.

Peter Hagboldt, "Achievement at the End of the Second Quarter Measured by the American Council Test," *The German Quarterly* (Nov. 1928), pp. 160–69. "Achievement after Three Quarters of College German as Measured by the American Council Test, Form B," *ibid.* (March, 1929), pp. 33–43, and articles referred to in Chapter II, pp. 38–39, note 1.

For mere reading, we need far less grammar study than is commonly believed.[1] As to vocabulary: within a Quarter (ten to eleven weeks) in college, one can read thoroughly, besides studying essentials of grammar, five small graded readers equal to 200 pages and containing a vocabulary of 875 stem words and 147 idioms.[2] Might not the same be done in one semester of high-school instruction? Could not the second and third Quarters in college, or the corresponding time in high school (second, third, and fourth semester) provide a background to enable the student to read several times more than heretofore?

3. "A high cultural aim cannot be achieved by mere contact with good books; it is reaction to good books that counts."

In a brief course we have no right whatever to set high aims which, as everybody knows, are unattainable. High cultural aims are the problem of advanced classes, if not of graduate study. In brief courses we can teach only a certain limited knowledge of *Realia* and *Kulturkunde*, no more (cf. Chapter IX).

4. "Extensive reading in high schools is not effective unless vocabulary, idioms, and grammar have been studied thoroughly."

Extensive reading need not imply, as in the past, unrestricted vocabulary; on the contrary, material for such reading should be provided with definitely controlled vocabulary and grammar. The student will derive both pleasure and profit if the words and forms are quite familiar to him. This is an ideal; the task which it implies must be faced soon.

These are four out of more than a hundred objections raised by teaching candidates at my request to jot down some criticism of reading courses. One might point out many inconsistencies and weaknesses in the reading approach. Yet, on closer analysis nearly all the weak points have one common basis: most of our reading courses, particularly for younger and less gifted students,

---

[1] James B. Tharp and Eloise Murray, "Grammarless Reading in Foreign Languages," *Modern Language Journal* (Feb.1928), pp. 385–90. To determine experimentally the exact amount of grammar required for reading at a definite level would be of great importance.

[2] Peter Hagboldt, "A Preliminary Experiment with Graded Reading Material," *Modern Language Forum* (Sept. 1935), pp. 77–83.

lack in detail, in system, in clear outline. They are undeveloped; they are in their infancy. We must work and develop them.

We shall now discuss some of the basic problems in reading courses: word meanings and their growth; material of familiar content; intensive and extensive reading; inference; the reading text in its relation to grammar; obstacles in the way of reading courses.

WORD MEANINGS. Every word has one, several, or many meanings. Röntgenſtrahlen means *x-rays;* auch signifies *too* or *also;* faſſen may denote *to hold, contain, comprise, include, grasp, seize, take hold of, apprehend, comprehend, understand, conceive,* and, besides, some other meanings confined to certain idioms. Fortunately not all words are as elusive as the verb faſſen, but each new meaning totally different from the one learned before requires attention.

I have stated that we generally learn one meaning at a time. Gifted students through the retentiveness of their memory retain several; and whenever the context permits them to use inference, they twist or expand one of the old meanings into a new one, fitting exactly into the passage they are reading. Thus arbeiten, *to work,* becomes *to labor* or *toil;* beginnen, *to begin,* fuses into *to start* or *commence;* bekommen, *to get,* is easily expanded into *to receive, obtain, acquire.*

THE GROWTH OF WORD MEANINGS. What we know about this fascinating problem is based on personal observation of scholars and teachers and will perhaps in time be developed, through ways and means as yet unknown, into much needed exact information. The quotations below apply to reading and speaking, to the native language as well as the foreign.

> We gain knowledge of native words by instinctive analysis. The first sentence we hear conveys to the mind an indistinct notion of the meaning of the word, the second makes its notion somewhat clearer, the third and a fourth render conjecture still more definite, until at length a last induction removes all doubt as regards the idea to be attached to it. In this manner we come, by almost imperceptible steps, to know the precise meaning of a considerable number of abstract terms which no definition could ever make us understand.[1]

[1] Claude Marcel, *The Study of Language Brought Back to Its True Principles, or the Art of Thinking in a Foreign Language.* Translated from the French edition (Appleton and Company, 1867), pp. 61 f.

The best way to get a reading vocabulary is just the way that the child gets his spoken vocabulary, by having the new words keep coming in context environment that is familiar and interesting, and by trying to use them as they will serve his purposes.[1]

„. . . die meisten Wortbedeutungen gewinnt das Kind gar nicht selbständig und auf Grund eigener Geistestätigkeit. Die werden ihm durch den Unterricht oder sonst im Verkehr mit Erwachsenen aufgedrängt und dadurch vom Kinde gedächtnis= mäßig angeeignet und gelernt . . . Freilich bleibt das anfangs ohne viel Ver= ständnis Eingeprägte nicht immer als leere Wortkombination bestehen. Mit der Zeit füllt sich die Form mit Inhalt: ,Es geht ihm ein Licht auf.'" [2]

The various stages of the growth of meanings have been described as follows: "(1) A feeling of familiarity with the word, that she (the subject) would know presently what it meant; . . . (2) she then felt she would know how to use it, that is, the actual meaning came before; (3) the images enrolled themselves in all their variety in the third stage." [3]

Grown-up people are in the same position with regard to words they do not know, but which they come across in a book or a news-paper, e.g., demise. The meanings of many words are at the same time extraordinarily vague and yet so strictly limited (at least in some respects) that the least deviation is felt as a mistake. More-over, the child often learns a secondary meaning of a word before its simple meaning. But gradually a high degree of accuracy is obtained, the fittest meaning surviving — that is (in this connection) those that agree best with those of the surrounding society.[4]

My own experience both as a student and a teacher has verified every detail of the above findings. A frequent objection is that the growth of meanings in a child is vastly slower than that in an adult, that a great difference exists in learning the native tongue on the one hand, and a foreign one on the other. Quite true, yet no one has been able to prove the non-existence of "reading into" a new language by familiar material, nor of the impossibility of

[1] E. B. Huey, *The Psychology and Pedagogy of Reading* (The Macmillan Company, 1919), p. 348.

[2] Hans Pohlmann, *Beitrag zur Psychologie des Schulkindes* (Dissertation, Leipzig, 1911), p. 252.

[3] Eleanor H. Rowland, "The Psychological Experiences Connected with the Different Parts of Speech," Monograph Supplements, VIII, No. 1 of the *Psychological Review* (Jan. 1907), p. 3.

[4] Otto Jespersen, *Language, Its Nature, Development and Origin* (London, 1922), pp. 126 f.

deriving meanings through inference, nor of the inefficiency of extensive reading when carefully supplemented by the intensive study of books.[1]

If I were to sum up the compound judgment of my students, beginners and advanced, young and old, superior and less gifted, I should say: "Word meanings are best learned through the wide and varied experience and practice in that activity in which students want to excel; in our country this usually is reading."

In a narrow sense, word meanings are, indeed, learned by the study of words; in a wider and more correct sense, they are the result of experiences such as have been described. Thus, word meanings are often the result of "reading into" a new language by familiar material, of inference, and extensive reading. We shall briefly describe each.

MATERIAL OF FAMILIAR CONTENT is particularly favorable for students anxious to read into a new language by practicing both reading intensively and extensively.

The learner knows, let us say, the foreign sound system, the elements of grammar, and a vocabulary of the thousand most frequent word stems. The latter he has acquired not through word lists but by reading. The student's purpose is to learn in the shortest time possible an adequate vocabulary in his chosen field. If he is a student of German literature he selects a standard literary work which has been translated into English. If he is a student in one of the sciences he takes an authorized English translation of a German scientist. Then he begins to compare the two versions of exactly the same literary or scientific content. Having studied other languages before, he knows how to analyze a sentence, how to single out certain grammatical and syntactical forms and constructions, and all those details which serve his purpose best. In the beginning his progress is slow, but soon he finds out by which method of comparing words, clauses, and sentences he advances most satisfactorily.

Speaking psychologically the student does not read meanings out of the text; he reads meanings into it. Nevertheless, by read-

---

[1] Compare, for instance, Eduard Prokosch, "Reading Knowledge by Self-Instruction," *Modern Language Journal* (May, 1922), pp. 446–52, a significant article by a great scholar and teacher.

ing precisely known meanings into foreign words, he associates these two elements — words and meanings — so frequently that the result is most gratifying. Even though there is not much experimental evidence for this statement, yet experience is the best teacher. Lehrend lernen wir. In an effort to learn more about the effect of reading familiar material I once tried an experiment, with most illuminating results.[1] The comment of an excellent student was:

> The reading of known texts should be done extensively and intensively so as to produce greater advantages than can be derived from either alone. It gives the student a feeling for idiom and grammar, and at the same time it is the best device for building a vocabulary. The text is read first in German, then in English, and last again in German. When easy, the reading and working unit is a paragraph or a page; when difficult, a clause or a sentence. The tendency of this method is to inhibit literal translation and to cause complete German sentences to stand for complete thoughts.

This procedure is obviously far more adapted to self-study than to class instruction, better for mature students than for beginners, and effective only if the learner is determined to learn.

INTENSIVE AND EXTENSIVE READING differ in both nature and effect. Intensive reading aims to explain every minute detail, the degree of intensity changing with the aim of the course. It may vary from sufficient detail for adequate comprehension to an exhaustive analysis of every prefix, suffix, word, idiom, sentence, thought, or thought group. Intensive reading is slow, exacting, and thorough. Usually it emphasizes language as such, more rarely the thought conveyed by language. Interest in the story is often lost in the mass of detail.

Extensive reading seeks not detail but the gist of the subject matter; not exact but more general comprehension. Allowing, as it does, each student to read books suited to his personal needs and, perhaps, to his taste, it is interesting. But it results in super-

[1] Peter Hagboldt, "An Experiment on Reading Known Material in Beginners' Classes," *Modern Language Journal* (March, 1925), pp. 345–52.

In this connection see Edwin H. Zeydel's review of Hauff's *Karawane*. Bilingual edition by C. L. Esborn. *Modern Language Journal*, XXI, 5 (Feb. 1937), pp. 370 ff. Compare the letters of C. L. Esborn and William Kurath, *ibid.*, XXI, 8 (May, 1937), pp. 617 ff.

ficiality in students interested neither in language nor in books. The success of extensive reading depends on the instructor as much as on the student. Instructors who have never experienced its effect because they are by nature inclined to scrutinize every detail of the sentence cannot and will not recommend this type of reading. If, on the other hand, the student cannot bring himself to read extensively in spite of his teacher's advice, or if he "reads" huge and impressive numbers of pages without adequate comprehension, extensive reading is a failure.

Neither type of reading alone gives best results; both types combined are very effective. Some time or other during the course the deliberate and careful analysis must be supplemented by collateral reading of easier books; and the sooner the better. Exclusive attention to analysis of difficult material soon leads to fatigue because it stresses unduly the somber side of learning; while the cursory reading of books easier than the class text is pleasant, and gives, moreover, the feeling of confidence and growth.[1]

In the interest of the pedagogy of reading and for a better understanding of extensive reading the instructor may find useful something like the following words to the class:

Extensive reading causes to pass through our mind an endless chain of words, word groups, idioms, and sentences, and at the same time an endless wave of sounds and rhythms. In studying a foreign language we vocalize inwardly. This is true even of reading English where we pronounce mentally all those words and sentences which we want to impress upon our mind. Through this continual inner speaking we gain something that intensive reading and the careful study of grammar can produce but very slowly. We gain comparatively early in the course one of our main objectives — a distinct feeling for the foreign language. In fact, even grammatical problems are much simplified through systematic reading. By finding and repeating the same construction again and again we establish within ourselves unconsciously, but without fail, a certain feeling whose definiteness grows in proportion to the extent of our reading. For practical purposes this feeling is more reliable than formal grammar which, when needed, may have been

[1] *Language Learning*, pp. 117 ff.

forgotten or may fail to function. In a certain sense extensive reading offers an actual substitute for all those activities of everyday life by which as children we learn our native tongue. This type of reading becomes effective through the constant repetition of foreign structural peculiarities and the repetition of all those elements which constitute the spirit of the foreign language.[1]

DIRECTIONS FOR COLLATERAL READING

Then the instructor might give some general directions for the practice of collateral reading. He might say:

Always gain a general idea of the book, its contents and purpose by reading the Introduction or the Preface.

The first pages ordinarily give the exposition of the story and the clue to the plot; read them carefully.

Do not look up more words than absolutely necessary for understanding the gist of the story.

Extract from each book a number of words of frequent occurrence and add them to your vocabulary; write down all words looked up.

If a word recurs frequently, look it up.

Be careful in the choice of material. The book must interest you. An uninteresting book for outside reading is harmful. What seems "uninteresting" is in most cases too difficult.

Read many easy texts before proceeding to more difficult ones. Difficult material in the beginning discourages; the reading of many simple texts gives confidence and power.

Be certain that your material is graded in such a way that the line representing the increase of difficulty is very long, ascending gradually. Consult your instructor.

Read by sentence rather than by word, and by paragraph rather than by sentence; but do not let a paragraph go by without understanding it as a whole.

The meaning of a sentence that is not clear may be inferred in many cases from the sentence that precedes or the one that follows.

If a paragraph is vague, rereading it several times will often make it clear.

Take notes on the action of the story as you go along, thus compiling material for your report on the book.

In preparing a book report, remember that your instructor wishes

[1] Peter Hagboldt, *How to Study Modern Languages in High School* (The University of Chicago Press, 1925), p. 20.

to find out the extent of your understanding. Your task in making a report is to show that you have absorbed meanings, not only covered pages.[1]

INFERENCE may be defined as a mental process whereby we are able to determine the meanings of unknown words by aid of those which are familiar. Inference utilizes all the known elements of the subject matter — story, plot, paragraph, sentence, or word — in such a way that the sum total of the known may elucidate the unknown. We may distinguish between various types of inference the use of which has proved effective in college teaching. Scholars often use inference to read themselves into a new language.

Unfortunately, inference has its dangers and limitations. Roots of words are frequently elusive; idiomatic expressions can rarely be understood without the dictionary or a note; unknown elements may abound to such an extent that no correct surmise is possible until a dictionary has cleared up the most important points in the chain of the unfamiliar. Therefore, texts used for collateral reading must always be considerably easier than those studied carefully in class. For younger students successful inference is probably confined to full and partial cognates and correct surmises involved in reading meanings into words, word groups, and sentences of familiar content. Inference is an excellent crutch, but a poor leg.[2]

Here is an example of how students of English in Germany might read extensively a passage from Mark Twain:

"Saturday morning was come, and all the summer world was *bright* and *fresh*, and *brimming with* life. There was a song in every heart; and if the heart was young, the music *issued at* the lips. There was *cheer* in every face and a *spring* in every step. The locust trees were *in bloom* and the *fragrance* of the blossoms *filled* the air."

— MARK TWAIN

(Italics are mine.)

When the German student reads this passage for the first time the expressions in italics — nine in six lines — may be unknown. What he gathers is this: It is a summer morning; a song is in

[1] Peter Hagboldt, *How to Study Modern Languages in High School* (The University of Chicago Press, 1925), pp. 22 f.

[2] *Language Learning*, pp. 121–25; or my article "On Inference in Reading," *Modern Language Journal* (Nov. 1926), pp. 73–78.

every heart; people see trees and blossoms; they sing and are happy. Reading this passage a second time he uses this information to supply the meanings of the unknown words:

If people were happy the world would probably look *bright*, hell, fonnig; *fresh* would suggest frifch. Since people were in the open air and happy, he infers that *brimming with* denotes voll von or gefüllt mit. Knowing *music* and *lips* he concludes that *issued at* means *came from*. *Cheer* he is likely to interpret as Glück or Frohfinn or Lachen; and being familiar with the word *step*, he will not mistake the noun *spring* for the "spring season," but assume that *spring* is related to German fpringen, here denoting Sprung. In the last sentence he knows "tree," "blossom," and "air"; trees with blossoms explain *in bloom* as in Blüte; *blossom, bloom*, and *air* in turn explain *fragrance* as Duft; *filled* he will interpret as füllte.[1]

Thus the essential gist of the passage may be adequately understood by a German student of English who has not made a systematic study of English vocabulary.

It is to be regretted that in high schools no experiments have been carried out to determine the extent to which inference, familiar material, and extensive reading may be made effective. Can none of these helps be used and must we, in regard to high-school pupils, rely solely on the learning of specific things? In all probability we must.

THE READER FOR BEGINNERS is a most important problem. In reading courses we have no time to go through the larger part of a bulky grammar before coming to the point. The point is to begin reading soon.

We have acclaimed a new aim; but we have not provided the means for achieving this aim. Most of our grammars are not in the least designed or intended for reading courses. While they do give a limited number of supplementary reading selections, these are, more often than not, completely inorganic: they neither apply the vocabulary used in the grammar nor the forms and constructions which the grammar lessons profess to exemplify. In other words, readings and grammar do have points of contact, but they are not obvious to the student; readings and grammar are

[1] *How to Study Modern Languages in High School*, pp. 19 ff.

not integrated, do not synchronize; they run parallel, and parallel lines do not meet.

Indeed, serious objections must be raised to unnecessary detail in grammars, which, claiming to be "complete," fail to stress basic essentials. A large grammar supplemented by a limited number of readings is uninviting, if not intimidating. Students and teachers are discouraged before they begin (see p. 121, Fig. I).

A far better procedure is to use a much shorter grammar and a reader, strictly correlated with one another. Figure 2 (p. 121) illustrates such an arrangement.[1] The reader is divided into thirty steps, each corresponding to one lesson in the grammar. Each reading selection applies and exemplifies the forms taught in one specific lesson. The gradation of grammatical difficulties has been found to be quite satisfactory; yet it appears impossible to prepare sufficient material for each of the thirty lessons, nearly all forms taught seeming to demand immediate application.

Figure 3 (p. 122) is an illustration of the graded readers. Each of the thirteen steps represents one reader. Beginning with 500 words and 30 common idioms the thirteen readers present a vocabulary of approximately 1800 words and 300 idioms. The words are counted as stems; derivatives are not counted. In each reader up to No. 12 there are numerous exercises with prefixes, suffixes, and word combinations. The thirteen readers are roughly divided into three levels, elementary, intermediate, and advanced. There is a definite scheme of gradation: Thus, Readers 1 and 2 contain mainly principal clauses in the present; Reader 3 adds short dependent clauses in the past tense; 4 and 5 principal parts of common strong verbs; 6–10 other verbal forms, but no passives or subjunctives; 11–13 passives, subjunctives, and participial clauses. A brief grammar of 116 pages contains 500 of the frequent words and idioms occurring in the first seven readers and all those forms which were found of frequent occurrence in the others.[2]

The proportion is no longer, roughly speaking, six parts of grammar to one part of reading; it is reversed: six parts of reading

[1] Cf. Peter Hagboldt and F. W. Kaufmann, *Deutsch für Anfänger* and *Lesebuch für Anfänger*. The Heath-Chicago Series. D. C. Heath and Company.

[2] Peter Hagboldt and F. W. Kaufmann, *A Brief Course in German*. The Heath-Chicago Series. D. C. Heath and Company, 1937.

to one part of grammar. While many will regard this as an indication of progress, there is much work to be done before we have a really good reading method for German.

FIG. 1

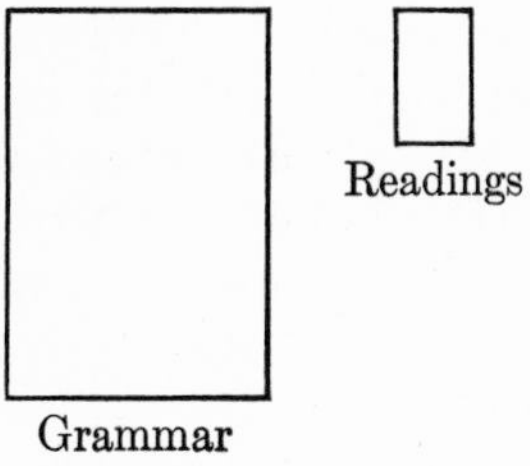

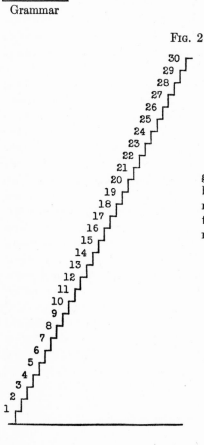

Readings

Grammar

A large grammar with a number of supplementary readings. Readings and grammar are rarely organically connected.

FIG. 2

Grammar and reader; each grammar lesson is supplemented by several reading selections; each reading selection stresses the forms taught in the grammar lesson.

Fig. 3

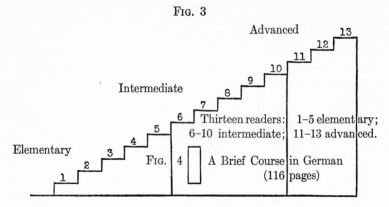

GRADED READERS. A word in regard to graded readers is desirable. Graded readers, to deserve their name, should approach a work of art in excellence of style and accuracy of technical detail. Their textual material should be interesting to students, and be constructed on the basis of a definite plan according to distinct levels of grammatical and structural difficulty. In the most meticulous manner they should record words and idioms with their best renderings. The number of repetitions should be so large as to have predictive value for the instructor, who must be able to say at a certain point: "My average student has read this text conscientiously. Words, idioms, and certain syntactical usages have occurred frequently enough to insure retention. Besides, we have studied carefully certain techniques of word building. Therefore my average student, after a thorough review and restudy, will pass a vocabulary and idiom test on this reader." And so he should be able to say of any book in a given series of graded readers.

There are two obstacles in the way of progress in development of reading courses; overemphasis on oral work and overlearning of certain problems of grammar. We have pointed out the necessity of distinguishing between two types of oral work (p. 110) and now come to

GRAMMAR IN READING COURSES. Tradition, habit, and fear of being superficial have caused us to waste an enormous amount of precious time on the study of grammar in brief courses. We have failed to ask in regard to each specific grammatical problem: What exactly will my student gain by a thorough study of these forms? Does he really need a mastery of, for instance, adjective declension, the use of prepositions, word order, or will it suffice that he recognize and interpret correctly the forms and constructions which he finds in his reading? In the following we shall distinguish between two types of problems: those which require careful and intensive study and those which are relatively speaking of minor importance. Fortunately, some of the greatest difficulties of German grammar are not very important, so that we need not stress them in the brief reading course:

1. Adjective declension means nothing to the reader. Its principle may be explained within a short time. The student, if time permits, may be required to write out several paradigms so as to gain a definite knowledge of the logic of adjective endings.

2. The comparison of adjectives is so closely related to English that it may be treated as vocabulary.

3. Adverbs, like gern and aufs beſte, and indefinite pronouns, like man, are vocabulary.

4. All the student needs to know about prepositions is their meanings plus the fact that they are capable of taking different cases; he does not need to know which cases they must take, except where the case following the preposition determines a part of the meaning: er ſchreibt über mich (mir).

Only a few prepositions which follow the noun (der Mutter wegen, den Umſtänden gemäß, dem Geſchmack nach) need special attention.

5. Coordinating and subordinating conjunctions are nothing but vocabulary as long as the student remembers that many conjunctions cause the finite verb to stand at the end of the clause or the sentence.

6. Numerals, expressions of time, and impersonal adverbs are vocabulary.

7. Inseparable and doubtful prefixes have no claim to careful attention; yet the former should be taken up in a systematic study of vocabulary as to their most frequent connotations.

8. Separable prefixes, while not requiring minute study, are often bothersome if the prefix stands unduly far away from the verb. A number of examples illustrating this difficulty will be in order.

These problems must be distinguished from others which need much more intensive study:

1. The definite and indefinite articles show gender and case, that is, the syntactical relationship of the various parts of the sentence. They are, moreover, fundamental for the inflection of pronouns. They are basic forms to be learned well.

2. The forms of possessives and demonstratives, of relatives and interrogatives, are of equal importance; they are easily learned on the model of the article inflection. The inflection of personal pronouns should also be learned carefully.

3. A study of the three hundred most frequent nouns and their division into four or five classes according to plural endings will help the student to deal more intelligently with other nouns as he meets them.

4. The auxiliaries fein, haben, and werden and several weak verbs should be written out and vocalized so frequently that the student's understanding of all the forms of the indicative is spontaneous and direct.

5. Strong verbs must be learned with their vowel gradation, for the student should be able to reduce a past participle or a form of the past to its infinitive so as to be able to interpret its meaning quickly. The nine irregular verbs and the modal auxiliaries with their meanings should also receive special attention. Nothing retards progress in reading more than a deficient knowledge of strong verbs.

6. The so-called double infinitive with modals and some other verbs in the perfect tenses needs careful illustration in many sentences, and careful translation into English.

7. The formation of the passive voice is important. Though less frequent in German than in English, it is, nevertheless, one of the major difficulties even for the reading student.

8. A thorough familiarity with the simple principles of the formation of subjunctive forms and tenses and their various uses and meanings is essential.[1]

I have tried to suggest a distinction in emphasis on problems of

---

[1] Compare Peter Hagboldt, "The Relative Importance of Grammar in a German Reading Course," *The German Quarterly* (Jan. 1928), pp. 18–21; the content of this article has here been somewhat modified.

grammar in reading courses. Some future committee will consider this interesting and important question. And perhaps the committee will conclude that in general reading ability in German depends very much on the knowledge of a large technical vocabulary in the reader's special field, and on a good knowledge of article and pronoun inflection, of strong and weak conjugations, of the forms and uses of the modals, passives, and subjunctives, and on the ability to analyze the structure of lengthy compound or complex sentences.

DEVICES FOR TEACHING AURAL COMPREHENSION. The fifteen pronunciation exercises (pp. 79–82) and also the seven techniques of giving dictation used in the different ways suggested (pp. 83–85) are specific means to develop aural comprehension. In addition the following are to be considered:

1. The instructor speaks the foreign language, always strictly within the limits of his student's comprehension. As a reward for a good recitation he occasionally tells an anecdote, supplying parenthetically the meanings of new words; or he discusses news from abroad, or interesting student customs.

2. The class has prepared thoroughly the home assignment. The teacher reads a number of correct and false statements based on this assignment. The students write on a slip of paper *correct* or *false*. The number of the student's incorrect answers subtracted from the right ones is the score.

3. A contest: Each student is assigned a page or two for fluent reading in class with proper intonation and expression. After a week all students are prepared. Each reads a sentence or two from his assignment. The winner may receive a book as a prize, and at some future time may perform again for the class.

4. A famous poem, ballad, or prose passage is read in class and studied thoroughly. The next day the students are given the text in mimeographed form and a phonograph record is played on which the text is spoken by an excellent reader. The instructor calls attention to difficulties and niceties in the artist's rendering. The text is then assigned for memorizing. The record is played in or after class as often as the students want to hear it.

5. Students listen to radio programs, lectures, and sermons; they report on their progress in aural comprehension. They visit

theater performances, clubs, associate with natives, reside with a German-speaking family or friend.

The main point is to give the student, in or out of class, as much opportunity to practice aural comprehension as circumstances allow. To a large extent this depends on the teacher, for it is difficult to remember approximately which units of speech have been taught in a given class, and more so to speak within these units.

DEVICES FOR TEACHING TO READ. The techniques and procedures listed under pronunciation and dictation (pp. 79–86) and those under words and idioms (pp. 94 ff.) and aural comprehension (pp. 125 f.) naturally play an important part in all reading courses. It is often difficult to decide whether a device should be mentioned under one skill or another. In the following I shall list only those which have not been discussed before [1]:

1. Intensive reading for grammatical analysis. In a reading course proper only those formal and syntactical problems should be singled out for careful analysis which prevent complete comprehension. In the beginning they usually are difficulties in recognizing the case or number of articles and nouns, the tense of strong verbs, the syntactical relationship of clauses. Later the difficulties change to the recognition of the passive voice, of subjunctive forms and their meanings, of participial clauses, of difficulties in interpreting long and involved sentences. If necessary, the class as a whole may receive supplementary instruction on specific difficulties, or individual students must be given corrective exercises to overcome their difficulties.

2. Reading for vocabulary expansion by means of induction (see pp. 96–99).

3. Reading for literal translation has as its sole object to ascertain quickly that all details have been completely understood. It may be used to advantage in sight reading, where the student is only concerned with the precise meaning of the page and not with its elegant rendering.

4. Reading to practice free translation, that is, to render a text into good literary English, is very important. The masterly

---

[1] Compare also Peter Hagboldt, "Making the Reading Lesson Effective," *Modern Language Journal* (Dec. 1926), pp. 129–32.

translation of a well-known speech, poem, short story, essay, or drama serves as a model. The model is studied and discussed. The result is that students come to look upon translation as an art, the secret of which is not to render the word but its concept, not the sentence but its thoughts, not the pages but their spirit, not the poem but the soul. The student sees that long, involved sentences are broken up into shorter ones which are clear and precise; that the word order is entirely changed, clauses transposed, the finished translation reading easily and smoothly, leaving no trace of the structural problems the translator has faced and overcome.

At least once in the course of study the student should be given the opportunity to try his power of interpretation and expression in this most difficult art. Even a little practice of this nature will make him more critical and cautious in the choice of expressions and more exacting in his demands on himself to use good literary English corresponding in style and in spirit to the original version.

5. Rapid silent reading in class can be used as a sort of a general test of the students' reading ability. The material must be new. After a definite period of time, ten to twenty minutes, the students are given a number of content questions on the blackboard or preferably in mimeographed form. Since the questions asked cover more pages than the best reader in the class can have read in the time allowed, the number of questions answered correctly may show two things: (1) the number of main points grasped and recalled; (2) the breadth and depth of the student's understanding.

6. The students' oral reading may be very informative for the instructor. If experienced, he can judge accurately each student's progress by the fluency or slowness of his reading, by his proper or wrong intonation, his false or right division into stress groups, and by the expressiveness of his reading. Yet caution is necessary; many students suffer from defective sight, or have bad reading habits in English.

7. "Read and translate" is a much overused and therefore much maligned exercise. Judged by its popularity one should think that no other devices existed. When based on prepared material, it can serve as a sort of comprehensive test on pronunciation, fluency of reading, and the student's ability to dig out the

meaning of a page with all the helps at his disposal — providing, of course, that he does not use the *pons asinorum* of interlinear translation or the printed "pony" provided by thoughtful publishers. Too frequently used, however, this convenient exercise becomes both a bore to the student and a dismal failure as a teaching device.

8. Each class has a certain tempo which is the result of three factors: the best student, the weakest student, and the teacher's attitude toward both. The teacher can sacrifice the best student to the weakest, the weakest to the best, or he can give individual assignments to either and devote himself to the average student in the class. Individual assignments are a solution for many problems created by the vast differences in native ability.

9. Rereading a book after studying it intensively is of the greatest benefit. In fact, rereading must be rated as the best way toward direct reading. The oftener one reads a thoroughly studied text the more direct his comprehension is bound to become. Words, word groups, and even whole sentences are finally anticipated and supplemented. The law of practice and repetition shows its results. Rereading has all the advantages of reading familiar material, only the meanings are more definite and precise, and retention is far more lasting. "If a book is worth reading once, it should be read twice," Benjamin Franklin once remarked.

In trying to find a solution for reading courses, we are not confronted by a theory but a fact, the fact of brief courses. However ardently we may long for a return of "the good old times," the truth remains that we have too confidently relied on the permanence of past conditions. In 1898 the trend of future instruction in our field was stated in unmistakable terms. Yet we waited thirty years, quoting untiringly European scholars whose findings did not then, and do not now apply to our specific conditions and necessities. The past is gone. Our task is to make a virtue out of distress. The sooner we are able to show that reading courses can be a success, the greater is the possibility that some day we shall be granted more time. Besides, we must never forget for a moment that even the modest fashioner of "mere tools" is thoroughly worthy as long as he strives not only toward mechanical perfection but, ultimately, toward fostering and furthering the great values of life.   Great values are stored in great books.   Great books will hardly be read in the original unless made more accessible by a greatly improved reading method.

For the present, until further progress can be made, I agree with Professor Werner F. Leopold who, after a fine and eloquent plea for the classics, states:

> In my opinion, what we should strive for is a rapid introduction to the grammar really reduced to minimum essentials for reading purposes; this should be followed by graded reading material, which quickly builds up a standard minimum vocabulary.   The next step would be a more extensive, unified text, which, building on the systematic base laid, would gradually shift the emphasis from tool material to content, at the same time increasing the vocabulary considerably without strict adherence to word counts.   All this should be done within the first college year or the first two high-school years.   After such preparation the student should be ready to tackle texts of real literary value and of increasing difficulty.[1]

That the reading of easy and carefully graded material can be introduced very early in the course seems conclusively proved by Professor C. R. Goedsche of Northwestern University who writes in a personal note dated October 7, 1939:

> During the winter semester 1938–39 I read ten of the Graded German Readers in a beginning class which met five times a week. After about two weeks of instruction in grammar, I began to assign eight to ten pages of reading, along with regular assignments in grammar.   Usually I asked my students to translate paragraphs, which I had carefully selected, amounting to three to five pages. Students answered questions concerning the remaining pages.   In order to secure a reliable check on correct understanding, I gave short written examinations once a week.

> Furthermore, after completion of each booklet, I gave a short vocabulary test of ten minutes, covering the new words and idioms found at the end of each booklet.   I insisted that at least 75 per cent of my class should make a perfect score.   Sometimes I was forced to repeat such vocabulary tests on the content of one booklet twice or even three times.   The result was very gratifying, however, because students were able to read successive booklets with much more ease.

[1] "Word-Counts and After," *Monatshefte für deutschen Unterricht* (Dec. 1936), pp. 355–62.

Compare also Alfred Charles Adler, "A Suggested First-Semester Course in German," *Modern Language Journal* (Nov. 1939), pp. 116–30.

BIBLIOGRAPHY

APPELT, E. P. "Die Privatlektüre im fremdsprachlichen Unterricht." *Monatshefte für deutschen Unterricht* (March, 1930), pp. 76–80.

BEARDSLEY, WILFRED A. "Simplifying the Classics." *Modern Language Journal* (March, 1937), pp. 396–97.

BOVÉE, A. G. "My Creed." *French Review* (March, 1931), pp. 397–406.

COLEMAN, ALGERNON. "A New Approach to Practice in Reading a Modern Language." *Modern Language Journal* (Nov. 1930), pp. 101–18.

DEIHL, JOSEPH DWIGHT. *The High-School Course in German.* Revised by B. Q. Morgan. Bulletin of the University of Wisconsin, 1928. No. 24. 59 pp.

FIFE, ROBERT H. "The Reading Objective." *German Quarterly* (May, 1929), pp. 73–78.

GEYER, HUGH E. "A Better Attainment of the Reading Aim." *Monatshefte für deutschen Unterricht* (Oct. 1934), pp. 197–200.

GOODLOE, JANE F. "The Technique of Reading German." *German Quarterly* (Nov. 1936), pp. 154–67.

HAGBOLDT, PETER. "The Work of Michael West." *Modern Language Journal* (March, 1938), pp. 411–19.

JACKSON, EUGENE. "Testing of Content in an Intensive Reading Lesson." *German Quarterly* (May, 1937), pp. 142–44.

JOHNSON, LAURA B. "Oral Work as a Prerequisite to Reading." *Modern Language Journal* (April, 1931), pp. 490–501.

KOISCHWITZ, OTTO, and HURD, ARCHER W. "Experimental Application of the Interpretative Reading Method." *Monatshefte für deutschen Unterricht* (March, 1935), pp. 92–96.

NEWTON, LESTER G. "Isn't This a Better Way?" *School and Society* (Oct. 28, 1933), pp. 569–71.

SPENDIAROFF, EUGENE. "Is Learning to Read an Easy Task?" *Modern Language Journal* (March, 1932), pp. 490–94.

STEINBACH, H. R. "The Problem of Extra Reading." *Modern Language Journal* (March, 1932), pp. 465–70.

THARP, J. B. "Popularity of Foreign Language Study." *Monatshefte für deutschen Unterricht* (Jan. 1936), pp. 21–26.

WEST, MICHAEL. "The Problem of 'Weaning' in Reading a Foreign Language." *Modern Language Journal* (April, 1931), pp. 481–89.

WEST, MICHAEL. *Learning to Read a Foreign Language: An Experimental Study.* London: Longmans, Green and Co., 1926.

SUPPLEMENTARY READINGS

BROWN, DONALD FOWLER. "A Grading System for the Stimulation of Outside Reading." *Modern Language Journal*, XXIII, 4 (Jan. 1939), pp. 270–75.

COENEN, F. E. "An Excellent Reading Method." *German Quarterly*, XI, 3 (May, 1938), pp. 139–41.

GAEDE, WM. R. "Some Guiding Principles for Outside Reading." *Modern Language Journal*, XXIII, 4 (Jan. 1939), pp. 251–55.

GEIGER, KAROLA. "A New Approach to Checking Outside Reading." *Modern Language Journal*, XXIV, 1 (Oct. 1939), pp. 28–30.

HEFFNER, R. M. S. "The Reading Objective and the Reading Method." *Monatshefte*, XXX, 7 (Nov. 1938), pp. 367–74.

HUEBENER, THEODORE. *The Reading Aim in Foreign Language Teaching.* Foreign Language Monograph, No. 6. Board of Education, City of New York.

MORGAN, B. Q. "New Hope for Learners of German." *Monatshefte*, XXX, 8 (Dec. 1938), pp. 454–56.

SOLDNER, DORA M. "A Test in Need." *Modern Language Journal*, XXIII, 5 (Feb. 1939), pp. 379–84.

SUGGESTIONS FOR DISCUSSIONS AND REPORTS

1. On the basis of Appelt's article prepare a list of collateral reading intended for first- and second-year high-school pupils (Juniors and Seniors).
2. A class discussion of Beardsley's article on "Simplifying the Classics."
3. What danger is there, if any, in Bovée's "eclectic" or "organized direct method" for two-year high-school courses?
4. Enumerate eight points in Coleman's article on reading a foreign language.
5. What does Robert Herndon Fife recommend in his article as to testing, the placing of students, and experimentation?
6. Describe West's idea of "weaning."
7. Analyze carefully the points of grammar which, according to your experience as a student and a teacher, need either more or less emphasis than suggested on pp. 123 ff.

8. Report on the following articles by: (*a*) Geyer; (*b*) Goodloe; (*c*) Jackson; (*d*) Johnson; (*e*) Spendiaroff; (*f*) Steinbach; (*g*) Koischwitz and Hurd; (*h*) Newton; (*i*) Tharp; (*j*) Hagboldt, the two articles mentioned on p. 110, n. 2.
9. Report on a number of articles dealing with the checking of extensive reading. See bibliographies.

CHAPTER SEVEN

GRAMMAR

BEFORE coming to the active phases of language study, we must discuss grammar, that important subject which for centuries has been both fervently blessed and bitterly cursed.

In 1904 Bagster-Collins wrote:

> One generation cultivates grammar as a precious thing in itself. The next generation says, "Away with grammar, we will have none of it." Still a third party, more thoughtful, says, "Grammar shall no longer be enthroned as a queen, but in the future shall serve as a handmaiden. We should no longer study grammar for itself alone, but as a means to an end, and not as an end in itself, as held generations ago." [1]

We are quite convinced that if grammar were enthroned once more as a queen it would speedily lead to a complete elimination of all modern language courses. Even yet, we have not been able to find for grammar the place which it rightly deserves. This is due, perhaps, to the utter complexity of the widely varying conditions under which we teach, to the indefiniteness of our aims which are definite in our printed catalogues far more often than in our practices, and to an endless variety of other factors which all contribute to the difficulty of determining the proper quantity of grammar given in the proper way at the proper time. Even though it is impossible to offer suggestions for every condition and situation, we shall attempt to clarify some fundamental con-

---

[1] *The Teaching of German in Secondary Schools* (Columbia University Press, 1904), p. 105. Bagster-Collins' statement of 1904 brings to mind an editorial in the *New York Times* of Sept. 12, 1938: "Down with Grammar." See *Modern Language Journal* (Dec. 1938), p. 219.

cepts implied in the teaching of grammar and thus, perhaps, throw light on its proper position.

FORMAL AND FUNCTIONAL GRAMMAR must be clearly distinguished. "Formal" means "according to form, or custom, or to established rules." Besides, "formal" has the connotation of "conventional, ceremonious, artificial." The latter meaning is strongly suggested in the expression "formal discipline."

During the Middle Ages formal grammar was used as a sort of gymnastic instrument to train the mind, to teach students to think clearly and logically, to give pupils the best training the schools had to offer at that time. In this spirit Comenius wrote: "I presume that no one can raise any objection to my placing (Latin) grammar first, since it is the key to all knowledge." Some years later John Locke stated that he would fain have anyone name that tongue that anyone can learn, or speak as he should do, by the rules of grammar. The Committee of Ten in 1893 seemingly reconciled these two conflicting views by saying that: "The study of formal grammar is valuable as training in thought, but has only indirect bearing on the art of writing and speaking." [1] In short, Comenius referred to formal grammar, while Locke had in mind not formal grammar but only the practical skills which no amount of formal grammar can give (cf. Chapter I, p. 8).

Functional grammar is grammar in function, in operation, in use. It is not content with stating rules, exceptions, and exceptions to exceptions, nor with listing lengthy paradigms of conjugations and declensions. It aims to limit grammar to that which is regular and fundamental, to minimum essentials, to a bare skeleton of forms which are most frequent and therefore most important and useful. The skilfully constructed devices invented in the course of time by generations of able teachers can set functional grammar into operation so effectively that the student, all things being equal, will really learn to use grammatical forms correctly. Formal grammar stresses forms and rules; functional grammar stresses the *use* of forms according to accepted standards, that is, language.

Nevertheless, it is advisable to remember the warning of

[1] Daniel Starch, *Educational Psychology* (The Macmillan Company, 1927), p. 262.

the Committee of Twelve who stated in their report of 1900, pp. 15 ff.:

> It [the grammar method] has, however, certain undeniable advantages. In the first place, it trains the mnemonic faculty; in the reaction against the hard, unattractive schooling of our fathers, modern pedagogical fashion has gone so far that the power of conscious acquisition and retention is hardly exercised at all; children go to college or out into life with an embryonic memory, and the teacher's task rivals the labor of the Danaïdes. Secondly, the careful study of grammatical rules and their nice application in translation and composition form one of the best possible exercises in close reasoning ... while devising a system more in accordance with the principles and possibilities of our time, let us not forget that the old-fashioned way had its good features.

INDUCTIVE AND DEDUCTIVE TEACHING OF GRAMMAR has been discussed ever since Viëtor started the reform in Germany. The terms need careful definition. "Inductive" is derived from Latin *inducere*, "to lead into"; its antonym is "deductive," from Latin *deducere*, "to lead out of." Inductive teaching leads the student's attention directly to specific points of language. For instance, a given coherent text uses forms and constructions of language which are to be taught. The instructor directs the pupil's attention to these forms and constructions by a number of carefully formulated questions arranged in a definite sequence. Each question forces the learner to direct his attention to a different aspect of the problem, and his own answers bring him step by step to the solution in the form of a grammatical rule.

Deductive teaching of grammar, on the contrary, directs the student's attention to a rule and points to several examples verifying this rule. Then, by means of this carefully and clearly stated rule and a number of words and phrases, language is constructed synthetically.

The advantages and disadvantages of the two procedures become plain after a moment's reflection. Induction gives the student the proper attitude toward language study. He finds that rules are derived from language, and that language is governed by rules. He recognizes that grammar is no more than an aid and a great simplifying force bringing order and system into a mass of seemingly arbitrary forms. He is compelled to scrutinize forms of speech, answer questions according to his own observations, and finally, with the help of his instructor, to state the rule. Induction is a safe and effective way of teaching grammar because of the careful observation of definite forms. Induction, therefore, is favorable particularly in reading courses, for reading depends largely on successful analysis. Deduction, on the other hand, appears to be more favorable in classes where a more active knowledge is sought, for deduction is based on synthesis, on executing a great many direct method exercises constructed and tested so carefully that the learner, provided he is interested and has time, may develop within certain limits the ability to express himself in the foreign language.

The case for induction is supported by a significant experiment which proves that an active attitude is approximately ten times as effective as a passive attitude.[1] It is remarkable how closely we attend to that to which we are told to attend, and how much our associations depend on comparisons we are told to make. Socrates, the wisest of the Greeks, never answered his students' questions. He always directed their attention to pertinent points of any given problem by questions of his own. Thus he forced the student to think clearly until the latter had solved the problem by his own efforts.[2] Socrates best exemplifies what Pestalozzi and Herbert Spencer urged in more recent times, namely, that we should not tell our student what he can find out by himself. Modern psychology speaks to the same end in saying: "It is not far from the truth . . . that any subject taught with a view to training pupils in methods of generalization is highly useful as a source of mental training and that any subject which . . . does not stimulate generalization is educationally barren." [3]

In all mental processes induction and deduction play an important part. We hear more about inductive teaching because it

[1] McDougal and Smith, "Some Experiments in Learning and Retaining," *British Journal of Psychology*, X (1919), pp. 204 ff., found students with an active attitude required nine to thirteen repetitions for retention, while those with a passive attitude required eighty-nine to one hundred.

[2] See *Plato, Gorgias*, translated by W. R. M. Lamb (G. P. Putnam's Sons).

[3] Charles Hubbard Judd, *Psychology of Secondary Education* (Ginn and Company), p. 432.

is as effective as it is difficult and rare. Our courses are usually so short that our breathlessness has become chronic. For this reason deductive teaching predominates. We do not develop the problems; we simply state them. In short courses this is inevitable and often advisable. Therefore, we must guard against considering inductive teaching the "only possible" way. Induction and deduction (analysis and synthesis) are merely two phases of the same process. Neither exists in an entirely pure form. They always interpenetrate. The example we shall give later shows how a lesson may be divided, more or less clearly, into analysis and synthesis. William James aptly says that these "incessantly alternating mental attitudes" are as necessary to mental processes as our two legs are for walking.[1] Goethe compared the two processes to inhaling and exhaling.[2]

A first example.[3] And now that we have explained induction and deduction as types of analysis and synthesis, let us give an example of a lesson in which induction is used to find the rule, and deduction to set the rule into practice. Suppose that the student has had five lessons and has learned the cases of the definite and indefinite articles, except the genitive; the present tense of sein and haben; the regular present tense endings; dative and accusative prepositions; and that he now comes to the genitive and the prepositions taking that case. We begin with a simple coherent text containing a number of definite grammatical problems:

Während des Sommers gehen wir zum Großvater aufs Land. Er wohnt nicht sehr weit von hier in einem Dorfe jenseits des Berges. Das Dorf liegt an einem Flusse oberhalb einer Stadt. Unterhalb des Dorfes liegt ein Wald. Der Wald ist groß und schön. Trotz des Alters ist der Großvater noch gesund und stark. Er bleibt wegen des Regens oder wegen der Hitze oder der Kälte selten zu Hause. Er will immer außerhalb des Hauses sein. Er sagt: „Innerhalb des Zimmers kann ich weder leben noch sterben." Seine Kleidung ist während des Sommers und des Winters sehr leicht. Auch im Winter trägt er einen Rock statt eines Mantels. Er arbeitet vom Morgen bis zum Abend im Garten oder auf dem Felde. Er liebt die Familie, und die Familie liebt ihn. Wir gehen gerne zu ihm.

[1] *Psychology* (Henry Holt and Company, 1915), p. 253. [2] *Language Learning*, pp. 70–75.

[3] Taken from Hagboldt and Kaufmann, *Deutsch für Anfänger: An Inductive Presentation of Minimum Essentials.* The Heath-Chicago Series. D. C. Heath and Company, 1930.

The instructor reads the selection to the class, pronouncing every word carefully and distinctly, and fluently enough to accustom the student to the sound and the rhythm of naturally spoken German. He rereads the passage in word and thought groups which are repeated by the class in concert. Then the words and phrases are explained and again pronounced by the instructor, by individual students, and in concert. Specific difficulties are singled out for special drill in an exercise called Übungen zur Aussprache (see Chapter IV, pp. 73 f.). The class in concert or individual students read words taken from previous texts or the present one.

The class has been reminded of certain words in previous lessons, and now it is time to lift the grammatical problems out of the text for examination. The problems in question are: (1) the genitive forms of the definite and indefinite article and kein; (2a) the genitive ending of most masculine and neuter nouns; (2b) the absence of inflection in feminine nouns; (3) the genitive of wer; (4) the prepositions with the genitive.

In a special section called B we print the problems and have them followed by questions which are not beyond the student's powers of analysis:

B. 1. *a.* des Vaters   des Hauses   der Mutter
      b. eines Vaters   eines Hauses   einer Mutter
      c. keines Vaters   keines Hauses   keiner Mutter

(*a*) What are the genitive forms of the definite article? (*b*) of the indefinite article? (*c*) of kein?

2. *a.* Das Haus des Vaters steht hier. Die Form des Balles ist rund. Die Farbe des Hauses ist weiß.

      b. Die Farbe der Tafel ist schwarz.

(*a*) What is the genitive ending of masculine and neuter nouns?
(*b*) Are feminine nouns inflected?

3. Wessen Haus ist das?
What is the genitive form of wer?

4. Anstatt eines Mantels trägt er einen Rock.
      Er will außerhalb (innerhalb) des Hauses sein.
      Er wohnt in einem Dorfe oberhalb (unterhalb) der Stadt.
      Das Dorf liegt diesseits (jenseits) des Flusses.
      Er geht während des Sommers trotz der Hitze aufs Feld.

GRAMMAR   139

What prepositions are always followed by the genitive? Give them with their meanings.

Since the forms and words asked about in B are printed in bold-faced type, the answers are easy. If time permits, the student may be requested to gather from his reading numerous examples bearing on the rule which is always stated for comparison and verification in a special section consistently called C in the exact order and arrangement of section B.

In section A the student worked through the text; in B he examined carefully forms and words lifted from the text, and by specific questions he was helped to formulate the rule; in C he was able to check and verify the rule; and now in D he is given exercises which he does in class and writes out at home. On the next day he is given exercise E, consisting of several reading selections based on the forms studied so far.

Then follows a purely deductive supplement of eight to ten direct method exercises designed to turn the student's knowledge into more active mastery. This supplement is called Übungen. It begins with questions based on the text, and continues by requesting the student to supply the definite article and endings, the indefinite article, appropriate prepositions. It presents, besides, a brief review by exercises with prepositions governing other cases; it requires the pupil to use each genitive preposition in a short sentence of his own making, and to formulate and answer questions with certain interrogatives which have occurred previously. Finally, the student is given an opportunity to apply the forms so far gained in a free composition, but not without having been warned to confine himself strictly to the forms which are taught in the present or previous lessons. Or, instead of a free composition, he may try his ability on a set of translation exercises consisting of short and easy sentences in the back of the book.

It has now become apparent, we hope, that inductive presentation need not be disorderly, as it has often been feared it might. It can and should be meticulously orderly and systematic. The greatest advantage of this sort of introduction to grammar is the clear division into two distinct parts, one inductive or analytic

(A–C), the other deductive or synthetic (D and Übungen). When the aim of the class is reading, the student may proceed to the next lesson after E; wherever it seems advisable to strengthen and fix grammatical forms by further exercises, he may take up a part or all of the Übungen.

A second example.[1] In the main, a deductive type of grammar presentation has grown naturally out of the constant pressure for time. This type of grammar omits the inductive feature entirely and begins with a simple statement of the rule. Then it proceeds to apply the rule in words and short sentences. Even the first lessons quickly lead up to coherent paragraphs. The technique of the exercises is that used in the direct method. The simple lesson structure is throughout as follows:

1. The grammatical part.
2. Exercises leading up to coherent, meaningful paragraphs on which, as a final step, questions are based.
3. A vocabulary in alphabetical order.

After a simple statement of the rules involved in the first lesson we continue with exercises:

Übungen (Exercises)

A. Give the following nouns with ein and kein:

EXAMPLE: ber Vater, ein Vater, kein Vater

ber Student, bie Mutter, bas Kind, ber Winter, bas Wort, ber Sommer, bie Dame, ber Herr, bie Aufgabe.

B. Replace the nouns in A by personal pronouns of the third person.

EXAMPLE: ber Vater, er

C. Conjugate: 1. Ich bin hier. 2. Ich bin nicht in Deutschland. 3. Wo bin ich?

D. Supply the definite article:

1. —— Sommer ist warm. 2. —— Winter ist kalt. 3. —— Kind ist jung. 4. —— Großvater ist alt. 5. —— Mutter ist hier. 6. —— Vater ist ba. 7. —— Herr ist in Deutschland. 8. —— Dame ist in

---

[1] Taken from Hagboldt-Kaufmann, *A Brief Course in German.* The Heath-Chicago Series. D. C. Heath and Company, 1937.

Amerika. 9. —— Wort ist leicht. 10. —— Übung ist schwer.
11. —— Vers ist dumm. 12. —— Esel noch mehr.

E. Supply the indefinite article in D, 3–12.

F. Supply kein, keine:

1. —— Sommer ist kalt. 2. —— Dame ist alt. 3. —— Kind ist
hier. 4. —— Student trinkt Bier. 5. —— Wort ist schwer. 6. Blau
ist —— Bär.

G. Supply the proper form of sein:

1. Wo —— wir? 2. Wer —— ihr? 3. —— sie da? 4. Sie
(*They, you*) —— in Amerika. 5. Du —— kein Bär. 6. Die Aufgabe
—— nicht schwer.

H. Answer:

1. Wie ist der Sommer? 2. Wie ist der Winter? 3. Wer ist jung?
4. Wer ist alt? 5. Wo ist der Herr? 6. Wo ist die Dame? 7. Wie
ist die Übung? 8. Wie ist der Vers?

The greatest single advantage of this type of presentation is the
gain in time. Instructors and students feel at ease with a grammar
of one-fourth or one-third of the customary length. They can
work through a short and concise grammar in college in approximately fifty class hours and read a number of graded readers
besides (see Professor Goedsche's note, p. 129). To insure correctness of grammatical detail, tests may be given at regular
intervals. In giving these tests, which are designed to measure
progress and accuracy, it is difficult to find just the most oppor-
tune time, so as to keep the class working efficiently without
creating the feeling of haste, anxiety, or displeasure.

We have discussed two ways of presenting grammar, one beginning with induction, one beginning with deduction. There is,
however, a third possibility, namely, to write a grammar based
entirely on the principle of recognition.

A RECOGNITION GRAMMAR had, until recently, not existed for
the teaching of German. Yet, for the student whose only aim is
reading ability, a grammar based on recognition deserves a

thorough test. Even though we have been told innumerable times that reconstruction is more favorable for learning than recognition, have we a right to assume that this holds true for language instruction of a specific nature in very brief courses? We know for certain that reconstruction of forms is many times more difficult than their recognition. And for this very reason we must determine once and for all by actual experiment what would happen if we were much more specific in our methods. Supposing we were to reverse the old procedure and make our student do exactly what he attempts to do in reading a foreign language, *i.e.*, analyze, recognize, and interpret forms and sentences he finds in reading; does it not seem that this procedure would correspond much more closely to the student's needs?

Yet, on the one hand it may be that the richness of inflectional endings might prove unfavorable for recognition; on the other, however, we may find that we have overstressed grammatical instruction and neglected vocabulary knowledge. This possibility is strongly suggested by an experiment carried out at the University of Chicago in 1933 for 1325 students whose tests showed an extremely high correlation between reading and vocabulary, namely, .82.[1]

Instead of theorizing we should as soon as possible make a series of experiments with two types of short grammars, one based on deduction (reconstruction), one based on analysis (recognition). Both grammars should have exactly the same vocabulary and the same amount of grammatical information. In the first type the student would be required to reconstruct forms, in the second to analyze and interpret them. If such texts were used in two parallel classes with students of approximately the same training and intelligence, and if both groups of students were required to read the same number of pages in carefully graded readers and to supplement their study of grammar, it could be established with considerable accuracy which presentation is more economical in terms of time, effort, and effect.

It is hardly necessary to state that a recognition grammar is probably advantageous in very brief courses of six weeks to one

---

[1] See *Language Learning*, pp. 129–33, or "Reading for Comprehension and its Testing," *German Quarterly* (March, 1933), pp. 68–76.

semester in college or wherever conditions seem to demand a rapid survey of the structure of the language for reading purposes which later may be followed by more detailed study of grammar for more comprehensive aims.

A third example. We give an example from *First Aid,*[1] a recognition grammar. The structure of the lessons is as follows:

1. The grammatical statement, but where possible in a reversed way, that is, from the standpoint of the reading student.
2. A vocabulary in alphabetical order.
3. (*a*) Exercises to be written out, intended for better retention of the forms studied.
   (*b*) Identification exercises checking the comprehension of these forms.
   (*c*) Coherent paragraphs for reading and translation.
   (*d*) Questions based on the paragraphs, but to be answered in English.
   (*e*) Review exercises.

Übungen

A. Give the principal parts of: Class 1*a*: ſchreiben, bleiben, ſchreien, ſchweigen, abſteigen; 1*b*: reiten; Class 2: frieren, fliehen, riechen; Class 3*a*: finden, ſingen, trinken, gelingen; anbinden, aufſpringen; 3*b*: ſchwimmen, beginnen.

B. Conjugate in the past: 1. Ich fror. 2. Ich ritt durch die kalte Stadt. 3. Ich fand ein Wirtshaus. 4. Ich ſchrie: „Feuer!" 5. Ich floh aus dem Gaſtzimmer.

C. Identify tense or mood, infinitive, and meaning.

   EXAMPLE: binde an, imperative of anbinden (*tie on*).

1. ich ſchrie. 2. du biſt geblieben. 3. er hatte geſchrieben. 4. wir werden ſchreien. 5. ihr werdet geſchwiegen haben. 6. ich ritt. 7. du haſt gefroren. 8. er war geflohen. 9. ich roch. 10. du wirſt gefunden haben. 11. ich ſang. 12. du haſt getrunken. 13. trinkt! 14. es war gelungen. 15. wir hatten angebunden. 16. ihr werdet aufſpringen. 17. wir werden begonnen haben. 18. ſie ſchwammen. 19. ſchwimmen Sie!

---

[1] By Peter Hagboldt and F. W. Kaufmann, as yet unpublished.

D. Identify as present or past participle, give infinitive and meaning.

EXAMPLE: eine lesende Dame (lesend, present participle of lesen), *a reading lady.*

1. ein angebundenes Pferd. 2. der schreibende Schüler. 3. ein schweigender Mann. 4. das geschriebene Buch. 5. der getrunkene Wein. 6. der beginnende Sommer.

E. Translate: 1. Der Winter war sehr kalt, und das Wasser fror auf den Flüssen. 2. Ein Soldat ritt über das kalte Land. 3. In einer kleinen Stadt stieg er am Wirtshaus ab. 4. Er band sein Pferd im Stalle an. 5. In dem warmen Gastzimmer fand er keinen Stuhl. 6. Viele Gäste sangen und tranken dort. 7. Er schwieg einige Sekunden. 8. Dann schrie er: 9. „Hier riecht es nach Feuer." 10. Da sprangen die Gäste von ihren Stühlen auf und flohen aus dem Wirtshause. 11. So gelang es dem Soldaten, einen Stuhl zu bekommen. 12. Er trank ein Glas Wein. 13. Er stieg auf sein Pferd und ritt weiter.

14. Hast du den Brief geschrieben? 15. Nein, ich bin durch den Park geritten. 16. Ich bin nicht zu Hause geblieben. 17. Denn die Kinder haben geschrieen. 18. Meine Schwester hat gesungen. 19. Mein Vater ist aufgesprungen und geflohen. 20. Da habe ich die Arbeit garnicht begonnen.

F. Give the infinitives of the verbs in E.

G. Answer in English: 1. Wie war das Wetter? 2. Wo stieg der Soldat ab? 3. Wo blieb das Pferd? 4. Wen fand der Soldat im Gastzimmer? 5. Was schrie er? 6. Wohin flohen die Gäste?

THE SEQUENCE OF GRAMMATICAL TOPICS seems important and yet there is little we can state with absolute authority. The puzzling questions are: How much grammar shall we teach? What is to come first? What next? What is to follow? How much space shall we allow for each topic? What is the most logical sequence of topics? Shall we make logic or utility the basis of the presentation of grammar? What phenomena are most frequent and therefore most important? Which ones are comparatively rare and hence unessential? How can we avoid the danger of dividing the grammar into too many lessons or too few? What is the best procedure for pupils of a specific age in high school in regard to the aim and the length of the course? What about the vast difference in maturity and attitude of high-school and college students? Is not an entirely different approach needed for each?

Since each of these vital questions is certain to be answered in different ways by different instructors, it is not surprising that every year sees a crop of new grammars on the market.

It is probably true that two authors will seldom agree entirely on a majority of the problems arising constantly in the construction of a grammar. Every author has a definite amount of experience around which he builds an ideology of a "perfect grammar" for his specific situation. Every experience differs, and, besides, every experience is interpreted in a variety of ways.

However, there are a number of simple principles which should be observed in the construction of any grammar:

The younger the pupil, the shorter must be the lesson. The more mature the student, the more he can assimilate in a given time. If the student is very young, grammatical terms must be either entirely avoided or explained with the utmost care. The number of lessons may vary between 14 and 60 or even more, according to the age of the student. The older the student, the more he is likely to understand the necessity of a more or less logical presentation in accordance with the scientific classification of grammar. The young pupil depends largely on learning specific words and forms. He is not likely to see the connection and interrelation of forms which is quite obvious to mature students. The sequence of lessons should be orderly, progressive, and logical for maturer students. There should be a definite connection between the old lesson and the new, and be it only — in the case of young students — by words and idioms identical in both lessons. When the length of the course permits of inductive presentation it should be used to the full extent of its possibilities. The words and idioms should be based on reliable word and idiom lists. In courses of three or four years the grammar should present interesting coherent texts, but strictly within the limit of the most frequent words and idioms. The exercises should be keyed to the length of the course, that is, consist of many recognition exercises in short courses, and many reconstruction exercises in courses of longer duration.

In view of the long experience in teaching German here and

abroad, it is strange that our empirical knowledge should not have resulted in a definite optimum lesson sequence. No doubt this is due to the infinite number of possibilities of combining one problem with almost any other. In the absence of definite knowledge of the frequency of grammatical forms, H. T. Betteridge [1] has made an interesting study of five grammars in which he naturally finds a wide divergence in regard to sequence of lessons. Concluding that in the initial stages "we must be guided by the criterion of sheer utility rather than by any logical scheme of classification," he takes Morgan's *German Frequency Word Book* as a basis for suggesting at least the first six lessons. Since the word ber is the most frequent German word, Betteridge recommends as the first lessons: (1) the definite article; third singular and third plural of fein, haben, and werden; (2) the indefinite article; (3) prepositions with dative only; (4) prepositions governing the accusative; (5) prepositions governing the dative and accusative; (6) review of all the prepositions from lessons 2–5. We welcome his insistence on the mastery of the article declension, his recommendation that the verb should be taught at first only in its most simple tenses, present and future, and that the noun in the plural should at first be taught as needed. We cannot follow his demand that the attributive adjective must receive attention from the outset. The treatment of adjective endings depends entirely on the aim of the course. When the aim is reading ability, it is quite inadvisable to devote much valuable time to the teaching of endings which play no important part in the interpretation of the text. But the author's recommendation is entirely justified in England, where the active phases of language study are emphasized.

A much more reliable guide for the sequence of grammatical topics in an elementary grammar for high schools and colleges will be available as soon as the *German Syntax Count* is completed. No doubt it will give us much valuable and long needed information.[2]

GRAMMATICAL TERMINOLOGY. In December of 1913 there ap-

---

[1] "The First Term's Work in German," *Modern Languages*, XVIII (Oct. 1936), pp. 26–32.

[2] The late Joseph Dwight Deihl wrote in 1923 a booklet entitled *The High School Course in German*, edited and revised by Bayard Quincy Morgan in 1928. Bulletin of the University of Wisconsin. Serial No. 1505, High School

peared the *Report of the Joint Committee on Grammatical Nomenclature*.[1] In the Preface to the first edition the committee states that the confusion in the use of grammatical terms is quite hopeless. For instance "good" in "John is good" is given nine different names in twenty-five English grammars, *i.e.: attribute complement, predicate adjective, subject complement, attribute complement* or *predicate adjective, subjective complement, complement of intransitive verb, predicate attribute, adjective attribute,* and *predicate.* The committee states:

> The situation as we now have it is wasteful from the point of view of accomplishment, pitiable from the point of view of the needless inflictions which it puts upon the unfortunate pupil, and absurd from the point of view of linguistic science ... A system for high-school instruction more flatly opposed to the modern demand for efficiency could hardly be devised.

We are extremely fortunate in having a document by which the harmful confusion of grammatical terms may be definitely avoided in the future. Yet, according to Professor F. W. Meisnest, the *Report of the Joint Committee* had gone unread until recently by all but four authors of German grammars. In 1933, at a meeting of the American Association of Teachers of German held at St. Louis, it was voted to have a committee investigate the problem of standardizing the grammatical terminology in the teaching of German. The chairman, F. W. Meisnest, submitted a report in two articles, the first containing the nomenclature in English and German with recommendations, the second setting forth arguments in favor of the report.[2] To my knowledge the report has not been accepted as final at this writing.

As a result of the *Report of the Joint Committee* a great effort has

Series 24. On pp. 38 ff. he gives a syllabus for a four-year course in German for high schools. Unfortunately, this booklet is now out of print.

See also E. W. Bagster-Collins, *op. cit.,* pp. 105–36, for a chapter on grammar which, though written in 1904, is still very interesting and suggestive.

[1] First printed in 1913; several times reprinted, with a total of nine thousand copies. Revised edition Oct. 1923. Reprinted Oct. 1929. The University of Chicago Press.

[2] F. W. Meisnest, "Report of the Committee on Grammatical Nomenclature in the Teaching of German," *German Quarterly,* VIII, pp. 66–71 and 110–18 (March and May, 1935).

But compare A. W. Aron, "Tense Terminology of the German Subjunc-

been made in recent years to bring order into the chaos of grammatical confusion. Unfortunately it was found that the real cause was simple ignorance on the part of the student of the meaning of the most basic terms. Luella and Sidney L. Pressey have made a systematic study of the number of concepts which should be known to college freshmen.[1] They examined eight widely used grammars — two of each for French, German, Latin, and Spanish — and found that 260 terms were used 1 to 120 times, of which one-third occurred so infrequently that the investigators struck them off their list. Only 65 terms appeared 10 times or more, and 45 of these, it was felt, the student should know regardless of his previous training. Forty-one concepts of an advanced nature were expected to be known by students with two or more years of training in a foreign language. On the basis of the two lists — 45 and 41 grammatical concepts — 1500 freshmen were given a test which resulted in a median score of 42, the range of errors varying from 7 to 80.[2]

We are not surprised, therefore, at the results of an experiment made at the University of Pennsylvania [3] about which Cole remarks:

> When to one student in six entering college, *easily* is an adjective, and *him* a reflexive pronoun; when to 10 per cent of the class *you* is a relative pronoun, and *it was snowing* is a transitive verb, what must the situation be in the first or second year of high school? Under such conditions, how can the modern language teacher be expected to secure satisfactory results? [4]

ERROR COUNTS. An experimental study was undertaken at the request of the American and Canadian Committees on Modern

---

tive," *Modern Language Journal*, II (Nov. 1917), pp. 78–83 and F. W. Kaufmann, "Erarbeitung of the Subjunctive," *German Quarterly*, III (March, 1930), pp. 41–46. Moreover compare Eugene Jackson, "Debunking the Subjunctive," *German Quarterly*, III (March, 1930), pp. 103–06.

[1] "The Language Concepts Needed by College Freshmen," *Modern Language Journal*, XIV (May, 1930), pp. 624–30.

[2] Robert D. Cole, *Modern Foreign Languages and Their Teaching*. Revised and enlarged by James Burton Tharp (Appleton-Century Company, 1937), p. 277.

[3] W. S. Jack, "The Modern Language Student *vs.* English Grammar," *Modern Language Journal*, XIV (Nov. 1929), pp. 95–102.   [4] Cole, *op. cit.*, p. 278.

Languages in order to provide material for the study of the frequency of errors occurring in the written work of German students in secondary schools and colleges.[1] B. A. Eisenlohr and C. M. Purin prepared a check list divided into 11 topics, each in turn subdivided into 1 to 25 items, the total list containing approximately 100 items. A wide variety of material was checked, for the most part German-English translation exercises taken from 29 different grammars and textbooks. Twenty-two cooperating teachers checked more than 10 exercises each. Careful directions were sent to these teachers who had volunteered to help. Unfortunately, the number of students taking part in the experiment could not be ascertained. In all, approximately 51,738 running words were examined for correctness. The errors were then classified and recorded on 20 different tables. Table I shows the errors occurring in the 11 categories on the German error check list arranged in order of descending frequency.

1. Verbs	16,435	6. Adjectives	4458
2. Vocabulary	8249	7. Prepositions	3413
3. Limiting words (ber=		8. Pronouns	3406
words, ein=words)	7151	9. Idioms	678
4. Spelling	6885	10. Conjunctions	422
5. Nouns	5889	11. Adverbs	280

The great number of verb errors (see item 1 above) are classified as follows:

1. Position of verbs	6790	5. Principal parts	1033
2. Active indicative	4512	6. Subjunctive	781
3. Modals	1391	7. Imperative	456
4. Use of tenses	1114	8. Passive indicative	359

We note immediately the high number of errors in verb position (6790) and in indicative forms (4512); the frequency with which wrong words are chosen (8249), and the total errors in the use of ber=words and ein=words (7151). Altogether, a total of 56,267 errors were recorded, and if the estimate of the number of the words checked for mistakes be correct, we have more errors than words checked for errors. The author justly warns us against

[1] Lillie Vinal Hathaway, "A German Error Count: An Experimental Study," *Modern Language Journal* (April, 1929), pp. 512–33.

taking this investigation as the final word on the subject of error frequency. She offers constructive advice in behalf of future experiments of the same nature. No definite conclusion can be drawn from the report about students' attainment at different semester levels. The fact that the number of students examined is not even known and that 109 persons promised help, while only 30 usable reports finally came in, is eloquent testimony that the task undertaken was far greater than anyone realized.

Error counts are valuable. The more exact the information about the points of grammar which are felt to be difficult and elusive by our students, the better we are able to revise our presentation and to meet their difficulties. But even assuming that we got perfect results from such an error count, the conclusions drawn by different teachers would vary widely.

One group, by far the greatest, would find nothing wrong with an error count based on composition and translation. They would insist on mastery of forms and prescribe more drill on those grammatical problems which had shown the greatest number of errors.

Another group, much smaller but — we think — more thoughtful, would say: "This error count is excellent for students who are ambitious to write and speak; but since more than 80 per cent of our students aim at reading ability, the count is quite inadequate. For we do not care to know how correctly a student can supply forms of grammar in a composition; what we want to know is how correctly and easily he can recognize and interpret grammatical forms when and where he needs them in his reading. Our task is therefore not to give more drill on problems which may add little to the student's reading ability, but to provide for more exercises in that function of language in which our student wants to excel, that is, analysis, recognition, and interpretation of grammatical forms in reading.

ENTRANCE EXAMINATIONS. The content and the nature of our language courses in high schools is largely determined by the examinations set by two examining bodies, the Regents Examinations of New York State and the College Entrance Examination Board. In the course of time a great many articles have appeared praising or condemning these examinations. In 1927 Ben D. Wood through the *Study* published his fine volume on *New York*

Experiments with New-Type Modern Language Tests. Part II of this volume deals with the Regents experiments with new-type examinations in French, Spanish, German, and Physics. In Part III the author states his conclusions. He finds

> that the new-type examinations are roughly twice as reliable and valid as the old-type examinations of equal time allowance; that the new-type examinations afford comparable measures for all classes in a given subject matter in the same and in different years and thus offer a means of eliminating overlapping of classes and variations in local school standards to a much greater extent than they are eliminated by the old-type Regents examinations; and that the new-type tests over a series of years will cost not more than 10 per cent as much as old-type examinations, as administered and read by the College Entrance Examination Board, cost.[1]

Nevertheless, when we keep in mind the pitiful findings of the Coleman Report — at least 50 per cent of the two-year group and at least 30 per cent of the three-year group could not use the foreign language for reading or for writing with even a moderate degree of ease; and when, furthermore, we bear in mind that a high-school C — this has been our experience at the University of Chicago — when given a college placement test often ranks D in comparison with college students of comparable preparation, we cannot help believing that Coleman is correct in assuming that our demands on the average high-school pupil are too severe.[2]

The role of grammar as a modest handmaiden to reading must and will remain a beautiful theory as long as examining bodies consider translation from English into the foreign language an important function of language instruction. Translation is, at best, an extremely difficult task, which can hardly be achieved by the average student in two years, except in its most simple forms. One cannot help feeling that some examiners are inclined to minimize unduly the difficulties implied in translation. If a simple sentence of twelve words requires twenty-one mental steps to make an imperfect translation,[3] how many steps will be required for a longer sentence containing real difficulties?

[1] The Macmillan Company, 1927, pp. 318 ff.   [2] Algernon Coleman, *The Teaching of Modern Foreign Languages in the United States* (The Macmillan Company, 1929), pp. 168 ff.   [3] For an example, see *Language Learning,* p. 26.

Would it not be the part of wisdom not to require greater accuracy than we can reasonably expect of our students? Might it not be advisable in view of the findings of the *Study* to base entrance examinations on one single ability, that ability which we are trying to achieve? If examination boards were to set one type of examination, of which the first part were based strictly on recognition (for two-year high-school pupils) and the second part contained a test on grammar of the multiple-choice type [1] (for three- and four-year high-school pupils), both students and teachers would be immensely benefited. Teachers would be able to turn to their task; there would no longer be special drill sections for students intending to take college entrance examinations. Students would feel free to devote themselves to their reading and interpretation of grammatical forms and their usages, and teachers would have more time to spend on the perfection of techniques and devices in reading courses.

WHAT MUST BE THE RESULT OF GRAMMAR STUDY? The net result should be, roughly speaking, one of two distinct abilities:

1. The learner should be able to analyze, recognize, and interpret correctly meanings of words, phrases, idioms, and sentences within certain definitely defined limits. (This is true of all short courses.)

2. The learner should have practiced the use of words, phrases, idioms, and sentences so conscientiously, frequently, and effectively by direct method exercises that he can actually use the simpler forms of the foreign language both orally and in writing. (This is an aim which, in my opinion, cannot be achieved by students of average ability in a brief high-school course. The student must have special aptitude for language study.)

Since it is quite impossible to predict for any learner the point at which passive knowledge will be converted into active ability, and since we must keep in mind our minimum aim, reading ability,

---

[1] The multiple-choice technique is important. Ben D. Wood found that correlation between grammar and reading is only .65 as based on the results of the Regents Examinations which use completion. Completion is more difficult for the "reading student" than multiple choice. The latter technique as used in the *American Council Test*, both forms, is easier and corresponds more closely to the actual situation in reading. Compare text to note 1, p. 142, and Ben D. Wood, *New York Experiments with New-Type Tests* (The Macmillan Company, 1928), pp. 124 ff.

it is imperative that during the first two years of high-school study the teacher be on his guard not to indulge in an overdose of oral and written composition. These activities should be postponed until the essentials of language have been thoroughly assimilated through the study of a short grammar supplemented by abundant intensive and extensive reading.

MEASURING THE WORTH OF BASIC TEXTBOOKS. Our eagerness to test the results of teaching has naturally led us to an attempt to measure the merit of elementary, basic textbooks. In 1917 J. D. Deihl published an interesting and still useful article on "Choosing a Grammar for Beginners."[1] Deihl's example was soon followed by others. Howard C. McElroy wrote "Selecting a Basic Textbook,"[2] Alexander Green, "The Measurement of Modern Language Books,"[3] and Emilie M. White, "The Selection of High School Texts in Modern Languages."[4] James B. Tharp, acknowledging his indebtedness to Deihl, McElroy, and White, prepared five scales for basic texts, ten for readers, and six for standardized tests.[5]

In 1926 Alexander Green had predicted an early "end to this passing vogue" of rating scales, but late in 1938 the passing vogue seems to have been suddenly revived.[6] Personally, I believe firmly that measuring the value of a basic grammar is infinitely more difficult than we are ready to admit. And strangely enough, the difficulty does not lie in thoroughly analyzing a given book, but in coming to an agreement in regard to one single aim to be reached in a definite time and, moreover, in regard to the means by which it is to be achieved. We did agree on the single aim long ago, but, unfortunately, with strong, though unconscious, mental reservations. As a group we have even been accused of rendering lip service to the reading aim, and justly so.

Yet we can never construct a fair score card for testing the merit of a grammar unless we have in mind a clear aim and also a clear idea of the means to this end. Our convictions as to aim

---

[1] *Modern Language Journal*, II (May, 1918), pp. 368–73.   [2] *Ibid.*, XIX (Oct. 1934), pp. 5–8.   [3] *Ibid.*, X (Feb. 1926), pp. 259–69.   [4] *Ibid.*, XIX (April 1935), pp. 481–88.   [5] Printed privately. Address Professor James B. Tharp, Ohio State University, Columbus, Ohio.   [6] *Monatshefte für deutschen Unterricht*, Wisconsin State Teachers Association, Meeting of the German Division, XXX (Nov. 1938), pp. 383 f.

and method inevitably color and determine our evaluations. If, for instance, we are convinced that reading should be the only objective in a brief course, we have no right whatever to expect of a grammar more than a brief statement of the rule, and a modicum of synthesis followed by abundant recognition exercises. If we believe in *realia* even in brief courses, we are certain to look for them. Unless we find them we shall be prejudiced against the book. Yet no one can tell us to what extent *realia* can be presented within the limits of our word and idiom lists. If we are committed to induction, we are certain to be prejudiced against a deductive presentation of grammar. And so, all along the line, our creeds inevitably form our judgments. Perhaps the best way to make a fairly good score card for a grammar is to present to the individual scorer as many and as strong arguments for such features as have been found most helpful according to actual experience, and which can be defended in behalf of our pedagogical conscience.

The main trouble with score cards for texts is that the profession as a whole is not able to state clearly and definitely in terms of percentages what values should be allotted to the features constituting a grammar.

Deihl, whose work on this problem still is highly practical, divides the values given to each feature of a grammar as follows:

1. Illustrative reading (meaning the reading in the grammar exemplifying the rules stated) 20 per cent
2. Exercises (meaning the devices used to drive home the rules) 30 per cent
3. Theoretical grammar (meaning the simple statements of grammar) 15 per cent
4. Length in relation to course — to this very important feature Deihl gives only 7 per cent
5. Logic and clearness of arrangement (Überſichtlich= keit would perhaps be the German word) 8 per cent
6. Vocabulary (doubtless includes idioms; frequency is probably meant; one should consider that many authors treat vocabulary in their readers) 10 per cent
7. Treatment of pronunciation 5 per cent
8. Illustrations; make-up; price 5 per cent

Total 100 per cent

Following Deihl's outline I suggest a simple score card in question form.

1. Is there ample illustrative reading material either in the book itself or in a reader devised for and intended to be used in connection with this text? Is the vocabulary in this material graded in regard to words, idioms, and sentence structure?

2. Are there sufficient direct method exercises? Have they been tested in class? Do they direct the student's attention to one point at a time? Do they stress the thought unit rather than the single word?

3. How are the grammatical statements? Simple, clear, concise? Neither too short for beginners nor too long for mature students?

4. Is the text short enough to be finished well within the time at your disposal? (Remember that in reading courses you cannot make a success of a bulky grammar.)

5. Is the sequence of the lessons orderly, clear, logical? Does one get the impression of Überſichtlichkeit? Are inductive features used, or is the book intended for brief courses, so that the omission of inductive features seems advisable or even desirable?

6. How many words are used? How many idioms? Compare the vocabulary with Wadepuhl and Morgan's *Minimum Standard German Vocabulary* or with Purin's.

7. Is the chapter on pronunciation clear? Are the explanations simple and to the point? Are the words given as examples actually used in the lessons which follow?

8. Are the illustrations interesting and attractive? Is the student helped by certain typographical devices? Is the text not too expensive in comparison with similar texts on the market?

9. Is the grammatical terminology in agreement with the recommendations of the *Joint Committee on Grammatical Nomenclature?* [1]

I do not know whether or not the values given by Deihl to each item will pass the scrutiny of a committee that may be appointed some day to fix a definite percentage to each feature. What I do know, however, is that a score card must be clear and simple. It must not expect of the scorer that he spend too much time in analyzing and evaluating a given text. And it must not be so detailed as to make it impossible to allow even 1 per cent to a single item mentioned under a specific feature.

[1] Even in recent articles in reputable journals I notice that writers on grammatical problems use misleading terms, such as "conditional," a term particularly unfortunate in German.

In preparing a score card, let us not forget the main thing, which is to direct the examiner's attention to the most important features of the book, to remember that the most excellent book in the hands of a poor teacher is ineffective, and that in the final analysis no uninteresting presentation, however perfect in technical detail, can arouse and maintain the student's interest.

DEVICES FOR TEACHING GRAMMAR are far too numerous to be listed. Specific devices and techniques are given with each topic in any elementary or review grammar. Lists of devices are often misleading, for they mention grammar under almost any caption: dramatizing, composition, conversation, reading, dictation, etc., etc. It is true that we cannot write nor speak nor engage in many activities which do not imply the use of grammar; it is equally true that devices for teaching grammar are most effective when they concentrate the student's attention on one point, or on several points involved in one complex of one grammatical problem. To be sure, we may occasionally combine the study of grammar with other classroom activities, but we must beware of tormenting our students with never-ending drill on grammar. The important thing to remember is that our aim should determine the nature of devices, that in grammar all devices should be functional, *i.e.*, that each device should further the students' ultimate aim. Among the most important difficulties of German grammar for whatever objective are the article and the strong verb. We shall give a few techniques for each:

The article, definite and indefinite, is usually justly treated with great care in the first lessons of any elementary grammar. An absolutely thorough grasp is imperative.

ber — ein (fein)

The teacher's direction may be as follows:

1. Reproduce from memory a paradigm of ber.
2. Reproduce from memory a paradigm of fein.
3. Identify as to case and number the 16 forms of the definite article: ber (4 possibilities); bes (2 possibilities); bem (2 possibilities); ben (2 possibilities); bie (4 possibilities); bas (2 possibilities).
4. Do as in 3 with fein; identify each of its 6 forms, or 16 potential cases.

5. Supply the definite article according to simple rules.
6. Decline the definite article with nouns in the singular and the plural.
7. Do as in 6 with fein.
8. Identify the component parts of contractions.
9. Contract article and preposition.
10. Give in dative plural a list of nouns.

Strong Verbs

A model for each type of the seven ablaut classes of strong verbs might serve as a basis for effective instruction of strong verbal forms. One or several classes may be taken up at a time.

Models:

1.	(a)	bleiben	blieb	ift geblieben
	(b)	beißen	biß	gebiffen
2.		fliehen	floh	ift geflohen
3.	(a)	binden	band	gebunden
	(b)	fchwimmen	fchwamm	ift gefchwommen
4.		helfen	half	geholfen
5.		bitten	bat	gebeten
6.		fahren	fuhr	ift gefahren
7.		laffen	ließ	gelaffen

1. Conjugate several strong verbs in the past: Jch bleibe zu Haufe. Jch fliehe aus dem Haufe. Jch fchwimme nicht gut.

2. Give the principal parts on the model of the verbs listed above:

1. (a) fchreiben, fchreien, fchweigen, fteigen, abfteigen
   (b) zerbeißen, reiten, fchneiden, ftreiten
2. fliegen, fließen, frieren, fchießen, verlieren, ziehen
3. (a) finden, gelingen, fingen, finken, fpringen, trinken
   (b) beginnen, fpinnen
4. nehmen, ftehlen, brechen, fprechen, fterben, treffen, kommen
5. fitzen, liegen, effen, geben, treten, lefen, fehen, fein
6. laden, fchlagen, tragen, wafchen, wachfen, backen
7. braten, fallen, fangen, halten, raten, fchlafen, laufen, rufen

3. Give the principal parts of the three irregular strong verbs.

4. Write out complete paradigms of several strong verbs in the six indicative tenses.

5. Give a synopsis of: (a) Jch bleibe zu Haufe. (b) Jch reite jeden Tag. (c) Jch verliere mein Geld. (d) Jch finde meine Bücher nicht. (e) Jch finge nicht fchön aber laut. (f) Jch gewinne immer. (g) Jch

fomme jeden Tag. (*h*) Was geschieht jetzt? (*i*) Ich fahre aufs Land. (*j*) Am Sonntag schlafe ich lange. (*k*) Ich gehe nach Hause. (*l*) Ich stehe vor der Tür. (*m*) Ich tue nichts.

6. Give a sliding synopsis of the sentences in 5.

7. Begin the sliding synopsis with any one of the six personal pronouns.

8. In any given text change all the verbs to the past.

9. Reduce the past and the past participle of strong verbs to the infinitive and state the meaning of the reduced form.

10. Assign a number of strong verbs for each recitation; or hold one student responsible for corrections of errors in one of the seven classes; or review according to classes, finally ending up with a general review of all strong verbs which have occurred.

BIBLIOGRAPHY

COFFMAN, BERTHA REED. "An Experiment in Motivation." *German Quarterly* (Jan. 1932), pp. 17–20.

CRANDON, LAURA B. "Daltonizing First Year German Classes." *German Quarterly* (Nov. 1928), pp. 55–59.

GOODLOE, JANE F. "An Outline of German Grammar on the Mnemonic Scheme of Three, Five, Eight." *Modern Language Journal*, XXIII, 2 (Nov. 1938), pp. 109–17.

HAGBOLDT, PETER. *Language Learning.* The University of Chicago Press, 1935.

HESS, JOHN A. "The bu=row in a College German Class." *Monatshefte für deutschen Unterricht* (Sept. 1915), pp. 216–20.

HOLLANDER, LEE M. "Aus dem Schulzimmer. Methods of Exercise Correction." *Monatshefte für deutschen Unterricht* (Oct. 1931), pp. 184–86.

LOHSTOETTER, LOTTIE OLGA. "A Device for Teaching German Nouns to Beginners." *Modern Language Journal* (March, 1927), pp. 359–64.
—— "Adverbs and 'Adwords' in German." *Ibid.* (Feb. 1937), pp. 339–41.

LUSSKY, GEORGE F. "A Simplified Method of Teaching the Inflection of Adjectives in German." *Monatshefte für deutschen Unterricht* (Jahrbuch 1922), pp. 13–19.

PFEFFER, J. ALAN. "Less Formal English?" *Modern Language Journal*, XXIII, 1 (Oct. 1938), pp. 3–5.

SCHROEDER, PAUL G. "Presenting Possessive Adjectives in German and the Romance Languages." *Modern Language Journal* (Jan. 1936), pp. 226–27.

SHARP, STANLEY L. "The Importance of the Strong Verb in Reading German." *German Quarterly* (March, 1936), pp. 43–48.

SHONFELD, SADIE S. *Non-essentials in the Teaching of the German Subjunctive with Reference to the Reading Objective.* Unpublished Master's thesis (College of the City of New York, 1933). 79 pp.

STECKELBERG, MATHILDE. "How Erratic is the Gender of German Nouns?" *Modern Language Journal* (April, 1937), pp. 519–21.

TAUB, L. LEO. "Das Buchstabenspiel." *German Quarterly* (May, 1929), pp. 95–99.

TEN HOOR, G. J. "On the Use of the German Relative Pronoun after Prepositions." *Modern Language Journal* (Dec. 1938), pp. 187–90.

VOWELS, GUY R. "Textbooks and the Living Language." *Modern Language Journal*, XXIII, 7 (April, 1939), pp. 537–43.

WALDMAN, MARK. "A Practical Way of Imparting the German Subjunctive." *Monatshefte für deutschen Unterricht* (Dec. 1932), pp. 252–57.

SUGGESTIONS FOR DISCUSSIONS AND REPORTS

1. Compare and report on Coffman's and Lussky's recommendations concerning adjective inflection.
2. Discuss Crandon's article with special reference to individual differences in high-school and college classes.
3. Report on Lohstoetter's and Steckelberg's articles on the German noun.
4. Discuss Shonfeld's Master's thesis (if not available see Coleman's *Analytical Bibliography, 1932–37*, pp. 162 ff.).
5. Compare Waldman's presentation of the subjunctive with Kaufmann's and Jackson's (see note 2, pp. 147–48).
6. Report on the articles of: (*a*) Lohstoetter, the second one; (*b*) Schroeder, (*c*) Sharp, (*d*) Taub, (*e*) Hollander, (*f*) Hess, (*g*) Goodloe, (*h*) Pfeffer, (*i*) Vowels.
7. Report on Chapter II of Hagboldt's book, pp. 56–99.

CHAPTER EIGHT

ACTIVE PHASES: SPEAKING AND WRITING
(ORAL AND WRITTEN COMPOSITION)

W E SHALL divide this chapter into three parts: I. A definition of the problems involved in the active phases; II. A discussion of the means by which the problem may be solved; III. Some practical attempts at a solution.

I. PROBLEMS INVOLVED IN THE ACTIVE PHASES

ACTIVE PHASES AS AIMS.[1] Professor O'Shea informs us that "about one-half of high-school and college graduates, as they run, will need foreign language for conversation, and at least a fourth of them will need it for correspondence. Only about a third of high-school or college graduates will go through life and have no need for the use of foreign language in any way." [2]

Even without this statement it would be easy to convince parents and students that language exists to be spoken, that speaking ability is advantageous for many people in social and diplomatic intercourse, in commerce and travel, and as a help to reading.

Extremists claim that in speaking ability lies our only salvation. They say: „Nur wer eine Sprache sprechen kann, versteht sie vollständig." [3] Similar statements contain much truth and an immense deal of cause for discouragement, for we know well that in school we cannot develop speaking ability except within rather narrow limits.

---

[1] Speaking and writing are considered as closely related activities. Writing is thought of as a precipitate of speaking. For obvious reasons I have not always referred to them in specific terms.

[2] *The Reading of Modern Foreign Languages,* United States Department of the Interior, Bureau of Education Bulletin (1927), No. 16, pp. 66 ff.

[3] Ernst von Sallwürk, *Fünf Kapitel vom Erlernen fremder Sprachen* (Berlin, 1898), pp. 31 ff.

First we must determine what extremists mean by "speaking ability." Do they mean speaking in the manner of a well-educated native? Do they refer to the rather fluent uttering of a set of short phrases and sentences needed for traveling abroad? Or do they think of speaking within a definite range of speech units which have been so carefully learned and so frequently applied and manipulated in an endless variety of ways that the learner can speak rather fluently within these units? Let us assume they refer to the latter, for to my knowledge, speaking ability has never been defined.

To define speaking in a simple way, let us consider the relationship between thinking and speaking. Thinking and speaking are two forms of one and the same function. When I think verbally or in terms of words, my speech organs remain inactive; my thoughts are not voiced; I am silent. When I think aloud my speech organs become active; I speak. Thinking aloud is speaking. How do we learn to think aloud or to speak?

THE IDEAL LANGUAGE STUDENT learns to speak with assurance and ease.[1] As an illustrative example we take a case from actual experience. Let us imagine a student in college whose native gifts seem to predetermine him for a career in language teaching. This student enters a German class for beginners. He has taken, we assume, two years each of Latin and French. He wants to take a Master's degree in German, teach several years in high school, and acquire his Ph.D. as soon as circumstances allow. His preparation under capable high-school teachers in addition to his superior native gifts enables him even during the first weeks of his study to accomplish infinitely more than his fellow students.[2] Soon he will have mastered the German sound system, the present tense of auxiliaries, of some weak and some strong verbs, the inflection of articles, and a number of nouns of different classes. His retentive memory allows him to recite the texts of the grammar lessons correctly, to manipulate the text easily and flawlessly, to answer questions, and to speak and write within the definite and specific forms and speech units he has learned. The obvious

---

[1] Types of memory in language learning are analyzed in *Language Learning*, pp. 88–99. The ideal type of language student is described on pp. 94 f.

[2] For individual differences, see *ibid.*, p. 88.

conclusion is that a brilliant student particularly gifted for language can learn to speak and write within the limits of those units of speech which he has mastered by practice.

SPEAKING ABILITY MAY BE DEFINED, then, as the skill to use with adequate pronunciation and perfect understanding a specific number of units of speech according to accepted standards. The extent of our speaking ability is always limited to the number of speech units at our command for spontaneous and correct use.

Assuming now that our student continues the study of German through three or four years of well given college courses, that he keeps in mind his ultimate aim, that he fully realizes that his own success will mean the success of his future pupils, then at the end of three years he is certain to have a remarkable speaking ability within definite limits. And if, besides, he should make the best of his opportunities in special courses for oral and written composition he will unfailingly continue to improve his oral ability.

Unfortunately, the ideal student of language is comparatively rare. Often there is one like him or nearly like him in a college class of thirty; sometimes there are two; and occasionally none. In other words, in a group of 100 selected students, one or two show brilliant talent for language. Among these 100 students there are twenty or more who are good (B) and may be called superior in so far as they rank above average.[1]

AVERAGE ABILITY. The possibility of learning to speak a foreign language even within narrow limits is extremely slight for students of average gifts. Assuming that we learn to speak by speaking, and that a high-school pupil of non-German parentage and average talents begins the study of German in the ninth grade, continuing through the twelfth, what would happen under the most favorable conditions imaginable? Let us see. The pupil would take four lessons a week during about thirty weeks in a year. Four lessons a week for thirty weeks are equal to 120 class hours a year, or 480 class hours in four years. Four hundred and eighty class hours at fifty minutes each equals 24,000 minutes or 400 hours of work in class. Supposing now that the instructor be extremely capable, very experienced, in excellent health, and that he should succeed in making his students speak alone for two

[1] This is my personal experience at the University of Chicago.

minutes during each class period, the net result would be that each pupil would actually speak 480 times 2, or 16 hours during the entire four-year course.[1]

No one can hope to learn to speak a new language in 16 hours. One may object: The above estimate is based on classes of 30 or more students; in many classes there are but 20 pupils or less, so that each is favored correspondingly. The class time alone is not a fair measure; the pupil studies also at home. Moreover, the time for practice in speaking is advantageously distributed over a period of four years, an important factor, which would decidedly work in favor of positive results. The pupil improves his oral ability by supplementary exercises, and besides, he is urged to seek other opportunities for speaking after class hours, *i.e.*, in the foreign language club, by conversing with classmates, etc., etc.

All of these objections undoubtedly carry some weight. However, these facts remain: There is no evidence whatever that four-year high-school classes have been a success in regard to speaking ability in any foreign language. There are no standardized oral tests,[2] and therefore we cannot say that after a given time the average pupil should be able to make a certain score on a standard speech test. Since no evidence exists except for a few schools with ideal conditions, we can only suppose that some teachers, blessed with robust health and boundless energy, have been successful in making a small number of superior students speak within narrow limits in spite of crowded classes, indifferent students, and heavy teaching loads.

SPEECH TESTS. Before we can gather positive evidence in regard to speaking ability we must if possible develop speech

[1] Michael West in his pamphlet *On Learning to Speak a Foreign Language* (Longmans, Green and Co., 1933), pp. 18 ff., finds that in the ordinary "Direct Method" lessons the teacher is asking questions half the time. The result of a forty-five minute lesson for the individual is forty-five seconds actual speaking practice per pupil.

[2] An "Aural Comprehension Test for German" is suggested by Josephine Martin, *German Quarterly* (March, 1932), pp. 72–75. Also see Olav K. Lundeberg and James B. Tharp, *Audition Test in German* (only in mimeograph form); also W. C. Decker, "Oral and Aural Tests as Integral Parts of the Regents Examinations," *Modern Language Journal* (March, 1925), pp. 369–71; and F. W. G. Heuser, "Regents Examinations in German," *ibid.* (Jan. 1921), pp. 186 ff.

tests which will force the student to use a definite number of words, idioms, and syntactical constructions, so that we can say a student has shown a definite speaking ability at the end of a given course. If it were possible to develop such tests for each year, actual progress in speaking could be measured with some degree of accuracy. To administer such tests, however, would require much of the instructor's time, for the only known and reliable way of giving speech tests is to call each individual student and to examine him by the carefully formulated questions of the test still to be developed.

In courses of longer duration, the student, after the first year of study, may be required to answer in complete sentences with adequate pronunciation and intonation this type of question:

1. Wie heißen Sie? 2. Wie alt sind Sie? 3. Wohnen Sie bei Ihren Eltern oder in der Nähe der Schule? 4. Seit wann lernen Sie Deutsch? 5. Können Sie zählen? 6. Zählen Sie von zwanzig bis dreißig. 7. Kennen Sie die Namen der Tage? 8. Welchen Tag haben wir heute? 9. Wie spät ist es jetzt? 10. An welchen Tagen kommen Sie in die deutsche Klasse? etc., etc.

The test would measure aural comprehension as well as speaking ability within a narrow range of words and forms. The student would be graded on pronunciation, intonation, fluency of expression, and correctness of replies. For the first year the questions should, of course, be limited to words and idioms of great frequency, not presupposing as yet the knowledge of words outside of a definite active vocabulary.

DIFFICULTIES OF SPEAKING AND WRITING COMPARED. In speaking there is no time for reflection at all. Either I am able to express myself at once, or the person I am addressing will ask me what other language I am able to speak. My hesitation may be caused by an endless variety of difficulties. I may not know a word or an idiom, the gender of a noun or the past tense of a strong verb. I may be in doubt about word order, an adjective ending, or the fittest expression for the occasion. Or several questions may assail me at the same time, adding greatly to my confusion. In short, I am not equal to the situation. My knowledge of grammar may be excellent; yet I am, as it were, too conscious of grammar. I am too close to it. I have not been able to put grammar in its proper place; that means, I have not applied its forms and usages so frequently that I can speak. John Locke was right: No one can speak by the rules of grammar. We learn to speak by applying rules so frequently that we may forget them with perfect impunity. Rules work least when they are needed most.[1]

Writing is ordinarily done at home in the familiar surrounding of our study where we are quite at ease and within easy reach of dictionaries, grammars, and all the helps we need for whatever we want to put down on paper. We are not pressed for time, not haunted by the necessity of uttering sentences as correctly as possible on the spur of the moment. We have time to reflect, to plan, to organize.

Speaking is likely to be found more difficult in the beginning; writing grows more and more toilsome in advanced study. While in speech our words are usually simple and of great frequency, in writing they are apt to be more uncommon, more carefully selected, more literary, and often longer. In conversation our topics are as a rule limited to everyday life; more rarely they deal with remoter subjects as they do in writing. In speech our sentences are short and to the point; the main clause predominates; dependent clauses and complex sentences are avoided. In composition our sentences are tentatively sketched, then rewritten and revised, filed and polished until at length they seem to express our thoughts concisely and elegantly.

We have attempted to explain simply the comparative difficulties of speaking and writing and now we shall discuss those seemingly unnatural and barren stretches in our efforts which every student of language knows to his regret.

DEAD POINTS. Even a good or a superior student of language comes at certain stages of his endeavor toward facile oral and written composition to a point at which his progress seems to halt suddenly. He has reached a dead point. He is tired, needs

---

[1] E. L. Thorndike in "On the Learning of Rules in the Study of a Foreign Language," *German Quarterly* (May, 1931), pp. 89–95, points out the danger of rules which have not been completely assimilated by application, and the "essential repugnance of the mind to rules."

a rest, and must consolidate his gains by other less strenuous exercises before he can make new progress. Particularly, reading seems to be effective to overcome these natural periods of fatigue, which in reality are mere pauses for further progress. As we know, silent reading is equal to silent speaking, and if our student reads drama he speaks mentally, getting at the same time an invaluable exercise and a much needed rest from his more active and more strenuous efforts.

As our good or superior student's studies progress and his reading widens, gradually becoming more advanced and serious, he may some day run across the work of Wilhelm Wundt, a distinguished scholar who explains most lucidly the intricate process of speaking.

WUNDT'S ANALYSIS OF SPEAKING

„Jn dem Moment, wo ich einen Satz beginne, steht das Ganze desselben bereits als eine Gesamtvorstellung in meinem Bewußtsein. Dabei pflegt diese aber nur in ihren Hauptumrissen einigermaßen fester geformt zu sein; alle ihre Bestandteile sind zunächst noch dunkel und heben sich erst in dem Maße, als sie sich zu klaren Vorstellungen verdichten, als Einzelworte ab. Der Vorgang gleicht ungefähr dem bei der plötzlichen Erleuchtung eines zusammengesetzten Bildes, wo man zuerst nur einen ungefähren Eindruck vom Ganzen hat, dann aber sukzessiv die einzelnen Teile, immer in ihrer Beziehung zum Ganzen, ins Auge faßt. Übrigens ist die alltägliche Erfahrung, daß der Redende einen zusammengesetzten Satz richtig von Anfang bis zu Ende durchführen kann, ohne über ihn irgendwie reflektiert zu haben, offenbar nur aus diesem Grunde erklärlich. Diese Tatsache würde absolut unverständlich sein, wenn wir mosaikartig aus einzelnen zuerst isolierten Wortgebilden den Satz zusammenfügen müßten." [1]

[1] Wilhelm Wundt, *Völkerpsychologie*, Erster Band, *Die Sprache*, Erster Teil (Leipzig, 1900), p. 563.

I add my free translation:

"The moment I begin to utter a sentence, the sentence as a whole is in my consciousness as a compound idea, formed, however, only in its main outlines. All its constituent parts are at first hazy, arising to definite words only in so far as they are condensed into clear concepts. The process resembles approximately a light, suddenly illuminating a complex picture and permitting at first only a rough impression of the whole, and then successively single parts in relation to this whole. The common daily experience that the speaker is able to utter a complex sentence correctly from beginning to end without

In other words, the sentence exists at first only as an idea or thought, quite hazy as far as details are concerned. In the process of speaking, as we come to each phrase and clause, we rely on spontaneous construction. Yet the sentence as a whole is uttered as fluently as though it were read from a book. How is this miracle possible? Wundt explains the process in the following words:

„In Wahrheit besteht alles Sprechen in fortwährenden Analogie= bildungen und Angleichungen ... Ohne Zaudern bilden wir in einer uns geläufigen Sprache die Kasusformen des Substantivs, die Abwandlungen des Verbums und selbst Wortzusammensetzungen, ohne sie uns im ein= zelnen Falle angeeignet zu haben. Wir tragen gewissermaßen parabigma= tische Vorstellungsreihen als latente Kräfte in uns, deren Latenz aber darin besteht, daß sie uns nicht, wie die Paradigmen der wirklichen Grammatik, in Gestalt bestimmter Einzelvorstellungen gegeben sind, sondern daß sie nur in der Form elementarer funktioneller Anlagen in uns liegen, von denen jeweils die aktuell werden, die durch die gegebene Bewußtseinslage begünstigt sind." [1]

In the light of the above analysis we now realize how immensely difficult it is to learn to speak a new language. To be able to speak a foreign language fluently and with perfect ease, we must rely on certain latent powers or predispositions developed through many years of hard work and faithful application. It is obvious that such ability can be developed within limits only by superior students who have set their hearts and souls on excelling in their

having in the least reflected about it can evidently be explained only in this manner. This fact would be quite incomprehensible if we were forced to construct the sentence like a mosaic from isolated words."

[1] *Ibid.*, p. 463.

Again I add my free translation:

"In truth, all speaking consists in continually forming analogies and assimilations ... In a language thoroughly familiar to us we form without hesitation the cases of nouns, the conjugation of verbs, and even word combinations without having learned them for the specific case. In a certain sense we carry within ourselves as latent powers paradigmatic series of concepts, the latency of which, however, does not consist in single concepts as presented by the paradigms of real grammar, but rather in the form of elementary functional predispositions. Only those functional predispositions become actual which are favored by the given condition of our consciousness."

future profession by speaking the foreign tongue fluently. The American scholar, not bilingual as a result of parentage or education, who lectures easily and eloquently in German on German literature, is likely to have long since forgotten every grammatical rule. Yet his secret is simple. He has learned to speak by speaking, either during a prolonged stay abroad or by untiring and intelligent devotion to the task.

THE WEAK STUDENT. It is needless to say that the slow student with poor ear, inadequate reading habits in English, and a defective memory for language in general cannot learn a foreign language at all. Much valuable work has been done to prevent weak students from registering in foreign language classes. Prognosis tests have been constructed by which we are able to predict more or less accurately the probability of success.[1] In college classes any experienced instructor can predict within a short time whether or not a student should be discouraged from continuing with the course (see Chapter XI, pp. 264 ff.).

Ideally speaking, we should help all students to success, even those below average. In actual practice this is quite impossible. The weak pupil is in constant need of assistance in all phases of language study. He makes the teacher's work strenuous and is harmful for the class as a whole. The crucial question is who deserves assistance more, the weak or the excellent student. If we remember that the teacher's time is limited and that the superior student will no doubt some time be a leader in whatever he chooses to undertake, the answer is easy: The weak pupil deserves sincere sympathy and the friendly advice to take up some other subject; the excellent pupil deserves more: help when needed and, besides, the stimulating influence of an occasional word of praise and encouragement.[2]

Whatever we may finally decide to do with sectioning classes,

[1] *Modern Foreign Languages and Their Teaching*, by Robert D. Cole. Revised and enlarged by James Burton Tharp (Appleton-Century Company, 1937), pp. 444–54.

[2] See in this connection Magna A. Gray, "An Experiment with a Modified Course in German," *German Quarterly* (March, 1937), pp. 89–90. Eugene Jackson, "An Adjustment Class in German in the Tilden High School," *High Points* (June, 1936), pp. 61–62. "The Proposed Syllabus in Modern Foreign Languages for Pupils of Lower Linguistic Ability," *ibid.* (Sept. 1935), pp. 5–32.

in no case should we permit the weak pupil to retard the progress of the excellent one.[1]

II. MEANS BY WHICH THE PROBLEM MAY BE SOLVED

TRANSLATION AND COMPOSITION. In 1882 Viëtor stated: „Das Übersetzen in fremde Sprachen ist eine Kunst, welche die Schule nichts angeht."[2] As late as 1904 Bagster-Collins, after a thorough investigation of modern language texts, finds that "to judge from these books, translation seems to have become almost universally regarded as the method *par excellence* of acquiring a language other than one's own."[3] The fact is that for more than a third of a century translation and composition have been considered as completely synonymous both in theory and in practice, as is proved even today by many "composition books."

There are three reasons for this: (1) A strong time-honored tradition formed in the course of centuries through instruction in Latin and Greek. Teachers naturally carry into modern language instruction the practices by which they themselves have been taught. (2) The Committee of Twelve, whose recommendations were considered the gospel for all language instruction during several generations, had emphatically stated in 1900 "that the old-fashioned way had its good features." (3) Interest in the merits of translation, such as there are, is kept alive by articles in defense or condemnation of this practice.[4]

The Committee of Twelve had urged in regard to "reproductive translation into German":

> It will be observed that the program of work for the second year of the elementary course provides for practice in the off-hand reproduction, sometimes orally and sometimes in writing, of the substance

[1] Much can be done by proficiency tests. Tharp states that 662 students saved in three years' time 950 semesters in terms of time or 3800 credits at a money value of nearly $27,000. Cf. Cole-Tharp, *op. cit.*, p. 454, n. 30.

[2] *Der Sprachunterricht muß umkehren; ein Beitrag zur Überbürdungsfrage* (Leipzig, O. R. Reisland, 1905), p. 33. First edition, 1882.

[3] *The Teaching of German in Secondary Schools* (Columbia University Press, 1904), p. 149.

[4] T. E. Oliver, *The Modern Language Teacher's Handbook* (D. C. Heath and Company, 1935), gives a great many books and articles dealing with translation; see pp. 669–76. Also see *Language Learning*, pp. 22–33.

of short and easy selected passages. This is what the Germans call "freie Reproduktion," and is one of the most profitable exercises possible. It teaches the pupil to give heed not only to the meaning but to the form in which it is expressed, to put thoughts in German with German as a starting point. The language of the original should, of course, not be memorized verbatim; what is wanted is not an effort of the memory, but an attempt to express thoughts in German, forms that are remembered in a general way but not remembered exactly. The objection to independent translation from English into German is that for a long time it is necessarily mechanical. The translator has no help except his dictionary and grammar. His translation is mere upsetting. In free reproduction, on the contrary, he instinctively starts from his memory of the original. His thoughts shape themselves in German form. In short, he learns to think in German.[1]

It is necessary to explain the means by which "reproductive translation into German" may become feasible. Reproductive translation or freie Reproduktion is absolutely impossible for the student unless he has worked over (verarbeitet) the text so thoroughly that he can easily change the form of each element of the sentence correctly according to whatever he may choose to say. Nouns, verbs, adjectives, prepositions, and other parts of speech must be singled out, explained, and drilled carefully by direct method exercises. Nouns are to be declined, verbs to be conjugated, sentences manipulated, until finally the text has been completely assimilated. All this should be preceded by first going over the text. Content questions must then bring about a complete comprehension of every detail. The net result should be that the student has actually done far more than memorize the text. He should be able to manipulate the text freely, which is the very skill required in free reproduction or reproductive translation.

This point is of basic importance. On it depends the success of all composition, written or oral. For composition means to construct phrases and sentences correctly according to the accepted standards of the foreign language, correctly in spite of the strong hostile influences of the native tongue. To be successful in composition we must rise above translation. We must begin with a

[1] *Report of the Committee of Twelve* (D. C. Heath and Company, 1900), pp. 69 f.

thought to be expressed, and then express it from within the spirit of the foreign language. In brief, we must rely not only on the model furnished us by the text, but also on the effect of our exercises which, in their totality, must bring about, in the words of Wundt, "latent functional predispositions."

The undeniable ADVANTAGES OF TRANSLATION INTO THE FOREIGN LANGUAGE (Hinüberſetzung) are easy to explain:

1. Translation can be used early in the course, provided that the sentences to be translated be simple and easy, that they resemble closely the constructions of the native sentence, and that they contain no difficulties in word meanings.

2. It can be checked easily since it presents the same difficulties to all students.

3. It is quite effective in bringing to light and emphasizing differences of idiom.

4. It is commendable also for more advanced students in certain phases of grammar review.

On the other hand its dangers are numerous:

1. Unless most carefully prepared and cautiously applied it is certain to create wrong attitudes toward language in general.

2. If overdone it encourages indirect associations.

3. It is too difficult for average students, except in the beginning, and then only in its most simple forms. As soon as complex and idiomatic sentences are involved, it is difficult for the instructor to give a sufficient number of explanatory notes.

4. In the hands of a poor teacher it easily degenerates into the solving of puzzles.

5. As a daily diet it becomes unbearably tedious.

6. It is too often used to hide the teacher's inability to use more effective devices.

7. For intermediate and advanced students carefully constructed exercises of a more direct nature based on supplementing, mutation, and completion appear to be more favorable in keeping the learner steeped in the foreign language.

The extent to which translation into the foreign language may safely be used depends in the final analysis entirely on the ability of the teacher. The way in which he himself has been taught, his competence in handling the foreign language, and last but not least, the convictions which have resulted from his teaching experience, will decide.

A safe way of avoiding excessive stress on translation into the foreign language is to be guided by these considerations: The sole purpose of translation is to compare thoroughly the vernacular structure with that of the foreign tongue. The more clearly we realize that the two structures differ and how they differ, the nearer we are likely to come to real translation, which has nothing whatever to do with literal translation, but is virtually a recasting of thought into molds and patterns peculiar to the foreign tongue. The ultimate aim of translation is to make it unnecessary. Translation is a bridge. On the other side lies direct expression.

ELIMINATING TRANSLATION. The principle of eliminating translation is the same for passive and active phases of language. In reading we first ascertain complete comprehension of each minute point of the textual difficulties, and then reread the whole frequently to make comprehension direct. In speaking we first aim at perfect understanding of each word, phrase, or clause in its relationship within the sentence, and then we proceed to exclude translation by manipulating each speech unit in actual utterance. In both cases we find a solution in the law of exercise or practice. In both cases the bond between concept and foreign expression (or idea and foreign sound sequences) is made direct by frequent use.

The difficulty of eliminating translation in speaking or writing lies not in finding enough exercises but in choosing the most effective ones in the immense variety of possibilities. All such exercises may be called practice in oral or written composition. As such we shall enumerate those which are most widely used. We shall discuss in turn: (1) functional grammar exercises; (2) the question; (3) memorizing; (4) object lessons; (5) dramatizing.

1. FUNCTIONAL GRAMMAR EXERCISES, usually called direct method exercises, are extremely effective, particularly when the directions are clearly given with a concise example in each case. For instance:

(*a*) Continue changing personal pronouns, possessive adjectives, and verb endings, progressively.

EXAMPLE: Ich gehe mit meinem Onkel in meine Schule, du gehst mit deinem Onkel in deine Schule, er geht mit seinem Onkel in seine Schule, etc.

(*b*) Give a sliding synopsis of es gelingt mir nicht. Change the personal pronoun and tenses progressively.

EXAMPLE: Es gelingt mir nicht, es gelang dir nicht, es ist ihm nicht gelungen, etc.

(*c*) Replace the participial constructions by relative clauses.

EXAMPLE: die aufgehende Sonne = die Sonne, die aufgeht; die aufgegangene Sonne = die Sonne, die aufgegangen ist.

das ruhig spielende Kind; die ins Meer sinkende Sonne; eine unbekannte Dame; ein in englischer Sprache geschriebenes Buch; ein aus dem Osten gekommener Freund; etc., etc.

(*d*) Formulate questions to which the following sentences are answers; use wo(r) with the proper preposition affixed.

EXAMPLE: Sie sprachen von interessanten Dingen. Wovon sprachen sie? — Er glaubt an nichts. Woran glaubt er?

Er denkt immer an seine Bücher. Aus Trauben macht man Wein. Durch diese Übungen lernen wir Deutsch. Ich spreche gegen den Krieg, etc.

(*e*) Continue:

Ich bin es, du bist es, er ist es, etc.
wegen meiner, wegen deiner, wegen seiner, etc.
meinetwegen, deinetwegen, seinetwegen, etc.
Ich tue es für mich, du tust es für dich, er tut es für sich, etc.
Ich freue mich über meine Ferien, du freust dich über deine Ferien, er freut sich über seine Ferien, etc.
Ich wasche mir die Hände, du wäschst dir die Hände, er wäscht sich die Hände, etc.

(*f*) Begin the following sentences with es.

EXAMPLE: Jemand klopft = Es klopft jemand.

Niemand ist dort. Jemand ist hier gewesen. Niemand ist zu sehen. Einige Bücher liegen auf dem Tisch. Etwas muß getan werden.

(*g*) Read the following sentences, placing the underlined words first.

EXAMPLE: Es ist kalt heute = Kalt ist es heute.

Wir warten seit einer halben Stunde. Er kommt nie zur Zeit. Er kommt immer zu spät. Er hat uns gewiß vergessen. Er hat zu lange geschlafen. Er macht es immer so.

(*h*) Read the words in quotations first.

EXAMPLE: Vater sagte: „Jetzt ist es Zeit." = „Jetzt ist es Zeit," sagte Vater.

Er sagte: „Die Kinder müssen zu Bett gehen." Die Kinder riefen: „Nur noch fünf Minuten!" Die Mutter antwortete: „Keine Sekunde mehr!" Der Großvater befahl: „Ins Bett, ihr kleinen Teufel!"

An endless number of similar exercises can be constructed for each grammatical difficulty. To provide a sufficient number of them is the task of the teacher. Usually they are given in abundance with every elementary or review grammar, but every experienced teacher can prepare his own, especially when he has in mind specific remedial exercises for individual students.

2. THE ART OF QUESTIONING. It is easy to recognize the teacher's ability by the nature of his questions. The question is one of the most important factors in language teaching. The learner's age and maturity, of course, must be taken into consideration. We may distinguish between many types of questions:

(*a*) Questions directed to forms and constructions intended to establish grammatical principles inductively (see pp. 138 f.).

(*b*) Questions referring to grammatical rules which should not be answered by the rule, but by its application in a phrase or, better, in a sentence.

EXAMPLE: When are descriptive adjectives not inflected? Unser Großvater ist jung. When are they inflected? Unser alter Großvater ist noch sehr jung.

(*c*) Questions intended to prevent common errors, particularly in written work: Did I capitalize all nouns? Did I use inversion whenever the sentence does not begin with the subject?[1] etc., etc.

(*d*) Questions concerning the various parts of speech.

EXAMPLE: Der Vater schreibt der Mutter schnell einen Brief, der schon morgen in Berlin ankommen wird.

Concerning the subject: Wer schreibt einen Brief?
Concerning the direct object: Was schreibt der Vater?
Concerning the indirect object: Wem schreibt er einen Brief?
Concerning the verb: Was tut der Vater?
Concerning the adverb of manner: Wie schreibt der Vater den Brief?
Concerning the adverb of time: Wann wird der Brief ankommen?

[1] For further examples see *Language Learning*, pp. 148 f.

Concerning the adverb or adverbial expression of place: Wo wird der Brief ankommen?

This type of question establishes beyond a doubt whether or not the student has completely grasped the meaning of the sentence. A great evil in speech courses is that the teacher does most of the talking. To avoid this, the names of the parts of speech may be written on the blackboard, the instructor points to one at a time and then calls on one student to formulate a question and on another to answer it.

(e) Content questions develop quite naturally out of questions concerning parts of speech. At first all questions must be based on very simple and easy sentences, preferably using only the present tense and the most frequent words. All questions should be for a considerable time text-reproducing, *i.e.*, they should be so worded as to contain the answer with no required changes, or with a minimum of changes.

(f) Content questions, the answers to which require a change in word order, should be avoided until the student is ready for them. The best way to prepare students for such questions is by direct method exercises on dependent word order.

(g) Content questions may be comprehensive in nature. Was geschah dann? may require the student to reproduce freely a number of sentences from the text, which, of course, should not be done before the class has dealt successfully with a great many functional exercises.

(h) Any resourceful teacher can formulate and arrange questions based on a given story so skilfully that the answers are a complete reproduction of the text.

(i) Before risking free reproductions it is advisable to facilitate it by giving the student key words which at first should allude to the structure of the sentence by connective words such as und, da, als. Later we should give only key words to refresh his memory.

(j) And finally, as a last step, we may risk freie Reproduktion, which is really equal to free composition.

Some teachers are convinced that speaking exercises cannot be too numerous. In a way they are right, in another entirely wrong.

All depends on what we intend to accomplish. The late Max Griebsch in his pamphlet *Zur Methodik des deutschen Sprachunter-richts* [1] gives several examples for the treatment of reading texts, showing how eight to ten lines of text can be worked over by questions. In each example the author devotes to a few lines more than two pages of closely printed questions and answers, so that presumably an entire class period would be spent on oral exercises, and yet the pages carry the caption Lefeunterricht. One might ask whether Lefeunterricht is equal to Sprechunterricht. There is no doubt that oral exercises contribute greatly to reading facility. But should we lead students to believe that Lefeunterricht is equal to answering questions in the foreign language? The age-old tradition of considering speaking ability the only true criterion of the student's accomplishment has certainly played an important part in the convictions of Max Griebsch, who, incidentally, as is well known, has done much in furthering the study of German in the United States.

3. MEMORIZING has been credited with being the only safe way of developing correct speech habits. This belief is both right and wrong. It is right in so far as some time or other we have learned everything we are able to say. It is wrong in so far as whatever we learn by heart remains rigid, fixed, and unchangeable unless and until we make it pliable by exercise and practice. Again we face the necessity of developing "latent functional predisposi-tions." For this reason memorizing cannot be enough. When, for instance, we memorize the idiom auf englisch, we are safe be-cause it happens to be of a rigid nature; but when we memorize es gibt, we still need to know es gab, es hat gegeben, es hatte gegeben, etc., es gebe, es gäbe, es habe gegeben, es hätte gegeben, etc., es werde geben, es würde geben, es würde gegeben haben, etc. The same is true of verbs and nouns, of adjective endings, of word order, in fact of all inflections and constructions which need changes the moment we begin to manipulate a memorized text.

Perhaps the best material to learn by heart is poetry. It seems best because we are not likely to use it for exercises for which prose offers a much more adequate means. Poetry is excellent

---

[1] Reprint from *Monatshefte für deutschen Unterricht*, Vols. XXII–XXVI, 1931–1934 (University of Wisconsin, Madison, Wis.), 56 pp.

mainly for acquiring fluency in pronunciation and intonation, particularly when the phonograph supplements the instructor's voice. Prose is far better for mutation exercises.

Memorized material impresses on the learner's mind definite forms in correctly constructed sentences. A memorized sentence has great value. It serves as a model for innumerable sentences of the same structure.[1] It is a safe way of gaining Sprachgefühl, which we have defined as "not a mysterious sort of linguistic second sight, but simply as the result of energetic, successful application, as exact knowledge merged in the subconscious." [2]

Like the Committee of Twelve, some instructors object to memorizing. They evidently fear that the forms and models memorized may become a hindrance rather than a help to the student. Personally I cannot see any harm in memorizing. On the contrary. Memorized material supplies the foundation for exercises in speaking and writing, in vocabulary and idioms, in the basic patterns for the construction of sentences. Perhaps there is only one means far better than memorizing, and that is to work over (verarbeiten) the material so thoroughly that by questions and by many of the devices we have discussed, the student can give in his own words a free reproduction of the memorized text.

4. OBJECT LESSONS, for which there is unfortunately little time in our courses, have undeniable advantages. They afford ample opportunity for thinking in the foreign language, for practice with words, idioms, and simple sentences, for presenting and working over thoroughly the material to be written down at home. They are excellent for bringing about aural comprehension and direct verbal expression. The mechanical aspect of translation is entirely avoided. Emphasis is where it belongs, on the foreign language itself. There is something natural and inevitable in their directness. In a sense they resemble learning the vernacular, even though we cannot hope to duplicate in the classroom the conditions of the nursery. Their danger is that, unless carefully planned, they easily degenerate into a hit-or-miss conversation in which the teacher is forced to do most of the talking. Young students as a rule react to them willingly and readily and find them interesting or even fascinating. College students are usually in a

---

[1] See *Language Learning*, Analogy, pp. 16–18.   [2] *Ibid.*, p. 156.

hurry and likely to resent this type of instruction as a waste of time.

5. DRAMATIZING. Pictures used in object lessons may be the basis for dramatizing. Max Walter describes how under his care young students made use of wall charts in connection with brief and logically arranged sentences in the manner of François Gouin (cf. pp. 12–13). He states:

> Ɉn den Köpfen unſerer Kinder ſteckt eben viel mehr Erfindungsgabe, als wir gewöhnlich annehmen. Es gibt für ſie keine größere Freude als ihrer Phantaſie nachgehen zu dürfen. Die Einbildungskraft ſollten wir als ein Mittel zur Förderung des Unterrichts weit mehr heranziehen. Machen die Schüler Fehler beim Sprechen, ſo iſt das nicht ſchlimm — wir Erwachſene machen ja beim ſchnellen Sprechen auch ſolche — wir dürfen nur die Kinder nicht immer gleich verbeſſern wollen, ſonſt nehmen wir ihnen den Mut, ſich in der Sprache auszudrücken und in ihr heimiſch zu werden. Wir ſollen ſie vielmehr zum Sprechen ermutigen . . . [1]

In our country dramatizing is sometimes used in courses of longer duration by able instructors who have a thorough knowledge of the foreign language and, besides, a special gift for encouraging their students to prepare text material for dramatization. The instructor may work up the material into simple dialogues in class, or he may turn the task over to a group of students who in special meetings divide up the various parts and prepare the text for the occasion. Most favorable to start with might be a short play, read in class with roles assigned. But also a fable, an anecdote, a *Märchen*, or, in fact, any short narrative containing dialogue can be effectively used.

In a paper read before the New York Teachers' Association in October, 1936, Professor F. W. Kaufmann discussed the interpretation of reading texts. From his own practice he cited many interesting examples. For instance, how he first made his students perform the more dramatic selections of an elementary reader, and then took up other materials, such as commonly known fables. For example, in performing "The Fox and the Raven," the student impersonating the raven wore a black tail coat and was perched on the back of a chair, while the fox addressed him with the well-

---

[1] *Zur Methodik des neusprachlichen Unterrichts*, Vierte Auflage, bearbeitet von Paul Olbrich (Marburg an der Lahn, 1931), p. 25.

known poem of Heine: *Du bist wie eine Blume.* The raven bitterly lamented the loss of his cheese by the song: *Ach du lieber Augustin, alles ist hin.*

During the second semester students wrote their own dramatic version of Kästner's *Emil und die Detektive,* also of *Pünktchen und Anton* by the same author. The best dramatic version was chosen for a public performance and was well received. In the course of the second and third year, students reduced *Hanns Frei,* a five-act comedy by Otto Ludwig, to one act, and prepared a dramatic version of Eichendorff's *Aus dem Leben eines Taugenichts.*

Kaufmann emphasizes important and familiar arguments for activity instruction. Through dramatization, a medium for oral expression is created between the book and its reader. The book comes to life. The passive attitude is overcome. All inhibitions to self-expression, which are certain to appear in language classes unless these are started while pupils are young, cease to exist. Associations between sequences of sound and meanings become firm and lasting, acquiring a much deeper significance than can be developed by reading alone.[1]

Charles E. Pauck reports in an article entitled "Producing a German Play"[2] interesting and favorable results with classes which by dramatic performances had improved their oral ability. He gives numerous suggestions for the selection and production of plays. A list of fifty German plays suitable for presentation by German classes or clubs is given by B. Q. Morgan.[3] T. R. Dawes describes a successful experiment in exchange visits of student-actor troupes from various countries under the auspices of the International Students' Drama League.[4]

III. PRACTICAL ATTEMPTS AT A SOLUTION

SPEECH COURSES. The most scientific and comprehensive speech course was written many years ago by François Gouin (see pp. 12 f. and 59 f.). As we know, the direct method, a greatly improved and refined version of several others, is still being used,

---

[1] Professor Kaufmann's article did not appear in print.
[2] *Monatshefte für deutschen Unterricht* (Nov. 1932), pp. 220–22.   [3] *Ibid.* (Feb. 1932), pp. 31–44.
[4] "The Drama and Modern Languages," *New Era* (Jan. 1933), pp. 25–26.

now as a means toward oral ability, now as reading approach. Many books for conversational German have been written. One of the most recent ones comes from the pen of Professor C. R. Goedsche who seems to have found a solution for a speech course as given in his classes at Northwestern University. His text, *Wie geht's?* [1] is intended purely for conversation, and presents lively, interesting dialogues dealing with student life under American conditions.

The newness of this presentation lies in two factors: first, in emphasizing the difference between spoken and written language; and second, in acknowledging the necessity of a technique quite different from that used in other courses.

The author at once comes to the main point of the problem by stressing the importance of the idiom and by rejecting the time-honored review grammar as a basis for conversation. He reasons: ". . . overemphasis on grammatical rules is a grave mistake in the teaching of conversation and is the chief reason for the student's failure to learn to speak idiomatically." By implication, not by actual statement, the author alludes to an element which every experienced instructor knows — suffering from an overdose of formal grammar, a condition which Professor Morrison was in the habit of calling "grammar bound." We become "grammar bound" by studying the rules of grammar instead of applying them, so that a veritable wilderness of rules and paradigms assails us when we try to utter the simplest sentence. Goedsche sees the fine and often imperceptible difference between grammar and idiom. To take a sentence at random from his book: Du haſt es doch nicht ſchon wieder vergeſſen. If we omit doch nicht ſchon the statement is simple, falling easily under a grammatical category. But as soon as we try to interpret the sentence as a whole we need the connotation of doch nicht ſchon, for the statement is entirely idiomatic. Strictly speaking it cannot be translated at all. It must be understood as a whole and used as a whole in the meaning: "I certainly hope you have not forgotten it again."

Since conversational German abounds in similar expressions, Goedsche is correct in concluding that fluent conversation depends to a large extent not on grammar but on memory; or to express

[1] F. S. Crofts & Co., 1938.

the same thought in different terms, not on formal but on functional grammar, supported by a retentive memory which is able to recall spontaneously a great many phrases and idioms needed in specific situations.

It is advisable to point out the difference between Goedsche's book and a review grammar. A review grammar, when good, emphasizes functional grammar and idioms. So does Goedsche's book, but it limits itself to the words, constructions, idioms, and rules involved in the dialogues. Most review grammars are extensive and general; *Wie geht's?* is concentrated and specific.

COMPOSITION COURSES. The number of articles on composition is so large that I must confine myself to discussing a few of more recent date.

Professor Lindsey Blayney reports on "The Prose Laboratory and Special German Sections at Carleton College," [1] which he himself instituted. He deplores the discouraging features of composition work, praises pleasant translation versus composition drudgery,[2] and fears that the prestige of language departments will suffer unless we give the student something more than only reading ability. Then the author makes a strong plea for translation into German. During the first year lengthy, involved sentences are translated into German at the earliest possible moment. During the second year translation is given in homeopathic doses every day. A rather long carefully prepared sentence is dictated in English. Ten minutes or less are needed for the sentence, and two or three questions in German based on the text which is being read are to be answered in German.

In the laboratory one problem (sentence) is given at a time. Students stand before high desks. Each is given a card with one problem. There is one assistant for every five students, a graduate assistant being in charge. When in trouble the student summons an assistant, who first tries to help him by inductive questioning. As soon as the student has completed the sentence satisfactorily, he is given the next problem. All the work done in the laboratory is voluntary and carries no credit.

The great advantage in such a procedure is that the weaker

[1] *Modern Language Journal* (May, 1935), pp. 596–603. [2] Translation from English into German is meant.

students are given individual help on their specific difficulties. The author does not give models of sentences to be translated at various stages of the course, but he does point out the genuine benefits derived from the course as a whole. A small class was organized in the History of Modern German Literature to meet three times a week. The text was in German, and so were the discussions. Yet, fifteen students volunteered to take the course, although no credit was allowed.

COMPOSITION SCALES were developed by the *Study* a long time ago, but in spite of their obvious usefulness they seem to be little used except with the American Council Tests for which they were constructed. In the last part of this test, the student is required to write a free composition on a picture which is printed in the test. The performance of each student was carefully recorded, and from an immense number of such compositions certain ones were chosen which represented certain specific qualities. These qualities are expressed in terms of numbers, 0 representing the lowest, 14 the highest quality. For the American Council Test as well as for rating compositions in general during the first two or three high-school years the scales are a contribution toward a more reliable judgment in regard to the students' written performance.

The laborious task of building the scales was carried out for German by Professor Elizabeth Rossberg of Milwaukee-Downer College. From one hundred to one hundred and fifty teachers aided in the work of rating compositions from which the scales were constructed.[1]

The authors give clear and concise information in regard to: (1) what the scales measure; (2) when to use them; (3) the unit of measurement; (4) measuring the quality of pupil's composition; (5) statistical treatment of scores. The scales themselves are given on pp. 509–30. The American Council Test has been administered to innumerable high-school and college students. It is to be regretted, therefore, that the correlation between reading

[1] M. A. Buchanan and E. D. MacPhee, *Modern Language Instruction in Canada*, Volume I of the Publications of the American and Canadian Committees on Modern Languages (The University of Toronto Press, 1928), pp. 506 ff.

ability and composition has not been established. If it had, we should know what quality of composition is most frequently linked with poor or superior achievement in reading.

ADVANCED COMPOSITION. The most competent though brief discussion of the problems of composition in advanced classes that has come to my notice in recent years is by Professor Ernst Rose.[1] He starts out with an observation, often verified by every instructor of experience, that students with an undiluted Anglo-American background can be more easily taught than bilingual students, who, convinced that they already know everything, ask the instructor for a course on style.

Rose has been teaching German Literature for more than fifteen years and also free composition to fourth- and fifth-year German classes, the latter designed particularly for the training of teaching candidates. Naturally he speaks from an abundance of experience. I quote a number of significant statements:

> The teaching of composition presupposes a mastery of grammatical fundamentals ... At all events the aim should be taken as modestly as is possible without boring the best minds of the class. A too ambitious composition teacher will defeat his own ends ...

> The English compositions of which translations are required are more or less "doctored" and carefully graded and so lead the student into the mistake of trusting too much to literal translation even when his own English models are not at all prepared for translation. At best, a strangely unidiomatic or else highly stilted German will result from leaning too much on the translation method.

> A consistently direct method seems to avoid some of the pitfalls of the translation method, ... yet, ... discussion of finer points in grammar is virtually impossible in a German that the student at this stage would understand ... More often than not a certain idiom or grammatical rule can be easily demonstrated by an application through translation where the direct method substitute would lack convincing force.

> Still, the use of English should never dominate a composition class, and should rather be the exception ...

[1] "German Composition in Advanced Classes," *Modern Language Journal* (Dec. 1938), pp. 163–67.

Actual classes and individual students have been found to vary so greatly as to warrant the construction of an independent course with each new term.

At the end of his article Rose summarizes the features he expects to find in an ideal composition book. He names four: (1) Presentation of the material in connected fashion, preferably a model composition. (2) Digestion of material by clever questioning, repeated reading, repetition in slightly altered form (different tense, indirect discourse, and the like). (3) Stimulation of associated words and ideas by drill on idioms, synonyms, antonyms, word formation, questions on related topics, and the like. (4) Exercises in free composition. Here Rose suggests three stages: (*a*) The free rendering of the model composition in slightly changed form; (*b*) the same made more difficult by addition of some new material; (*c*) for the most advanced students an entirely free composition on a new subject based on presented material.

On the whole, I find myself in agreement with the author. The basic problem in all composition is the difficult and despairingly slow process of freeing the learner from the influence of his native tongue. To achieve this the instructor must use whatever means seem best for the class, now direct method exercises, now translation, here a paraphrase, there mutation and supplementing. Ideal courses hardly exist. What is perfect in one situation is a failure in the other. What is modern today is, perhaps, old-fashioned ten years hence. In the end, not the little unimportant detail counts, but the large important principle. The large principle by which we learn is the same for all human efforts. We learn by practicing, by making mistakes, by correcting mistakes which we ourselves have made, and by avoiding them if we can forever.

A different type of course, although one with the same objective, is described by F. W. Kaufmann.[1] The author based his course on lectures given to high-school teachers and later to college students with one or two years' preparation. The lectures were founded on standard works of the history of German art and the richly illustrated Knackfuß monographs dealing with Richter,

---

[1] "Some Experiments in the Advanced Practice Course," *German Quarterly* (Jan. 1933), pp. 23–27.

Schwind, Böcklin, Thoma, and others. Interest was increased by a reflectoscope which projected slide pictures as well as postcard illustrations. Throughout the course as many questions as possible were asked about the pictures, so as to give students a chance to develop speaking ability and, moreover, the power of observing and analyzing pictures. One lecture out of three was devoted to the history of art, the others being used for a survey of German history and the discussion of themes proposed by the students.

My own experience leads me to believe that, once the fundamentals of grammar have been mastered, surprising results in composition may be obtained by lectures. It is important for the lecture technique not to overwhelm the student with words, expressions, and idioms which he is not likely to know, nor to speak in lengthy, complex sentences. In the beginning it is even advisable to write the lectures out, to see to it that each sentence is well constructed, short and clear, to underline all words and idioms the student cannot know, and, before class, to write them on the blackboard.

We have briefly defined the problems implied in oral and written composition, discussed the means by which the problems may be solved, and, finally, given some practical suggestions for types of courses. Only a few words remain to be said. Success in composition, oral or written, depends on three things: practice, experience, and theory; practice must result in experience; practice and experience must be directed and controlled by theory. For experience alone lacks the calming authority of theory, and theory alone comes to life only through practice and experience. The three combined are certain to prove effective.

BIBLIOGRAPHY

Anon. "Aids to Conversational Skill." *Bulletin of the Institute for Research in English Teaching* (Japan), No. 90 (Jan. 1933), pp. 1–2 and 5.

BRAUN, WALTER. "Zur Kritik neusprachlicher Unterrichtsziele." *Zeitschrift für französischen und englischen Unterricht* (Nov. 1932), pp. 311–13.

CHEYDLEUR, FREDERIC D. "The Use of Placement Tests in Modern Languages at the University of Wisconsin." *Modern Language Journal* (Jan. 1931), pp. 262–80.

CLARKE, F. "In Defense of Translation." *Modern Languages* (March, 1937), pp. 115–16.

CORBIN, ALBERTA L. "Special Promotion for Superior Students." *Modern Language Journal* (Nov. 1927), pp. 115–17.

DIRKS, H. G. "Briefwechsel mit deutschen Studenten." *German Quarterly* (May, 1937), pp. 130–36.

ENGEL, E. F. "The Broadcasting of Modern Foreign Languages in the United States: A Survey." *Modern Language Journal* (March, 1936), pp. 356–58.

GINSBURG, EDWARD B. "Foreign Talking Pictures in Modern Language Instruction." *Modern Language Journal* (March, 1935), pp. 433–38.

JONES, N. A. "A School Holiday in Germany." *Modern Languages* (Dec. 1936), pp. 89–90.

LENZ, HAROLD. "Dramatics in the German Club." *German Quarterly* (May, 1937), pp. 123–29.

PALMER, HAROLD E. "Sentences Worth Memorizing." *Bulletin of the Institute for Research in English Teaching* (Japan) (Feb. 1933), pp. 1–2.

THARP, JAMES B. "How Shall We Section Beginning Foreign Language Classes?" *Modern Language Journal* (March, 1929), pp. 433–44.

WARSHAW, J. "Prognosis and the Open Door." *Modern Language Journal* (Jan. 1931), pp. 253–61.

WEST, MICHAEL. *On Learning to Speak a Foreign Language.* London: Longmans, Green and Co., 1933.

SUPPLEMENTARY READINGS

FUNKE, ERICH. "Sprechkultur in England." *Monatshefte*, XXXI, 6 (Oct. 1939), pp. 302–03.

GOEDSCHE, C. R. "German Composition and Conversation." *Monatshefte*, XXXI, 1 (Jan. 1939), pp. 46–49.

HOLZMANN, ALBERT W. "A Decade of Declamation." *Modern Language Journal*, XXIII, 2 (Nov. 1938), pp. 133–36.

HUEBENER, THEODORE. *The Use of Dialogue in Foreign Language Teaching.* Foreign Language Monographs, No. 3, Board of Education, City of New York.

—— *Can the Slow Pupil Learn Foreign Languages?* Foreign Language Monographs, No. 2, Board of Education, City of New York.

—— *Modern Languages and the Pupil of Lower Linguistic Ability.* Board of Education, City of New York.

—— *Dialogues, Songs, and Projects for Pupils of Lower Linguistic Ability.* Board of Education, City of New York.

RADIMERSKY, GEORGE W. "An Introductory Study of German Idiomatic Speech." *Modern Language Journal*, XXIII, 2 (Nov. 1938), pp. 137–46.

RILEY, THOMAS A. "Übungen machen den Meister." *Monatshefte*, XXXI, 3 (March, 1939), pp. 143–46.

SOKOL, A. E. "The Questionnaire as a Teaching Aid." *Monatshefte*, XXX, 1 (Jan. 1938), pp. 16–19.

SUGGESTIONS FOR DISCUSSIONS AND REPORTS

1. Discuss the possibility of learning to speak a foreign language at school for: (a) the superior, (b) the average, (c) the weak student of language.
2. Compare the difficulties in speaking with those in writing.
3. Report on individual differences. Use your own experiences as a teacher.
4. Report on devices which may be used both for speaking and writing.
5. Enumerate advantages and dangers of translation.
6. Discuss devices for eliminating translation.
7. Compare Wundt's analysis of speaking with your own experiences in learning to speak foreign languages.
8. Discuss Michael West's book, especially in regard to speaking vocabulary.
9. Report on the articles by: (a) Anon and Palmer; (b) Cheydleur; (c) Warshaw; (d) Corbin; (e) Tharp; (f) Braun and Clarke; (g) Dirks and Jones; (h) Ginsburg and Engel; (i) Lenz.

CHAPTER NINE

CULTURAL MATERIAL

IN CHAPTER TWO we briefly discussed cultural aims in relation to short courses. We pointed out the general difficulty of achieving cultural aims, and the more particular problem of combining the teaching of minimum word lists with an early presentation of cultural material. We now come back to the same problem in order to see how German scholars and teachers have struggled to reconcile a high ideal with stern reality, and to discuss some important American attempts at a final solution. But first let us be clear about our terms.

WHAT IS CULTURAL MATERIAL? We refer to it by a variety of names: *realia, Kulturkunde, Deutschkunde, Volkskunde*. Of these *realia* is, perhaps, the most modest term, and *Kulturkunde* the most pretentious. According to Webster, *realia* means "real things, realities." In a narrow sense we frequently construe it as denoting "visible things," such as coins, pictures, and maps; rivers, countries, and boundaries. In a broader sense *realia* may denote anything which is characteristic of a nation's real thought and life: its history, literature, and science; its institutions, manners, and customs; its noblest productions in art, science, and philosophy. In this broader sense, then, *realia* is synonymous with *Kulturkunde*, a term which has found wide acceptance in the teaching of all modern foreign languages. *Deutschkunde* is a term referring to *realia* or *Kulturkunde* in regard to Germany alone. *Volkskunde*,[1] a somewhat unfortunate term, is easily mistaken for "folk-lore" as which, in fact, it is given in many dictionaries (compare, for instance, Heath).

---

[1] Compare Walther Hoffstaetter und Ulrich Peters, *Sachwörterbuch der Deutschkunde* (Leipzig und Berlin: Teubner, 1930), Vol. II, see under *Volkskunde*.

For practical purposes we may distinguish between *realia* and *Kulturkunde*, naming as *realia* the visible, simple, and more obvious facts of German life which can be taught in a two-year high-school course, and considering as *Kulturkunde* all those elements of cultural information which clearly belong to advanced study.

Generally speaking, no simple outline of characteristic traits can be valid for an entire nation. All such outlines are misleading, unless supplemented by lectures and books dealing with each trait more extensively. The only reliable way of getting at the real essence of a foreign civilization and culture is not the presentation of a simple scheme of characteristic traits, but a prolonged and intimate contact with the highest cultural achievements the foreign nation has produced in the various fields of endeavor. Yet the thorough understanding of a single great work of literature like Goethe's *Faust*, or a single great composition of Johann Sebastian Bach, may do more for a just appreciation of German cultural achievements than a casual acquaintance with a number of national characteristics. Nevertheless, we think it desirable to give at this point a brief summary of those character traits which are most frequently presented as typically German.

Typical German Traits (Deutsche Wesenszüge)

1. The German is fond of speaking of Gemüt, Stimmung, and Innerlichkeit, words whose exact connotations are translatable only in part; they are typically and specifically German. They find expression in an intense love of nature (Naturschwärmerei) and in lyrical poetry, the richest genre of German literature. Innerlichkeit does not necessarily manifest itself outwardly; it is rather a certain inner feeling, not expressible at all, save in poetry or in music. Gemüt, Stimmung, and Innerlichkeit are superbly expressed by the great masters of music: Bach, Händel, and Haydn; Mozart, Beethoven, and Schubert; Schumann, Mendelssohn, and von Weber; Wagner and Liszt; Brahms and Bruckner; Reger, Wolf, and Strauß.

2. The life of feeling (Gefühlsleben) is closely related to the life of will (Willensleben). Yet it has neither the explosive *élan* of the Frenchman nor the practical energy of the Englishman or American. The German is slow, but tenacious. His achievements are

the result of untiring zeal and industry. The typical hero of German literature is the man of will power whose motives do not always seem clear. Clear to us is only ber bunfle Drang, that vague but imperious urge to act, to accomplish, to achieve. Examples are *Siegfried, Parzival,* and *Simplicius; Wilhelm Meister* and *Faust; Wallenstein* and *Der grüne Heinrich.* Freytag's *Soll und Haben,* the great cultural-historical novel of the nineteenth century, is a hymn to the German people at work.

3. Gemüt and feeling play an important part in German life; reason is relegated to a less important role. The German has neither the practical worldly wisdom (Weltflugheit) of the English nor the clear rationality of the French. He is inclined to distrust pure reason and to permit phantasy free play, particularly where feelings are concerned. But he is self-critical. He tries to compensate for his inclination to feel by fostering a tendency to think and to reason, thus making a conscious effort to develop a "balance of forces" within himself. But he does not always succeed in compensating nor in avoiding over-compensation. Hence on the one hand extreme phantasy, on the other blind devotion to theoretical laws even in the fine arts (Dürer, Goethe, Wagner). Fear of vagueness in the sciences leads him to develop order, method, system. Gründlichkeit, often referred to as "German thoroughness," eingehend, "thoroughgoing" or "searching," and Wesen, "innermost essence," are typical German words. The German's longing for absolute personal freedom is overcome by voluntary submission to authority.

4. The German is individualistic to the extreme. In social life this is manifested by an effort to be original (Eigenbrötelei), in politics by separatist movements (Partifularismus). In art it is shown by strong personalities who are, more often than not, difficult to group according to definite trends or schools. In language individualism has long prevented absolute norms. German is even now far less standardized than French (but see Chapter IV, pp. 69 f.).

5. The strong tendency toward individualism produces a definite lack of uniformity and, at the same time, a versatility capable of the most diverse and the widest intellectual interests. Germany is the land of universal minds (Leibniz, Herder, Goethe, Alexander

and Wilhelm von Humboldt) as well as the home of one-sided specialists.

6. „Der Deutsche ist nicht, er wird" (Nietzsche). He has never finished, never is through. He does not finish a book, he "concludes" it in the conviction that it can and must be improved later. He always strives toward self-betterment. Hence his keen interest in all questions of education, in the phenomena of evolution and growth in nature, in history, in the universe. German philosophy does not conceive of man and the world as static; it conceives of all things as growing, as always in the process of evolution. The Entwicklungsroman is Germany's particular contribution to the types of the European novel: *Parzival, Simplicius, Agathon, Wilhelm Meister, Der grüne Heinrich.*

7. Critics speak of German "formlessness," contrasting it with the perfect form and taste of the French. The typical German form is dynamic (ever-changing) and shows itself in an eternal striving toward the infinite. This Unendlichkeitsstreben, often called das metaphysische Bedürfnis, finds expression in German architecture and literature, religion and science, philosophy and music.

8. Mechanical skill, devotion to the minutest detail in mechanics (Präzisionsinstrumente), a great and extraordinary talent for organization (Organisationstalent), and also an unfortunate tendency toward abstruse and impractical research — all these traits are frequently mentioned among the characteristics of the Germans.[1]

THE STRUGGLE FOR *Kulturkunde* as an integral part of foreign language instruction has been going on in Germany ever since 1882, the year of *Quousque tandem.* The struggle grew more bitter after the World War. When the new general directions (Richtlinien) appeared in 1924 a great many scholars and teachers resented the demands for *Kulturkunde* as far too rigid and too severe.[2] As late as 1928 Hans Strohmeyer stated: Wir befinden

---

[1] For fuller treatment see Hoffstaetter and Peters, *op. cit.,* Vol. I, article under "Deutsch (Psychologie des Deutschen)" by R. Müller-Freienfels.

[2] Ludwig Faser, *Lehrverfahren und Lehraufgaben für Französisch und Englisch* (Marburg a. d. Lahn: 1926), pp. v ff.

The most recent Richtlinien appeared in 1938. For the first part of an account see *Deutschunterricht im Ausland.* Zeitschrift des Goethe-Instituts der deutschen Akademie (München: Verlag von R. Oldenbourg), Heft 10,

uns alſo noch im Kampfe um das kulturkundliche Problem.[1] Strohmeyer
demanded, as others had done before him,[2] an entirely new orientation toward language teaching, maintaining that the war had
proved conclusively the urgent necessity of *Kulturkunde* as a
science, and as the only science which might draw the European
nations closer together, and thus promote peace and international
understanding. The "cultural penetration of foreign language
instruction" (die kulturkundliche Durchdringung des Sprachunterrichts)
was categorically demanded. He and other writers admit that the
presentation of cultural material is one of the most intricate and
baffling problems ever faced by the profession. Strohmeyer
defines *Kultur* as a state of development which a nation has reached
in an intellectual, spiritual, and economic respect. Nothing is
more dangerous, he says, than misjudgments and prejudices in
regard to cultural traits. Only complete fairness of evaluation
will do. To determine the peculiar essence (das besondere Weſen)
of a people is so difficult that we are bound to err grievously as
soon as we construct a definite scheme into which we try to force
the Frenchman, the Englishman, or the German on the basis of
hasty observations made here and there in our reading. The
problem is to build strong and reliable bridges toward mutual
understanding. This is the noblest task of the language teacher.

We cannot hope to draw a complete picture nor to form complete
judgments. In *Kulturkunde* it is a question of presenting the
most essential as far as we can. A solid foundation within the
limits of possibilities is more important than a mere superficial
mention of this and that. It is, in fine, more a matter of ſich
Hineinfühlen than of factual information. To ignite the inner fire
for understanding is the great art of the teacher.

Discussing "Cultural Readers," Strohmeyer believes that a
clever teacher can do without them, but that such readers are
urgently needed in most German schools. The highest principle
in our schools, he states, is education in a positive sense, a principle which may not be shaken by anything on this earth.

pp. 13 ff. But compare Wm. R. Gaede, "German Modern Language Journals
in 1938," *Modern Language Journal*, XXIV, 1 (Oct. 1939), pp. 3–14.

[1] *Methodik des neusprachlichen Unterrichts* (Westermann, Braunschweig:
1928), p. 200.

[2] For instance, Ernst Otto and Walter Hübner (cf. page 107, note 3).

The "Cultural Reader," he says, must never become the class text; it should always play the role of a supplement to other valuable reading materials. The cultural elements must be a natural and inevitable outgrowth of class or outside reading, but they should never take on the appearance of something forced, didactic, or narrowly pedantic. Materials taken from the "Cultural Reader" should be thoroughly prepared at home and then serve as a basis for class discussions in the foreign language.[1]

The latter recommendation is not valid for our conditions except, perhaps, in somewhat advanced classes, particularly in college.

One cannot read recent German works on linguistic pedagogy without realizing how strongly their authors have influenced our thinking in regard to cultural content. No doubt their basic argument is correct. Education is the first and foremost concern of the schools, here as everywhere. And yet, this argument raises extremely difficult problems for which we have as yet found no solution: (1) The necessity of offering cultural material in adequate form within two years in high school; and (2) the fact that we cannot present such materials within a definitely limited vocabulary. These are our most baffling puzzles.

AMERICAN ATTEMPTS TOWARD A SOLUTION of the problem have resulted in three different plans: (I) to present cultural material in English; (II) to utilize textbooks containing satisfactory amounts of cultural material, having previously ascertained the cultural content by proper measuring devices; (III) to integrate language courses with other subjects in such a way as to make them more effective and more meaningful for the student. We shall briefly discuss all these commendable attempts toward a solution of our problem, trying to evaluate each in turn.

I. CULTURAL MATERIAL IN ENGLISH

Professor E. H. Zeydel in his *Beginners' German* was the first, to my knowledge, to supplement the cultural background presented in German by collateral readings in English.[2] His ten well chosen

[1] Strohmeier, *op. cit.*, pp. 199–239.
[2] D. C. Heath and Company, 1933. A more recent German grammar for beginners which offers cultural material in English is *Language, Literature,*

selections are these: (1) The German Language; (2) The Geography of Germany; (3) The Geography of Germany (concluded); (4) German History to 1700; (5) German History after 1700; (6) The Constitution of Republican Germany; (7) Education in Germany; (8) German Literature; (9) German Music and Painting; (10) The German Character. These English selections, even though in part now obsolete, due to the changes in Germany, are undoubtedly a welcome supplement to the German texts with cultural content, numbering about thirty. Zeydel evidently felt keenly the impossibility of reconciling the presentation of cultural material with the *Minimum Standard German Vocabulary*. Nevertheless, his preface simply states: "The first 250 words of the Morgan list are all used without exception, while the average for the next 750 is quite high." The total number of words used is, unfortunately, not given.

Zeydel's book was followed in 1937 by Professor Charles H. Handschin's *Introduction to German Civilization, an Outline*.[1] This book, written in English and divided into three chapters, is intended to promote among Americans an understanding of German civilization. In the preface the author deplores the fact that "in modern language instruction no systematic knowledge of the foreign civilization is given," and that "material of a most elementary and inconsequential nature is read." The writer states further that the material offered "may be used to supplement any course of study in German, or may be made the basis for a separate one- or two-hour course for the year." The contents are:

  I. German History: Technique and Sources — Map Drawing — The German Stems — Topography — Switzerland and Austria — Syllabus of German History from 375 to 1934 — Exercises.
 II. Institutions and Life: Governmental Institutions — Economic Institutions — Religion and the Churches — Education and the Schools — Recreation — Exercises.
III. German Culture: An Orientation — Great Men and Women — Exercises — Great Literary Men and their Works — Problems on Important Literary Works — Notes on Important Literary

---

and Life, German Book One, by Dorothea Davis and P. S. Allen (Scott, Foresman and Company, 1938).

[1] Prentice-Hall, Inc., 1937. 235 pp.

Works — Art and Architecture — German Music — German Philosophical and Scientific Thought — The German Character and Mentality — The Future — Exercises.

Suggested Readings.

Another attempt toward a solution of the cultural content problem in German instruction was made by Professor C. M. Purin through a pamphlet, *Germany and the Germans, Suggested Topics and Sources for a Year's Course in Secondary Schools*. Like Handschin, Purin sees a solution in presenting cultural content in English. The pamphlet was first sent out in mimeographed form, and later published in the *German Quarterly*.[1] Purin's basic idea is thoroughly sound. As long as the course suggested does not curtail the language courses proper, it deserves the most hearty support. Details about the purpose and scope of the course appeared in the *Monatshefte*.[2] The only difficulty that strikes one after a careful study of the suggestions is that few if any teachers are prepared to give such a course. Either special training must be given as part of a "Teachers' Course," or preparation must be provided in special courses dealing particularly with all those points which lend themselves to a presentation of clear-cut connections between German and American cultural life. This deficiency, however, can be easily remedied through special courses offered during summer sessions.

In the same vein as Zeydel, Handschin, and Purin, Professor E. Heyse Dummer in an article "The Teaching of German Civilization in First- and Second-Year College Classes"[3] describes a course given at Elmhurst College, Illinois, since 1934. The old practice of discussing from time to time cultural elements for ten or fifteen minutes before the bell interrupted had been abandoned. Through cooperation with other departments — the social sciences, history, religion, philosophy, music, science — the course became both more significant and more popular. The classes met four times a week. Every other week a full-period lecture was devoted to an illustrated exposition of German life. Well qualified

[1] University of Wisconsin, University Extension Division, 623 West State Street, Milwaukee, Wis.; also *German Quarterly* (May, 1939), pp. 117–39.

[2] *Monatshefte für deutschen Unterricht* (Feb. 1939), pp. 96–103.

[3] *Modern Language Journal* (Dec. 1936), pp. 179–85.

members of the German department discussed the following topics: Important Men and Events in German History; Touring Germany; German Society; The German System of Education; Customs and Manners; *Handwerk;* Germany, the Land of Music, etc. During the second year these lectures were supplemented by "cultural texts" in German and, moreover, by an extended reading list. Besides the materials read in German, students were required to read in English a minimum of 500 pages each semester.

II. CONTRIBUTIONS OF THE *STUDY*

Long before these suggestions had been made, the *Study* and, before it, the Committee of Twelve had sanctioned the use of cultural material. As one of the immediate objectives in a two-year course the *Study* had stipulated "Progressive development of a knowledge of the foreign country, past and present, and a special interest in the life and the characteristics of its people." As immediate objectives of the third and fourth year the *Study* had urged "an increased knowledge of the foreign country and its people and their achievements in various fields of activity." The ultimate objective of a four-year course was to be "Especial interest in the foreign country and its people, considerable knowledge of its past and present, and a broadened attitude toward other civilizations than our own. Increased ability to understand and to enjoy the literature (in the original or in translation) and the art of other nations, and greater curiosity about such matters." [1]

While these statements give us a general idea of what is to be achieved, they leave us at sea as to exact details. Coleman asks: "Through what means can this aim be realized?" And he answers his own question:

> Through the kind and the extent of reading matter, of course, through the information and comment that comes from the teacher, and through the interest aroused by the course which leads the student to learn about the foreign country in other ways ... Reading matter that is primarily informative or moral or didactic or too

[1] Algernon Coleman, *The Teaching of Modern Foreign Languages in the United States* (The Macmillan Company, 1929), pp. 107 f.

remote from the habits of mind of students will fail of its purpose, and for conversational purposes *realia* that are entirely external — coins, models of grocery stores and railway stations, and the like — can probably contribute to the objective only to the degree that they serve to stimulate interest in the foreign people and to hold attention.[1]

Even supposing the teacher to be full of information about the foreign country and eager to comment on it, how can he manage in a short course, where every minute counts, to find time to present enough cultural material to hold the students' attention? How can he give information in the foreign language strictly within the most frequent words and idioms? How can he avoid being too informative, too moral, too didactic, too remote from the habits of mind of the students?

Indeed, the question of cultural material bristles with unsolved problems.

If we keep in mind that in 1929 a group of selected teachers reported 56 to 60 pages of reading for the first year and 186 to 190 for the second, at best 250 pages in two years,[2] we have little cause for optimism. Besides, cultural content found in elementary texts is, as a rule, extremely meager. Coleman remarks:

> In order to fill out the picture, to supply the information needed to make allusions comprehensible, the notes and the instructor must do a large share. If they do not, there is little likelihood that the objective will be attained as the result of the modern language course ... teachers who fail to equip themselves to discharge the responsibility that is so evidently theirs must cross this objective from their list.[3]

Not long ago, before the cry for cultural content had reached its height, our problems were comparatively simple. Here was language, there cultural content and literature. Now that we have definitely gone on record as professing to a cultural aim even within two years, we find ourselves unprepared for a task so

---

[1] *Ibid.*, pp. 100 f.   [2] *Ibid.*, p. 101.

[3] *Ibid.*, p. 102. Some interesting attempts have been made to construct tests on the knowledge of literature and culture. See, for instance, Waldo C. Peebles, "A Test on German Life and Culture," *German Quarterly* (Jan. 1937), pp. 22–26; James B. Tharp, "A Test on French Civilization," *French Review* (March, 1935), pp. 283–87.

difficult and complicated. Listless pupils, unprepared teachers, crowded classes, heavy teaching loads and, besides, curricula hard to reconcile with a changed and restless world — all these factors were instrumental in spurring the *Study* into action even ten years ago.

MEASURING CULTURAL MATERIAL will seem impossible and, in a way, ludicrous to many, and yet, as we shall presently see, it has helped us to realize clearly the necessity of coming to an understanding of the problems involved in this basic point which may be divided into three questions: (1) Exactly what kind of cultural material should be presented? (2) When should it be presented? (3) What is the best way of presenting it?

MISS GILMAN'S INVESTIGATION. In 1929, Miss Gertrude Marcelle Gilman attempted to define anew the objectives of foreign-language teaching and to put the question of cultural content on a strictly scientific basis.[1] Advised by Algernon Coleman, she tried to evaluate the amount as well as the character of cultural material which she found presented in twenty-two French texts widely used in Illinois. Cultural she defines as informational and suggestive material bearing on the foreign civilization as distinguished from that of America. She analyzes the degree and the value of cultural material by the aid of eight key words which are: "note," "suggestion," "allusion," "mention," "statement," "picture," "description," "explanation or exposition." These key words are carefully defined as to their exact meaning and function within the experiment.

Then, after the material of the text had been gathered and appropriate key words applied to it, the material was divided and classified under fifty-one categories, namely: art, benevolent and moral institutions, Bible, bridges and highways, building, burial, business and professions, canals, Catholic church, city plans, civic improvement, classical antiquity, clothing and dress, cost and standard of living, customs-duty-tariff, directions, education, finance, food, geography, etc., etc.

---

[1] Her study, "The Cultural Material in the French Curriculum of Illinois High Schools," was first prepared as a thesis for the Master of Arts in the Department of Romance Languages of the University of Chicago. Cf. *Studies in Modern Language Teaching* (The Macmillan Company, 1930), pp. 225–77.

The net result of Miss Gilman's study can be briefly summarized as follows: The most frequent subject category is geography; next come history, marriage rites, and customs. One is surprised at the rare occurrence of certain categories, for instance, art, business and professions, clothing, dress, and education, food, law, politics, and government. The most frequent key word is "mention," outweighing "statement" and "note" by 16 to 1 or 2.

THE KURZ INVESTIGATION. Another inquiry into the cultural content of French texts was made by Professor Harry Kurz and Grace Cook Kurz.[1] They studied the contents of ten books, all widely used in college. Following Miss Gilman's technique, though with some curtailment of the many topical categories, the authors come to conclusions which deserve to be quoted:

> Tabulations, figures, and totals are always impressive and sometimes misleading. There is peculiar danger in any attempt at forcing numbers to measure that delicate mental experience which we call culture. Matters of style, of emotional content such as humor, pathos, irony, the *esprit* of an author or a book, these are all implicit and to be appraised or enumerated according to individual taste and apprehension. There can be no assumption, therefore, that the final cultural value of a French text depends upon the number of explicit *realia* contained in it ...
>
> Our tabulations offer no infallible guides ... It does not follow from them that the book having the greatest number of entries for cultural content is necessarily the best book, even for cultural influence; nor that notes offering the greatest amount of information are, *ipso facto*, the best notes ...
>
> Ultimately, the cultural influence of any class book must be checked or stimulated by the spirit of the teacher.[2]

The authors close with a number of highly stimulating questions suggested in the course of their experiment. They ask how far books of fairy tales and children's stories promote culture among college students. They inquire whether a humorous book chosen for young adolescents satisfies also the more mature mind of the college student. They wonder whether or not poetry should re-

---

[1] "The Realia Found in the French Readers Used in College Courses," *Studies in Modern Language Teaching* (The Macmillan Company, 1930), pp. 281–324.   [2] *Ibid.*, pp. 322 f.

ceive more attention in cultural readers. Other questions concern the variety of materials offered, the inclusion of *realia* in the exercises, the distribution of cultural and informational material so as to prevent overemphasis on fiction, the lack of materials dealing with art and music and, finally, the periods of civilization which are most desirable for students in two-year courses in college French.

THE VAN HORNE INVESTIGATION. A third experiment of the same kind was made by Professor John Van Horne and Margaret Varney Van Horne.[1] They followed the technique worked out by Miss Gilman under Algernon Coleman's guidance. The sources used in their investigation were twenty-one widely read Spanish texts.

The authors take pains to explain that they make no claims whatever as to the correctness of the results. At the end of their task they are still not convinced that they have been on the right road. They speak frankly of the immense difficulties they have encountered in the course of their investigation. And they are meticulously conscientious:

> Let no one imagine that real objectivity has been attained. The road still bristles with difficulties. It is often doubtful whether we should include a certain reference under one or the other category. *Religion* overlaps *education* and *social life* and *customs; art* overlaps *buildings, institutions* and *monuments.* Again uncertainty arises in the matter of weighing. Is a specific case a "mention" or "allusion," a "statement," a "description," or an "exposition?" . . .

> In general, the numerical count lists the obvious commonplaces of life. It catches the distinctive features of clothing, food, law, worship, art, geography, history, and the like. It misses the subtleties. It fails to record pathos, tenderness, character, humor, adventure, style. It seizes the local and the spectacular, and misses the exotic and the universal and the inherent. It favors prepared informational readers, realistic novels of manners and customs, propagandistic works and detailed annotations. It neglects adventure stories, novels of character, and plays.[2]

[1] *Studies in Modern Language Teaching* (The Macmillan Company, 1930), pp. 327–63.

[2] *Ibid.*, p. 361. For a discussion of these experiments see also Coleman, *op. cit.*, pp. 117–19, and Robert Herndon Fife, *A Summary of Reports on the Modern Foreign Languages* (The Macmillan Company, 1931), pp. 175–78.

At the end of their study the authors briefly summarize their findings in regard to each of the ten texts, expressing the hope that later investigators of cultural material will achieve superior results and conclusions.

Lest we be overcritical of these experiments we should realize that there is a lesson to be learned from them: (1) To measure cultural material is infinitely more difficult than has been supposed. (2) In an overwhelming number of cases the reference consists of a mere "mention" of a name or a fact. (3) A knowledge of the foreign civilization can be taught only if the teacher is anxious and prepared to explain from an abundance of study and experience all points which need explanation. (4) The distinction between *realia* and *Kulturkunde* seems to be absolutely necessary, because geography, the category most frequently occurring in the experiments, is far away from *Kulturkunde* which deals with the thoughts, creeds, beliefs, and attitudes in literature, art, and science.

It is interesting to note that this distinction is at least hinted at by several German authors who would first take up *realia* and *Land und Leute*, and much later, after the main linguistic difficulties had been cleared away, *Kulturkunde*.

An inquiry into the amount of cultural information contained in German reading texts was undertaken by Virginia Stockhausen in her article, "The Cultural Content of Reading Texts." [1] She followed Miss Gilman's technique, omitting, however, most of the categories. Coleman who discusses this article very briefly in his *Analytical Bibliography*, Vol. II, remarks: "The author's warning concerning the intangible literary qualities of these works and the highly subjective character of final estimates is given point by the fact that W. Leopold considers *Emil und die Detektive* interesting but not valuable culturally, while Miss Stockhausen considers it good." [2]

H. G. Shapiro's article, "A Method of Presenting Cultural

---

[1] *Monatshefte* (Oct. 1936), pp. 255–60.

[2] Published by the University of Chicago Press, 1938, p. 352. Coleman refers to Werner Leopold's article "Realia, Kulturkunde, and Nationalism," *Monatshefte* (Jan. 1937), pp. 17–24, which is a continuation of his previous article published earlier in the same journal. See "Word-Counts and After" (Dec. 1936), pp. 355–62.

Material," suggests ways to correct the usual haphazard methods of developing interest in a foreign civilization.[1]

A carefully prepared Master's thesis deals with the same problem. Henry Nashorn examined thirty-two readers on the Approved List for High-School German for New York City according to the technique of Miss Gilman's inquiry.[2] Among the most frequent categories, he found, were geography, social life and customs, and literature, and under these, in order of importance: cities, authors, Rhine, family life, and Christmas. The statement that "no book had a 1 : 1 ratio of textual and editorial treatment" leads one to believe that the author holds such a ratio advisable; why is by no means clear. Carl A. Krause's *Deutschkunde* [3] was found to have the highest average rate of cultural information, namely 4.04. It is noteworthy that at least seven of the approved readers show a vocabulary altogether out of proportion to the length of the actual text. One reader has a vocabulary of not less than 79 pages for only 71 pages of reading matter.

One of the most illuminating articles about the historical aspects as well as the present status of *realia* is by J. Alan Pfeffer.[4] The author studied carefully the course outlines of 109 universities and colleges with a total registration of more than 1000 each. Of the schools offering German, only 23 per cent listed courses in the civilization of Germany. In spite of claims to the contrary, the author found that 73 per cent of the institutions include no course on German *realia* whatever. An abyss separates theory and practice: a wholehearted acclaim of the cultural aim on the one hand, its complete neglect on the other.

The author goes on to depict the complete and hopeless confusion which exists in this important phase of language study. He cites an instance in which a committee of the New York Regents Examination Board tried to make a modest beginning with *realia*

[1] *High Points* (May, 1933), pp. 62–65.   [2] "The Culture Content of German Readers Used in the High Schools of the City of New York." Unpublished Master's thesis (College of the City of New York, 1933), 146 pp. Briefed in Coleman's *Analytical Bibliography*, Vol. II, pp. 349 ff.

[3] Charles Scribner's Sons, 1929.   [4] "Realia in American Modern Language Instruction," *German Quarterly* (Jan. 1937), pp. 1–11. Briefed in Coleman's *Analytical Bibliography*, Vol. II, pp. 277 ff.

by incorporating one question. A vigorous protest was the result. With justice he points out that as long as this chaos continues to exist, we cannot hope to attain any cultural objective whatsoever.

In 1929 Algernon Coleman proposed: (1) to establish by a consensus of the best opinion what our students should come to know of a given country and its civilization in order to understand better what they read and to add to their general education, and (2) to analyze books that are usually read in the different stages of the secondary-school course for explicit and implicit content of such material.[1]

We have tried the latter. The results have been commendable in so far as we have learned from these pioneer studies. But we have as yet not attempted to carry out the first suggestion which is even more important. For, indubitably, a yard of agreement is infinitely better than a mile of difference. May we hope, perhaps, that just as frequency counts of words and idioms have brought at least a degree of order into our reading, so similar counts of cultural allusions classified under certain (not too numerous) categories will some day bring order into the intricate problems of cultural content? However great the difficulties may be, hard work, willingness to compromise, and devotion to the task should finally arrive at a solution. We certainly feel that an early solution is imperative as we pass in review some of the outstanding articles of writers who are more or less closely connected with the movement of progressive education.

III. INTEGRATION OF LANGUAGE COURSES
WITH OTHER SUBJECTS

It is a matter of general knowledge that the great American philosopher and educator, John Dewey, has influenced educational theories far beyond the boundaries of his native land. As early as 1901, in an essay on *The Child and the Curriculum* he used the term "new education," [2] and ever since then he has, in books and

---

[1] Coleman, *The Teaching of Modern Foreign Languages in the United States* (The Macmillan Company, 1929), 118 pp.

[2] Cf. *Contributions to Education*, No. 5 (The University of Chicago Press, 1901), p. 23.

essays read throughout the civilized world, expounded the fundamental theories of this "new" and, as it often came to be termed,
"progressive" education. It would be interesting and instructive
to trace the basic ideas of John Dewey through his important
works [1] and to find the central thought in all his utterances in regard
to the social aspects of language teaching. For obvious reasons
we must limit ourselves to stating that the progressive education
movement is largely influenced by Dewey's writings. The old
traditional scheme and the new progressive one are contrasted by
Dewey as follows:

> The traditional scheme is, in essence, one of imposition from
> above and from outside. It imposes adult standards, subject matter,
> and methods upon those who are only growing slowly toward ma-
> turity. The gap is so great that the required subject matter, the
> methods of learning and of behaving are foreign to the existing
> capacities of the young . . .
> To imposition from above is opposed expression and cultivation of
> individuality; to external discipline is opposed free activity; to learn-
> ing from texts and teachers, learning through experience; to acquisi-
> tion of isolated skills and techniques by drill is opposed acquisition
> of them as means of attaining ends which make direct vital appeal;
> to preparation for a more or less remote future is opposed making
> the most of opportunities of the present life; to static aims and
> materials is opposed acquaintance with a changing world . . . [2]

THE PROGRESSIVE EDUCATION MOVEMENT AND INTEGRATION.
In the new or progressive education movement nothing has played
a more important role than the theory of integration. Integration
does not merely mean "to bring the various phases of language
together in a unified whole by the separate training of each
phase," for instance, speaking, writing, hearing, and reading.[3] In
progressive education, integration is used in a much wider and
more inclusive sense. To integrate here means to make entire,
to complete, to round out, to perfect, to unite parts or elements

---

[1] *School and Society* (The University of Chicago Press, revised ed., 1932);
Democracy and Education (The Macmillan Company, 1926); *Human Nature
and Conduct* (Henry Holt and Company, 1922).

[2] *Experience and Education* (The Macmillan Company, 1938), pp. 4 ff.

[3] Compare *Language Learning*, pp. 43–47.

with something related so as to form a whole, or in the words of Wilford M. Aikin, "to find ways of breaking down the barriers which artificially and harmfully separate subjects of study and the work of teachers in various fields, and to discover how to make breaches in the walls which have so separated school from community life as to make school life sterile and relatively insignificant." [1]

In 1929 a Progressive Education Conference was held, and a discussion group dealing with the problems of progressive secondary education asked for a "Commission on the Relation of School and College." Mr. Aikin was made chairman of this commission which was to experiment with schools altogether freed from any and all predetermined requirements. More than 280 colleges agreed to the plan, and thirty secondary schools were finally selected to take part in the experiment. The experiment was to extend over a period of eight years, and later became known as the "Eight-Year Study." Professor Ralph M. Tyler, of the University of Chicago, agreed to direct the efforts of a staff of young workers whose task it was to help teachers devise tests and measurements to evaluate the results they would attain under the new plan of instruction. Professor Paul B. Diederich represented the foreign languages. Aikin stated the principle of the experiment as follows:

> We are trying to develop students who regard education as an enduring quest for meanings rather than credit accumulation; who desire to investigate, to follow the leadings of a subject, to explore new fields of thought; knowing how to budget time, to read well, to use sources of knowledge effectively and who are experienced in fulfilling obligations which come with membership in the school or college community.[2]

In 1936 the National Education Association held a meeting at St. Louis and there discussed "The Place of Foreign Language Study in an Integrated Secondary School Program." Dean Henry Smith of Indiana University, after consulting with twenty deans

---

[1] Cole-Tharp, *Modern Foreign Languages and Their Teaching* (Appleton-Century Co., 1937), p. 214.

[2] "The Purposes of the Eight-Year Experimental Study," *Educational Record* (Jan. 1935), pp. 114 ff.

of other Schools of Education, summed up the consensus of opinion as follows:

> It seems to be almost a universal opinion in Schools of Education that the study of a modern language does have a place in the integrated secondary school program (not justifiable for all, but elective for a part). It is quite possible, then, that at least one of the modern languages should be offered in every high school curriculum.[1]

Professor Diederich, who for many years visited the schools directed according to the principles of progressive education, points out the relationships between foreign languages and other parts of the curriculum.[2]

What are possible relationships of foreign language study with other parts of the curriculum?

(a) With English: natural extension of reading habits and interests; study of words and their relationships.

(b) With social science: current and source material in other languages; travel, applying the social experience of other nations to our own problems.

(c) With natural science: reading scientific reports in other languages (possible only with advanced students).

(d) With visual arts: illustrations of the life and art of the foreign people.

(e) With music: folk songs, opera, biographies of musicians.

In 1935 the campaign toward integration, toward gathering all elements of language study under one common educational objective, was at its height. Professor Walter V. Kaulfers, a most able student of the problem of integration and a frequent contributor to many journals, wrote a series of invaluable articles in which he described and outlined the language courses of the future. Kaulfers, it seems, has made the most intensive and thorough study of the curriculum in regard to language. In 1937 he and his colleague, Holland D. Roberts, published a book containing sixteen articles which give the most thorough information on the

[1] The meeting was reported by J. B. Tharp in "Can Foreign Languages Integrate?" *Monatshefte für deutschen Unterricht* (March, 1936), pp. 124–27; *Modern Language Journal* (Nov. 1936), pp. 115–22; (Dec. 1936), pp. 196–203.   [2] Cole-Tharp, *op. cit.*, p. 217.

varied problems of integration available at the present time.[1] The authors discuss with vigor and clarity every conceivable angle of their subject: from the revolt against excessive departmentaliza- tion in the high schools to the development of a creative American- ism, from objections raised against a wider differentiation of educational opportunities to the cooperative approach to the problem.

The first article of their book is entitled "Integrating the Lan- guage Arts for Social Purposes."[2] It pleads for: (1) evaluating the contributions of European, Asiatic, and African peoples to American life and culture; (2) understanding America's part in the cultures of other peoples; and (3) sympathetic understanding of the world's major civilizations. Coleman fears that the impli- cations of their program would lead to a complete elimination of foreign language teaching.[3]

In the concluding paragraph Kaulfers quotes from his article "The Foreign Language Curriculum of the Future"[4]:

> Although the horoscope for the future does not presage the advent of the millennium, it serves quite adequately to reveal the lines along which frontier workers in the language arts will seek to find a solution to present problems. In so far as the efforts of these pioneers are

[1] *A Cultural Basis for the Language Arts* (Stanford University Press, 1937), 115 pp. The book contains twelve articles by Kaulfers, three by Kaulfers and Roberts, one by Roberts. Their study was issued in connection with the "Stanford Language Arts Investigation."

[2] By Walter V. Kaulfers and Holland D. Roberts, published first in *Edu- cation* (Dec. 1935), pp. 239–45.

[3] Cf. *Analytical Bibliography*, Vol. II, p. 40.

But note the following reply of Professor Roberts in a personal letter dated May 1, 1939:

Fears that an integrated cultural program, based upon the needs of students, will lead to the elimination or minimizing of foreign language teaching, are groundless. Experience has proved the reverse to be true. Carefully con- sidered work in the San Mateo High School, over a period of years, has demon- strated that the provision of a cultural basis roots the teaching of language far more firmly than traditional procedures. Other schools have had a similar experience. Many young people — and this is especially true in America — have not had their imaginations stirred by the emotional meaning of language. They see no relationship between the needs of their daily rounds and reading, speaking, or writing another language. An acquaintance with the lives of a people, different from those of their own community, and a study of the contributions of that people to our own culture, frequently arouses inter- ests which would not otherwise exist.

[4] First published in *Hispania* (Feb. 1936), pp. 13–24.

based on realities of present-day life, on an appreciation of the history and philosophy of American education, and upon first-hand knowledge of the abilities of youth, their labors are destined ultimately to triumph, for current professional literature is replete with evidence that they will have the support of administrators and curriculum specialists, and of that large majority of foreign language teachers whose professional vision is fully commensurate with the possibilities of the present and the opportunities of the future.

Kaulfers' articles have been frequently misunderstood and misinterpreted. In a personal letter of April 4, 1939, he writes:

My philosophy, in brief, is that language can and should be taught from the very start in and through content of significance in terms of the ultimate objectives of education. If this is done, integration is inevitable, though certain methods of approach will obviously lead to more effective results than others.

I do not know of a statement that is more crisp and to the point, and moreover is quite in agreement with the rigid demands of the Richtlinien of 1924.

Other writers, too numerous to be mentioned here, have shown a keen interest in problems of integration. James B. Tharp, convinced that the main concern of language study is to make the student's experience immediately vital and meaningful, urges that the training of teachers be improved so as to enable them to offer an integrated program of study.[1] B. Q. Morgan, in a brief discussion of "Language and Integration," [2] comes to the conclusion that primary stress should be placed on language itself, and not on specific cultural facts which the pupil can obtain for himself through reading outside of the class. Matthew H. Willing in a stimulating article proposes an orientation stage in the form of a "Language Arts Survey." [3]

[1] "Can Foreign Languages Integrate? A Report on the St. Louis Panel Discussion," *Modern Language Journal* (April, 1936), pp. 416–19. "Foreign Language Integration; Extended Remarks of the St. Louis Panel Members," *ibid.* (Nov. 1936), pp. 115–22; *ibid.* (Dec. 1936), pp. 196–203. Also: *Monatshefte* (March, 1936), pp. 124–27, and "Foreign Languages and the Social Sciences," *The Educational Record* (Oct. 1938), pp. 449–62.

[2] *School and Society* (July 4, 1936), pp. 12–13.   [3] "Present Trends in the Secondary School Curriculum and Their Implications for the Teaching of Modern Foreign Languages," *Monatshefte* (Oct. 1937), pp. 275–84.

A letter to me from Professor Diederich, dated April 4, 1939, unfortunately cannot be quoted in full. Diederich states that no significant improvements in the content or methods of foreign language instruction should be expected from the "Eight-Year Study." He says that for a long time the secondary schools have been taking orders from colleges as to what they shall teach and that the results have been satisfactory neither to the colleges nor to the high schools. He continues:

> Whatever may be the fact, secondary school faculties have come to feel that the study of foreign languages has been over-emphasized in response to college requirements. They point out that it occupies more time in the program of pupils who are preparing for college than any other field in the curriculum. While they do not dispute its value for properly qualified pupils, they question whether it is of more value than any other field of study, as its present position implies . . .
>
> This trend has thrown foreign language teachers on the defensive which has led many of them to oppose new developments in the curriculum and to regard themselves as conservatives. This, in turn, has led many to cling to the "rigor" of their traditional methods of instruction to symbolize their opposition to what they regard as "soft pedagogy" in the newer courses. This attitude is reflected in the journal articles and convention addresses of recent years in which passionate protest has often been substituted for reports of significant research and new developments in the teaching of foreign languages. This is undoubtedly a passing phase, but an unfortunate one . . .

THE RESULTS OF THIS DISCUSSION

What have we found in the course of our inquiry?

1. The study of *realia* and cultural material is undeveloped, its present demands probably dating back not farther than 1882. In the brief period of sixty years we have come to realize clearly the immense importance of an understanding of cultural relations between peoples, an understanding which may, in the future, decide between peace and war, progress and decay. This is our greatest gain.

2. We have rapidly passed in review the various attempts toward a solution of this most elusive problem. Beginning with the simplest solution possible (Zeydel, Handschin, Purin, etc.) we

proceeded to a description of a more difficult one (Gilman, Kurz, Van Horne, etc.) and, finally, we set forth various possibilities suggested by representatives of the progressive education movement (Kaulfers, Roberts, Diederich). In passing we noted with regret the abyss between theory and practice, the utter confusion and helplessness in dealing adequately with the problem as a whole, and also the lamentable difference of opinion between language teachers and educationists. This is our greatest disappointment.

3. There is, however, one comforting reflection. There is hope in what we can, must, and, in the end, shall do to overcome our difficulties: effect a compromise and come to a solution. All solutions are but temporary. Each solution is valid only for that situation for which it is found. At any rate, we cannot believe that two groups of people who strive or should strive toward one great educational objective — language teachers and educationists — should not be able, by means of friendly discussions, to come to an agreement satisfactory to all concerned.

4. In the course of our discussion we have noted an imposing number of possibilities, all of which might be used in one form or another as potential means of integration. But no single person can determine the nature of cultural material to be taught, nor when and how it should be taught. This can only be determined by effective cooperation. At some future time, not too distant, we hope, the nations of Europe will turn away from strife and struggle to more peaceful pursuits. An international commission will meet somewhere. Their conviction will be that the real values of life begin where the greed for power, land, and gold ends. They will attempt to find a solution for this all-important and basic question.

In the meantime we can do much to promote the solution of our problem. We can profit greatly from a thorough study of all the sources mentioned and from Moreno-Lacalle's "Report of the Committee on Realia." [1] We can, through local discussion groups,

---

[1] *Hispania* (March, 1922), pp. 96–102.

An interesting booklet in mimeographed form, entitled *A Foreign Language Program for Progressive Secondary Schools*, was prepared under the chairmanship of Paul B. Diederich. The first article by Diederich bears the title of the booklet (86 pages). The third article "A Suggested First-Year Course in

throw much light on the exact details of the feasible ways and means toward integration, thus preparing ourselves for effective participation in future national conferences which are certain to come.

But by far the most important necessity is that each individual teacher carry the question in his heart and, if possible, make his own contribution to the subject.

And now, finally, we must turn from theoretical discussions to information of immediately practical value.

SOURCES OF REALIA are given in an important book, *The Modern Language Teacher's Handbook* by Thomas E. Oliver.[1] A number of Service Bureaus for the different modern languages are ready to help teachers secure necessary information on all sorts of problems.[2] Numerous articles contain suggestions in regard to the formation and the administration of German clubs.[3] The literature dealing with dramatic performances is abundant.[4] Phono-

German" is by Alfred Adler of the Francis W. Parker School in Chicago. For permission to quote from this booklet address the Progressive Education Association, 310 West 90th Street, New York City.

[1] D. C. Heath and Company, 1935, vii + 706 pp., $3.60. Look under Realia, Art, Cards, Charts, Costumes, Films, Flags, Games, Informational Readers, Maps, Newspapers, Photographs, Pictures, Prints, Posters, Slides, Songs, etc., etc.

[2] For German write to The German Service Bureau, University of Wisconsin, Madison, Wis.

[3] J. A. Hess, "A Guide for German Clubs," *Modern Language Journal* (Jan. 1927), pp. 213–36. Reprints may be secured from Professor J. A. Hess, Ohio University, Athens, Ohio.

See also the article by Myrtle J. Joseph, "Club Work and Activities in the Field of German," *High Points* (Jan. 1933), pp. 39–47.

Miss Mariele Schirmer is the secretary of The Interscholastic Federation of German Clubs. Address: State Teachers College, Milwaukee, Wis. See her article, "The Significance of the Modern Language Club," *Modern Language Journal* (Nov. 1922), pp. 93–98; also her "Bibliography of Articles on German Clubs," *Monatshefte* (March, 1928), pp. 86–90.

[4] Marian P. Whitney, "German Christmas Play at Vassar," *Modern Language Journal* (Feb. 1929), p. 399.

Ernst Feise has published a number of articles on plays in the *Jahrbuch der Monatshefte* for 1921, 1922, 1924, 1925. See also his "Choice and Staging of a German Christmas Play," *Monatshefte* (Oct. 1928), pp. 169–72.

E. P. Appelt, "Programmvorschläge für Weihnachtsfeiern," *Monatshefte* (Oct. 1929), pp. 164–67.

E. A. Philippson, "Deutsche Spiele für die Schulbühne," *Monatshefte* (May, 1929), pp. 138–41.

graph and radio have been used to supplement class instruction.[1]
Films, slides, and postcards are important in visual learning.[2]
Maps, wall charts, and posters are able to serve the same purpose.[3]

B. Q. Morgan, "Theaterstücke für die Vereinsbühne," *Monatshefte* (Feb. 1932), pp. 33–44. Also "Deutsche Gedenktage: A Calendar for the German Club," by B. Q. Morgan and Stella M. Hinz. *Modern Language Journal* (Dec. 1938), pp. 250–64. Also see Oliver, *op. cit.*, pp. 516–20.

[1] Phonograph:

E. P. Appelt, "Das Grammophon im Sprachunterricht," *Monatshefte* (Oct. 1928), pp. 166–69.

Emma Gertrude Kunze, "The Use of the Phonograph in Language Work," *Modern Language Journal* (April, 1929), pp. 538–49. Gives sources for records, omitting, however, Otto Sperling, Stuttgart, Germany.

John Whyte, "On the Use of Phonograph Records in the Teaching of German Pronunciation," *German Quarterly* (Nov. 1931), pp. 170–74. Oliver, *op. cit.*, lists many firms dealing in phonographs as well as in records; cf. pp. 497–500. The German records of the Linguaphone Institute, 30 Rockefeller Plaza, New York City, are splendid, according to personal experience.

Radio:
W. S. Hendrix, "Foreign Language Broadcasting in the United States," *Modern Language Journal* (Nov. 1932), pp. 91–96; a list of broadcasting stations is given.

J. Sandreau, "La Radiophone et l'étude de l'allemand," *Revue de l'enseignement des langues vivantes* (Nov. 1928), pp. 390–95.

Der Schulfunk, the only radio magazine for schools, is published twice a month by the Zentralstelle für Schulfunk, Berlin.

The National Broadcasting Company, Inc., RCA Building, Radio City, New York, issues weekly *Short Wave News*, a paper listing daily radio programs, including *Die deutsche Stunde*.

An interesting account of late developments in radio broadcasting in the interest of students is given by James B. Tharp, the reviser of Cole's book. See Cole-Tharp, *op. cit.*, pp. 570 ff.; also their chapter on *realia*, pp. 223–58.

[2] Films and Slides:
Silent films, and slides for the cost of transportation may be obtained from the German Tourist Information Office, 665 Fifth Ave., New York City.

For films of Germany, address Dr. Max Winter, 102 E. 15th St., New York City.

Films and slides can be secured at nominal cost from the Federation of German Clubs or from the Service Bureau at the University of Wisconsin, Madison, Wis.

For films, see Oliver: *The Modern Language Teacher's Handbook*, pp. 205–07, for slides, pp. 600–01, for postcards, p. 529.

[3] Maps:
See Professor Lilian F. Stroebe's note, "New Maps of Germany for the Classroom," *Modern Language Journal* (April, 1923), pp. 442–43.

Werner Neuse, "Wie sollen die Deutschlandkarten in unseren Lesebüchern aussehen?" *Monatshefte* (April, 1935), pp. 143–46.

Foreign newspapers and magazines have long been considered effective helps.[1] School and college publications written by the students themselves under the supervision of a faculty member are even more effective.[2] Correspondence with students of other countries has been mentioned before, but may well be referred to here.[3] Songs, music, and art play an important part in presenting *realia* to the student in a most pleasant way.[4]

The Kramer Publishing Company, Westmoreland Ave., Syracuse, N. Y., carries an inexpensive map of Germany by Kullmer; 75 cents. Other sources of maps are J. Nystrom and Co., 536 Clark St., Chicago, Ill. Consult also Oliver, pp. 398–400.

For charts see Oliver, pp. 86–87. For posters write to the German Tourist Information Office (cf. p. 212, note 2).

[1] The best German newspaper published in this country is probably the *New Yorker Staatszeitung*. The *Frankfurter Zeitung* and the *Berliner Tageblatt* are among the best printed in Germany. *Die Woche, Über Land und Meer, Die Berliner illustrierte Zeitung* are excellent illustrated weeklies. *Das deutsche Echo*, an illustrated monthly (nine issues), published by Westermann, is widely used in this country. American representatives are F. S. Crofts & Co.

[2] See Maurice Friedman, "One Outlet for the Exceptional Language Student," *Modern Language Journal* (Jan. 1929), pp. 289–93; T. Hirshman, "Unser Eckchen," *High Points* (Dec. 1929), pp. 50–52.

In 1937 there were four publications written by students of high schools and three by college students: *Hier und Da*, Jamaica High School; *Plaudermäulchen*, James Monroe High School; *Das Eckchen*, Walton High School, all published in New York City. Also *Das Shortridge deutsche Echo*, Indianapolis, Indiana, edited by Dr. Lester Groth.

Der Spiegel, Deutscher Verein of New York University; *Der deutsche Gesellschafter*, Northwestern University, Evanston, Ill.; and *Bulletin of the Modern Language Club*, Marquette University, Milwaukee, Wis.

Jugendpost, Verlag der Rochester Abendpost, 237 Andrews Street, Rochester, N. Y. Editors: Dr. E. P. Appelt, Dr. A. M. Hanhardt, University of Rochester, Adelaide Biesenbach, Madison High School, Rochester, N. Y.

[3] H. G. Dirks, "Briefwechsel mit deutschen Studenten," *German Quarterly* (May, 1937), pp. 130–36. Kurt Horn, "Bemerkungen zum Schülerbriefwechsel mit Frankreich, England und Amerika," *Die neueren Sprachen* (April, 1933), pp. 154–159.

See also the publications of "The National Bureau of Educational Correspondence," *Modern Language Journal* (Oct. 1925), pp. 39–42, and Jan. 1928, pp. 279–80.

[4] Songs and Music:
Erich Hofacker, "Volkscharakter und Lyrik; Deutsche Abend- und Nachtlieder," *Monatshefte* (Nov. 1929), pp. 219–24.

B. Q. Morgan, Max Griebsch, and A. R. Hohlfeld, *Neues deutsches Liederbuch* (D. C. Heath and Company, 1931), v + 162 pp. Contains music and words of 140 songs: *Volkslieder, Studentenlieder*, and *Wandervogellieder*, with explanatory notes.

BIBLIOGRAPHY

APPELT, E. P. "Deutsche Zeitungen als Lesestoff." *German Quarterly* (May, 1932), pp. 131–39.

COLE, R. D. *Modern Foreign Languages and Their Teaching.* Revised and enlarged by J. B. Tharp (New York: Appleton-Century Co., 1937), Chapters VII and VIII.

ENGEL, E. F. "The Broadcasting of Modern Foreign Languages in the United States: A Survey." *Modern Language Journal* (March, 1936), pp. 356–58.

GINSBURG, EDWARD B. "Foreign Talking Pictures in Modern Language Instruction." *Modern Language Journal* (March, 1935), pp. 433–38.

HANDSCHIN, C. H. "An Introductory Course to German Civilization." *German Quarterly* (Nov. 1935), pp. 169–76.

HINZ, S. M. "German Service Bureau Notes." *Monatshefte* (March, 1934), pp. 81–84.

JOHNSON, EDGAR G. "The New Curriculum Challenges the Modern Foreign Language Teacher." *Modern Language Journal* (March, 1937), pp. 387–95.

—— "A Contribution to International Attitudes." *Journal of Educational Sociology* (March, 1936), pp. 421–25.

KAULFERS, WALTER V., and ROBERTS, HOLLAND D. *A Cultural Basis for the Language Arts* (Stanford University Press, 1937), 115 pp.

—— *A Visit with a Teacher of First-Year Foreign Language.* School Publication 314 of the Los Angeles City School District, Secondary Curriculum Section (June, 1938).

LEOPOLD, WERNER F. "Realia, Kulturkunde, and Nationalism." *Monatshefte* (Jan. 1937), pp. 17–24.

SAMMARTINO, PETER. "Language Work at the New College Community in the Mountains of North Carolina." *French Review* (April, 1934), pp. 402–05.

C. M. Purin and E. C. Roedder, *Deutsche Gedichte und Lieder*, illustrated (D. C. Heath and Company, 1912), vi + 154 pp. Music and words of twenty favorite songs.

B. J. Vos and others, *Treasury of German Song*, A collection of lyrics and ballads (Henry Holt and Company, 1924), 81 pp.

The Thrift Press (Ithaca, N. Y. and Chicago, Ill., 1866 Howe Street) publishes many excellent booklets at five and ten cents each, including three booklets of songs. General editor and owner, Professor Jacob Hieble.

The catalogue of the German Service Bureau at the University of Wisconsin, Madison, Wis., contains suggestions for Christmas songs, music, plays, and programs. See also Oliver under Songs, Christmas, and Music. For Art, see Oliver, pp. 48–49.

SCHLIMBACH, ALICE and JORDAN, EMIL L. "The German Language House: A Successful Educational Experiment in Modern Language Teaching on a College Campus." *Modern Language Journal* (March, 1936), pp. 347–52.

SCHMALE, FLORENCE E. "Some Approaches to German." *German Quarterly* (Jan. 1933), pp. 8–18.

SCHMITZ, MATTHIAS F. "Wir veranstalten ein deutsches Rundfunk-programm: Ein Beitrag zur Deutschkunde." *German Quarterly* (Jan. 1935), pp. 27–36.

SPRINGER, OTTO. "German Kulturkunde." *Monatshefte* (Oct. 1933), pp. 168–75.

TAUB, LEO L. "The Inter-High School German Glee Club of New York as a Cultural Project." *High Points* (May, 1934), pp. 47–53.

SUPPLEMENTARY READINGS

APPELT, E. P. "Der Deutschlehrer und die Volkskunde." *Monatshefte*, XXIX, 5 (May, 1937), pp. 211–18.

—— "Literatur zur deutschen Kulturkunde." *German Quarterly*, XI, 3 (May, 1938), pp. 126–32.

—— "Wortschatz und Kulturkunde." *Monatshefte*, XXX, 5 (May, 1938), pp. 264–67.

CARLSON, HAROLD G. "Namenkunde und Kulturkunde." *German Quarterly*, XI, 1 (Jan. 1938), pp. 29–35.

ENGEL, E. F. "The Future of Modern Language Instruction by Radio." *Modern Language Journal*, XXIII, 6 (March, 1939), pp. 412–17.

GREINER, OTTO A. "The Main Objective in the Study of Foreign Languages." *Modern Language Journal*, XXIII, 3 (Dec. 1938), pp. 209–13.

ROEDDER, EDWIN. "Was will Volkskunde?" *Monatshefte*, XXX, 3 and 4 (March–April, 1938), pp. 136–43.

STEINHAUER, H. "Entertainment or Culture?" *Monatshefte*, XXXI, 4 (April, 1939), pp. 184–86.

TAUB, LEO L. "The German Club Radio Hour." *German Quarterly*, XI, 1 (Jan. 1938), pp. 37–41.

WILLING, M. H. "Social Functionalism in the Secondary School Curriculum and Its Implications for the Modern Foreign Languages." *Modern Language Journal*, XXIII, 7 (April, 1939), pp. 527–33.

SUGGESTIONS FOR DISCUSSIONS AND REPORTS

1. Study the book by Kaulfers and Roberts carefully. Keep in mind the basic idea of integration (see Kaulfers' statement, p. 208). Read, if

available, his article, "A Visit with a Teacher," etc.   Then prepare a program for a first-year course in German.

2. Analyze:
   (a) The main points in Leopold's article.
   (b) The article of Schmitz; dwell on advantages of radio programs.
   (c) The article of Otto Springer.
   (d) The articles of Taub (for the first one, see *German Quarterly*, March, 1937, pp. 68–86).

3. Discuss the following articles:
   (a) Appelt; emphasize the advantages and disadvantages of reading German newspapers.
   (b) Johnson in reference to the new curriculum and the failure of language teachers to meet its demands.
   (c) Ginsburg.   Ask yourself: "What sort of talking films should be produced?" (history, geography, *Land und Leute*, manners and customs, drama, great music, etc., etc.)

4. Report on:
   (a) Chapter VIII of Cole's book (pp. 223–56).
   (b) The articles of Engel and Hendrix.
   (c) Sammartino's article.   Use his various recommendations for students of German.   Give exact detail.

5. From Miss Hinz's article and the suggestions contained in this chapter, compile a reading list (English and German) for first-year college students.

6. Study Handschin's article and his book (page 194); show in how far his book is, or is not, an elaboration of his article.

7. Discuss some of the difficulties which Kurz and Van Horne found in their investigations.

CHAPTER TEN

THE TRAINING OF TEACHERS

THE TRAINING of teachers presents us with one of the gravest of all educational problems. On it depends the future of our students and with it the whole cultural future of the nation. For this reason school authorities strive to establish definite standards for teachers in every secondary-school subject concerning the mastery of the subject and ability to teach it. For only one branch of studies do no such standards exist: the modern languages.

If we study the puzzling questions involved in the training of modern language teachers we are struck by the widely differing practices in our schools, colleges, and universities. What is praised as the best practice in one school, city, or state is frowned upon in the next. What is law in one part of the country is considered malfeasance in the other. All in all, existing conditions give us the impression of endless variety, but not of the sort of variety which makes for order and harmony.

There are two ways of looking at the problem of teacher training — the one idealistic, the other practical. The first describes in general terms desirable abilities resulting from academic and professional training regardless of time. The second states in terms of semester hours and of specific courses the total amount of such training. Our problem is to scrutinize these two possibilities and reconcile them if we can.

I. IDEAL PREPARATION

In 1898 the Committee of Twelve formulated the best possible preparation for modern language teachers as follows:

To be ideally prepared for giving instruction in a modern language, even in a secondary school, one should have, aside from the ability to

217

teach and the general personal culture necessary to secure the respect and attachment of pupils, a thorough practical command of the language to be taught, a solid knowledge of its literature, and a first-hand acquaintance with the foreign life of which the literature of the language is the reflection. To be decently prepared, he should at least have read so much in the recent literature of the language that he can read about as easily as he would read matter of the same kind in English. He should have studied the principal works of the great writers, and should have taken a course in the general history of the literature. He should know thoroughly the grammar of the language in its present form. If he has some knowledge of the historical development of forms, such knowledge will help him in his teaching, especially in the teaching of French to pupils who have studied Latin. He should be able to pronounce the language intelligently and with reasonable accuracy, though he may not have the perfect "accent" of one who is to the manner born. He should be able to write a letter or a short essay in the language without making gross mistakes in grammar or idiom, and to carry on an ordinary conversation in the language without a sense of painful embarrassment. Even this degree of attainment will usually require residence abroad of those for whom English is the mother tongue, unless they have enjoyed exceptional opportunities in this country. In any case, the residence abroad is greatly to be desired.[1]

Closer analysis of this eloquent statement shows four essential points.

1. Practical and theoretical command of the language to be taught:

(a) pronounce with reasonable accuracy;

(b) read about as easily and fluently as English;

(c) write a letter or a short essay without gross mistakes;

(d) speak with considerable ease;

(e) know present as well as historical forms of grammar.

2. A thorough acquaintance with the literature and life of the foreign people, with the principal works of its great writers, and its literary history.

3. Ability to teach.

4. Personal culture.

[1] *Report of the Committee of Twelve* (D. C. Heath and Company, 1900), pp. 31–32.

What serious objections can we raise against this proposed ideal preparation? None whatsoever! An ideal is an image of perfection. Perfection exists nowhere but in thought. Perfection, always ardently sought by the best, is partly achieved by few, and fully realized by none.

Yet, on the practical side we may object that each of the points enumerated involves skills so difficult to master and issues so teeming with unsolved problems that a lifetime will hardly suffice for dealing with them all. An adequate preparation for a career in language teaching is not a matter of serving time, but of accomplishment and merit. Any attempt to set a definite time limit for acquiring even a modest degree of mastery of subject matter and of teaching techniques is likely to be misleading. The teacher's growth must never end; if it does, the teacher is intellectually dead.

A great many books and articles have been written on the training of language teachers.[1] The general tenor of these is that no one can teach without loving his task; that the one and exclusive sign of thorough knowledge is the power of teaching; in short, that no stream can rise higher than its source.

Professor Hayward Keniston states that the most important contributions made by the graduate school to the welfare of the future teacher or scholar are a knowledge of the background (linguistic, cultural, and bibliographical) and a vision of the entire field of work. Like every able scholar he thinks of graduate work as professional education in its widest and best sense, not to be done grudgingly as a chore, but in anticipation of a growth which constantly advances the realization of an ideal.[2]

Professor Albert W. Aron, taking for granted the practical command of the language of the foreign people and an acquaintance with its literature and its institutions, emphasizes an acquaintance with the most important phases of linguistics: phonetics, principles and history of language, and psychology. He demonstrates

---

[1] For a bibliography consult T. E. Oliver, *The Modern Language Teacher's Handbook* (D. C. Heath and Company, 1935), pp. 665–69. Also Coleman, *An Analytical Bibliography of Modern Language Teaching* (The University of Chicago Press), Vol. I, pp. 260–76; Vol. II, pp. 473–514.

[2] "The Role of the Graduate School in the Training of the Modern Language Teacher," *Modern Language Journal* (Oct. 1922), pp. 1–4.

lucidly that the linguistically untrained teacher is helpless. Of special interest are his felicitous examples for arousing interest in the study of linguistics and the proof that only mastery of the subject can bring the standard of the profession to a higher plane.[1]

Peter Hagboldt tries to analyze the processes and problems involved in language teaching and to divide them into elements of art and science.[2] Professor Ernst Jockers' article deals with (1) extramural activities (language clubs, dramatic performances, films, etc.); (2) subject matter and methods (a deluge of publications); and (3) the teacher. He concludes with the observation that interest in German can be furthered by the personality of the teacher who, as has often been stated, is the only safe guarantee of success.[3] Professor Lilian L. Stroebe stresses the fact that methods, however excellent, cannot function without content. Constant self-improvement and uninterrupted professional growth are imperative. She recommends a list of inexpensive books for self-study of language, the history of German literature, German art, and novels of the nineteenth century. The idea of self-improvement will certainly persist as long as there are teachers.[4] Two articles by Professor George H. Danton treat of general and specific ways of teacher training.[5]

Professor Philip H. Churchman makes a strong and eloquent plea for a graduate school of teacher training.[6] "Methodology without scholarship," he says, "drills the mediocre, chills the ambitious, and inspires nobody." The hope expressed in this interesting article is:

... that graduate school teaching may so shift its emphasis in the training of teachers ... as to include complete mastery of those

[1] "The Linguistic Background of the Modern Language Teacher," *Modern Language Journal* (Nov. 1922), pp. 75–83.

[2] "Elements of Art and Science in Modern Language Teaching," *Modern Language Journal* (Dec. 1928), pp. 192–96.

[3] "Lehren als schöpferische Tätigkeit," *German Quarterly* (March, 1937), pp. 60–67.

[4] "Self-Improvement and Inexpensive Books for the Teacher of German," *Modern Language Journal* (Jan. 1932), pp. 289–98.

[5] "Training German Teachers for the New Era," *Monatshefte* (Jan. 1931), pp. 1–11; "An Experiment in a Methods Class," *Monatshefte* (Nov. 1934), pp. 223–30.

[6] "Wanted: The Graduate School of Teacher Training," *Modern Language Journal* (Oct. 1926), pp. 1–11.

subjects and some interest in the art of teaching, and that therefore many more of our secondary school teachers and absolutely all of our college teachers will come to our graduate schools, sure that they will there be trained in essentials and helped to study the problems of teaching, but eager also to drink deep draughts of a "scholarship" that will now be kept in its true perspective.

Professor Laura B. Johnson analyzes the various possibilities in teacher-training courses.[1] She shows that neither teaching candidates instructing their fellow students will do, nor candidates teaching an elementary course for a brief period under the supervision of an experienced teacher. She recommends admitting prospective teachers into various elementary classes, not as ineffective practice teachers, but as well-prepared participants in all classroom activities. Miss Johnson speaks from a rich and valuable experience in training future teachers in her own classes. She shows that the student teacher by coaching an individual student during a class period, or by working with a small group of pupils for a few minutes at a time, may get many chances to do real teaching and to gain vital experiences for self direction and self criticism. The dearth of articles on the training of student teachers makes one wish for a whole series of essays, equally clear and concise; for the training of language teachers through participation is one of our unsolved problems.

Professor Frank Mankiewicz, in a welcome and timely article on the "Training of Teachers in Service"[2] gives us the benefit of observations made in preparing young teachers for their future profession. He discusses in turn the problems of the student teacher, the teacher in training, and the regularly appointed teacher. The student teacher (upper senior or young graduate) is assigned to the department of German in a high school so as to get experience through observation and actual teaching. The requirements vary from 20 to 200 hours, according to the city or the state. The student teacher spends at least three class periods daily, two in observation, one in teaching under supervision. In addition he takes subject courses at his college or university and a course in special methods. He learns to observe,

[1] "Teacher Training Through Participation," *Modern Language Journal* (Oct. 1922), pp. 28–37. [2] *German Quarterly* (May, 1938), pp. 142–52.

to look at problems from the teacher's point of view, and gets acquainted with the organization of the department and the school. Moreover, he attends general and departmental conferences, corrects test papers, and makes ample use of the departmental library. He is given his first opportunity to do actual teaching in conformity with a careful plan, thus supplying for his supervisors a basis on which to judge his own personality and his merit.

The student teacher then is required to pass an examination on this experience and, after passing it, is appointed to a school to serve for one year as a teacher in training. He has to teach two or three classes daily, assuming full responsibility. Once a week he is visited by the head of his department for a full lesson period, after which his performance is carefully discussed and all problems cleared up. He continues to take courses and in various ways tries to perfect himself in the oral use of German. "Whether the teacher in training will develop into an outstanding member of the teaching body, or remain just a mediocre member of it, or become definitely a detriment to it, is largely determined" during this period.

As a last step the teacher in training has to pass a rather difficult examination in subject matter, in methodology, and in classroom teaching. Then after three years of probationary teaching, provided that his work has been satisfactory, he is finally given a permanent certificate.

The author is justly convinced that the future of modern language teaching in this country depends entirely on our ability to make the subject serve important social ends. The members of our profession, he states,

> must acquire on the basis of their individual capacities, not only large factual knowledge, which has been welded into a harmonious, educational background, but also certain intellectual and emotional attitudes, which train them to think independently, to reason carefully, to judge objectively, to acquire a social point of view, and to respond with an emotional and esthetic understanding to the events and questions of our many-sided civilization.

So much for ideal training and the various efforts to bring it about. We shall now enumerate, as briefly as we can, some of the high points of the Purin Report.

II. THE PURIN REPORT

In an effort to determine the status of the training of modern language teachers, the *Study*, through its Committee on Investigation, sent out numerous questionnaires. One, concerning teacher training, was addressed to 776 college and university departments of modern languages. Another, on observation and practice teaching, was sent to 405 institutions. A third one, on the training and experience of teachers in secondary schools, was sent to more than 1200 public and private schools, representing approximately 70 per cent of all schools where foreign languages were taught. A special questionnaire was sent to 1560 selected teachers with the request to answer significant questions in regard to objectives, attainments, content of courses, etc. Moreover, an important book on the training of modern language teachers in France and Germany [1] facilitated useful comparisons. The mass of these data was then supplemented by the Acker-Manahan investigation concerning state certification of modern language teachers.[2] On this compound picture of fact and opinion the Purin study is based.[3] Volume XIII of the *Study*, bearing the title *The Training of Teachers of the Modern Foreign Languages*,[4] is often referred to as the "Purin Report."

In the public schools, teachers of modern languages, as a body, have on an average devoted 4.6 years to the study of the language they teach. Slightly more than one-fifth of them have enjoyed training in graduate courses, and almost one-third have had less than three years of teaching experience.

California leads in strict requirements for the training and the certification of language teachers.[5]

[1] Ruth Emily McMurry, Max Mueller, and Thomas Alexander, *Modern Foreign Languages in France and Germany. The Training of Teachers and Methods of Instruction.* Teachers College, Columbia University, 1930.

[2] This inquiry was undertaken under the sponsorship of the *Study;* a mimeographed copy is available for consultation at the University of Virginia.

[3] The replies were analyzed and tabulated by Hugh Stuart in his monograph *The Training of Modern Foreign Language Teachers for the Secondary Schools of the United States.* Teachers College, Columbia University. Contributions to Education, No. 256, 1927.

[4] The Macmillan Company, 1929. 112 pp. For sources and materials of Purin's book, see pp. 1–8. [5] Purin, *op. cit.*, pp. 9–28.

Professor Fife remarks:

> Modern language teachers in secondary schools are, as a class,
> engaged in teaching a language in which they have a briefer prepara-
> tion than many seniors in the better colleges who study modern
> languages simply as a part of a liberal education, and . . . within a
> period of less than three years one-third of the entire teaching staff
> has to be renewed from the ranks of inexperienced college graduates.[1]

THE ORGANIZATION OF TEACHER-TRAINING COURSES.[2] The part
played by normal schools and teachers colleges in preparing candidates for teaching positions in modern languages is insignificant.
The type of school most frequently attended by the secondary-
school teacher is the liberal arts college.[3]

The *Study*, through its Committee on Investigation, urged
that normal schools should cease trying to achieve in two years
what can barely be accomplished in other institutions in four
years of intensive and concentrated study, and then only after
a two-year preparation in the subject in secondary school.

The liberal arts colleges have often reproached normal schools
and teachers colleges for being more interested in the technique
of presentation than in the mastery of the subject. The latter
have replied that college graduates frequently are completely helpless before their pupils. Certain it is that both educationists and
teachers in liberal arts colleges can only gain by complete and
sympathetic collaboration. Their common interest is that of raising the standards of secondary education. Moreover, mastery
of subject matter and mastery in presenting it are inseparable.
Neither can exist without the other.

SUBJECT MATTER OF TEACHER-TRAINING COURSES.[4] Purin
discusses critically, partly in the light of the recommendations of
the Committee of Twelve, types of courses ordinarily offered to
language teachers, courses in pronunciation, in grammar review,
composition, oral and aural training, literature, civilization, and,
finally, in the history of the foreign language. He also deals with
the question of residence abroad during undergraduate years,

---

[1] Robert Herndon Fife, *A Summary of Reports on the Modern Foreign
Languages* (The Macmillan Company, 1931), p. 56. The Purin Report is
discussed on pp. 53–68.   [2] Purin, *op. cit.*, pp. 29–36.   [3] Fife, *op. cit.*, p. 56.
[4] Purin, *op. cit.*, pp. 37–56.

and with the problem of the technique of teaching a modern language.

In regard to the latter, Purin aptly remarks that for the young teacher

> teaching consists merely in following as best he can the methods to which he has been exposed without a critical test of their quality. He sets his own standards on arbitrary grounds, emphasizes his special preferences, and ascribes failure to indifference or lack of application on the part of his pupils.[1]

This important and correct observation is closely bound up with the question as to whether or not the prospective teacher should receive instruction quite different from that given to other students. When we read that as a rule the future teacher sits beside other students not majoring in the subject,[2] we realize how important, considering the above statement, is the question of specific techniques for specific aims.

REQUIREMENTS FOR THE MAJOR AND THE MINOR [3] in a modern language vary all the way from 6 to 12 semester hours (in 27 colleges) to more than 48 hours (in 3 colleges), the median requirement being 24 semester hours, which means the equivalent of a three-hour course extending over four years. The Committee on Investigation finally made a compromise, recommending that the minimum requirement for a major be fixed at 30 semester hours following two years of the foreign language in secondary school.

The Committee recommended furthermore that of this time 16 hours be devoted to language and 14 to literature, the latter mainly in the nineteenth and twentieth centuries.

Conditions in our public schools demand that we prepare future teachers for at least two subjects. Fourteen semester hours were found to be the median requirement for a minor subject (three hours a week extending over two and one-half years) which, of course, is quite inadequate. The Committee therefore recommended a minimum of 20 semester hours based on two years of study in secondary school as the smallest amount of time admissible for teaching a second language.

Of more than a thousand teachers in public schools 71 per cent

---

[1] Purin, *op. cit.*, p. 53. [2] Fife, *op. cit.*, p. 59. [3] Purin, *op. cit.*, pp. 57–62.

were found to be teaching one foreign language, nearly 28 per cent two, and slightly over 1 per cent three. According to this specific inquiry, history was the subject most frequently found in combination with foreign languages.

REQUIREMENTS IN EDUCATION.[1] The college curriculum consists as a rule of 120 semester hours, of which 20 to 30 semester hours used to be required in education and psychology alone. The Committee on Investigation, profiting by the results of experimental data and by the advice of educationists and psychologists, agreed that a total of 15 semester hours might be considered adequate preparation, provided that the following subjects receive proper attention: principles of secondary education or educational psychology; psychology of high-school subjects; tests and measurements; technique of teaching the major and minor subjects; and observation and practice teaching.

Concerning observation and practice teaching, Purin says that both have the same function as laboratory work in the study of the physical and biological sciences or as hospital service in a medical course.

In 1926 an inquiry revealed that of 321 colleges nearly one-half offered neither observation nor practice teaching and that only about one-third required both.

Courses in observation were found to be nearly always conducted by members of the department of education, yet 40 per cent of these departments reported that so far as they knew no help or advice had been offered by language departments "toward making observation work yield the highest possible returns."

The main obstacles in the way of observation and practice teaching were found to be:

inadequate training-school facilities; low salaries for supervising teachers; insufficient training of supervisors; transportation difficulties, and a disinclination on the part of the parents to have their children used for practice teaching.[2]

CERTIFICATION AND PLACEMENT.[3] Purin observes that "in American secondary education we attach almost as little importance to intensive preparation and specialization as we do in

[1] Purin, *op. cit.*, pp. 63–72.   [2] *Ibid.*, p. 71.   [3] *Ibid.*, pp. 73–88.

our political life." As a natural result, the teacher, however well prepared, cannot be certain that he will teach the subject to which he has devoted his major efforts.

> Approximately 9 per cent of the teachers who majored in French are teaching either German, Spanish, or some other language. Fifty-eight per cent of the teachers that majored in German are teaching either French, Spanish, or some other language ... Fifty-two per cent of the teachers that majored in Latin now teach no Latin ...
>
> The highest percentage of misplacement is found in the cases of German and Latin majors.[1]

In 1916 Professor David Snedden made some excellent recommendations for the New England states in regard to minimum requirements to be applied to the certifying and the approving of teachers of modern languages. Yet ten years later it was found that not less than 28 states were in the habit of issuing "blanket" certificates, covering all subjects and specifying not any. Objections to this evil practice are too obvious to be enumerated. The "blanket certificate" encourages the idea that the teacher should be a "Jack of all trades" with very strong emphasis on the rest of the proverb.

Equally bad is the practice of putting graduates of four-year colleges on the same level with those who have had only two years of preparation, allowing the latter to teach in secondary schools, a practice persisting in 20 of our states.

Purin then discusses the first years of experience, which are likely to be the most distressing for the young teacher. He describes probationary service for young teachers and supervision of teachers in service, and he leaves no doubt that there is but one solution, namely, at least one year of probationary service as described by Professor Mankiewicz (pp. 221 f.).

POST-COLLEGIATE TRAINING.[2] The great majority of American summer schools confer on students after completion of certain graduate courses the degree of Master of Arts. In many cases teachers attend summer sessions for self-improvement, in others in the hope of an increase in salary. Five hundred forty-nine high schools were sent questionnaires to ascertain whether or not salary

---

[1] Purin, *op. cit.*, p. 76.   [2] *Ibid.*, pp. 89–94.

increases were granted in recognition of the teachers' effort to supplement their previous training. Less than one-quarter of the schools answered "yes." In spite of this lack of official encouragement, the number of high-school teachers who have studied abroad is relatively great in certain states. The District of Columbia was found to lead with 47 per cent. Purin is emphatic in his recommendation of adequate encouragement:

> For those who have given proof of competency in their subject and of faithful service, a sabbatical year with at least half pay should be granted, so that they may have sufficient time to come into close contact with the foreign country, its people and its language.[1]

As for the graduate school, Purin finds that three distinct groups of students must be trained: (1) for university positions and research; (2) for positions in colleges; (3) for positions in secondary schools. He states:

> ... university professors look upon all their students as potential investigators and fail to realize that all of them will become teachers — if they receive appointments. If we wish to make the graduate school as broadly useful as possible, we must not overlook the fact that graduate students need much and continuous training in the foreign language; that they will, if properly prepared, profit far more from courses conducted in the foreign language than from those presented in the mother tongue; that they need courses in advanced composition, conversation and phonetics, and that a course in methods of teaching, if it did form a part of the undergraduate course, is alike valuable for those who will teach in college and in secondary school, since it is only reasonable to insist that college instructors should have as thorough a pedagogical training as their colleagues in the high schools.[2]

We have attempted to describe briefly ideal preparation and the various suggestions for bringing it about. We have given a short summary of the high points of the Purin Report, and we now come to the fifteen points suggested by the Committee on Investigation as a compromise, not the ideal plan; as a practical move toward higher standards in the American secondary school.

[1] Purin, *op. cit.*, p. 92.   [2] *Ibid.*, p. 94.

III. RECOMMENDATIONS OF THE COMMITTEE

The fifteen recommendations of the Committee are the following [1]:

1. In so far as facilities permit, modern foreign language departments in the colleges of liberal arts and in teachers colleges should, together with the departments of education, organize curricula and courses specifically designed for the training of teachers of modern languages.

Professor Fife, no doubt, voices the consensus of opinion by saying:

> ... the secondary school teachers must be developed into a professionally minded body, a matter of great difficulty on account of the elasticity of the American social and economic order, but a prime necessity unless secondary education is to continue to flounder in a morass of inefficiency and dilettantism. [2]

Since this statement contains a truth of basic and far-reaching importance, it is to be hoped that professors of education and those in language departments may work in harmony toward higher standards in the professional training of modern language teachers.

2. The aim of these courses should be to give prospective teachers adequate training in the language, the literature, the history of the foreign civilization and of the foreign language, and in education and psychology.

The main difficulty lies in reconciling the manifold and severe demands which must be made on the prospective teacher in the interest of his future pupils with the time and the means at the candidate's disposal. But other elements enter into the problem: security, prestige, and the desirability of becoming a member of the profession. Other countries have gone much farther in making positions in secondary schools attractive. McMurry, Mueller, and Alexander remark:

> The sole reason that France and Germany can enforce the high standard of preparation is that they have made the secondary teach-

[1] For the fifteen points see Purin, *op. cit.*, pp. 95–97. They are numbered 1–15 and quoted on the following pages by special permission of the Macmillan Company.   [2] Fife, *op. cit.*, p. 54.

ing profession highly desirable ... to bring about similar conditions
in America which will make a high-school teaching position so desirable that candidates will spend the requisite amount of effort and
money to meet the standards equivalent to those of France or Germany, is a very difficult problem whose solution can be approached
only very slowly.[1]

The first steps toward a solution of the problem have already
been taken. In several states candidates are not admitted for
teaching positions in high schools without a year of post graduate
work or a Master's degree (see pp. 237 f.). Professor William S.
Gray, executive secretary of the committee on the preparation of
teachers at the University of Chicago, informs me that more and
more young candidates in education are taking their Master's or
Doctor's degree even for high-school positions.

3. In order that their courses may be properly planned, students
   intending to teach a modern foreign language should be advised
   to announce this fact at the beginning of the Sophomore year.

Considering the magnitude of the student's task as a whole,
this is sound advice. An early decision is certainly highly desirable.

4. Since in many schools teachers are required to teach more than
   one subject, candidates should be advised to prepare to teach at
   least two subjects. Placement bureaus should ascertain which
   subject combinations are in greatest demand in the secondary
   schools of the particular territory.

Everything possible should be done for the prospective teacher
to facilitate the finding of a position. All larger institutions maintain placement bureaus which keep in close touch with the local
and national needs for modern language teachers. At the University of Chicago the function of such a bureau is to help both undergraduate and graduate students to find part-time and permanent
positions for Bachelors, Masters, and Doctors, young and old.
There are numerous publications by which administrative officers
of placement bureaus inform themselves as to all kinds of pertinent
matters, from the best possible combination of subjects to laws

[1] McMurry, Mueller, and Alexander, *op. cit.*, p. 491.

governing the certification for positions in the schools of the United States Possessions.[1]

5. For the major language, in addition to two years of high-school work, not less than 30 semester hours should be required, of which approximately 16 hours should normally be devoted to the language and 14 hours to literature. For a teaching minor in a modern foreign language, approximately 20 semester hours following upon a two-year high-school course should be required, of which 12 hours should normally be allotted to language and 8 hours to courses in literature. An attempt should be made to measure the attainment of various skills on the part of prospective teachers by a more scientific and accurate method than merely by the completion of a certain number of semester hours of work.

Abilities and knowledge gained within a definite period of time naturally depend entirely on the individual student's native gifts and on the way he has applied them. In recognition of this fact, 83 per cent of the colleges replying to a questionnaire demanded that all candidates for teaching positions show a grade of "good" or better, an excellent practice which most certainly should be rigidly upheld.

In several passages of his book Purin expresses the hope of the committee that tests may soon be developed to measure the knowledge as well as the skills of prospective teachers. Even now Professor Ben D. Wood, Director of the Cooperative Test Service, is preparing for the National Committee on Teacher Examinations a battery of tests which will soon be available.

As far as courses in literature are concerned, the main difficulty

[1] A small but useful pamphlet by Clem O. Thomson entitled *Problems of Beginning Teachers*, 12 pp., can be obtained from the University of Chicago Bookstore.

A book on the *Requirements for Certification of Teachers and Administrators* by Robert C. Woellner and M. Aurilla Wood is published from time to time by the University of Chicago Press. Fourth edition 1939.

The North Central Association Quarterly gives information regarding requirements for certificates and the most favorable combinations of subjects.

The College of Education of the Ohio State University publishes monthly the *Educational Research Bulletin* containing all kinds of valuable information for the prospective teacher.

See also Geo. W. Cox and W. H. Jones, *How to Get a Position in School or College*, published by the Southern Teachers' Agency, Columbia, S. C.

is that students as a rule are not able "to read about as easily as he would read matter in the same kind in English," as the Committee of Twelve had recommended.

An invitation to college departments to make suggestions for improvements of courses in literature only brought evidence that present courses were felt to be unsatisfactory.[1] This is by no means surprising. Successful study of literature depends wholly on the ability to read with complete comprehension, or, as Lanson puts it, to find in a given text "ce qui y est, tout ce qui y est, rien que ce qui y est."[2] Yet, nearly 500 college departments estimated that a reading knowledge of a foreign language could be acquired in about five and a half college semester hours of study following a two-year secondary-school course.[3] When one finds in official syllabi how little is actually read during the first years in high school or college one must doubt that reading ability as thought of by the Committee of Twelve can be achieved in the time estimated by the 500 college departments. Ability to read a foreign language can be developed only by very extensive requirements beyond those usually set up. The acquisition of any specific reading ability is not a question of time to be spent in courses, but of adjustments to be made while actually engaged in the ability sought. Claude Marcel was correct (see pp. 11 f.).

German departments made many mutually contradictory suggestions for the improvement of courses in literature, and thus confirmed the aptness of Purin's quotation: "Who shall decide when doctors disagree, and soundest casuists doubt, like you and me?"

In discussing literary courses Purin suggests:

The presentation of literary material known in France as *explication de textes*, and used in this country with marked success by some teachers, is particularly well adapted to our needs, provided that each student be asked to take his turn in preparing to interpret a passage of prose or verse and in presenting the results of his analysis to the class without too many notes.[4]

[1] Fife, *op. cit.*, p. 61.   [2] Robert Vigneron, *Explication de textes* (The University of Chicago Press, 1934), p. 5.
[3] Purin, *op. cit.*, p. 45.   [4] *Ibid.*, p. 47. Vigneron's excellent booklet will repay careful reading; cf. note 2 above.

The next three recommendations are closely related.

6. An adequate oral command of the language should be required of all major and minor students in a modern foreign language who plan to teach the subject.
7. Whenever feasible, colleges should make arrangements to permit students who elect a major in a foreign language to study abroad in their Junior year under the proper supervision and to receive academic credit in all subjects thus completed.
8. Extracurricular opportunities for practice in hearing and speaking the foreign language should be provided by language departments through the organization of French, German, and Spanish houses, language clubs, etc.

Again and again individual writers and committees throughout the country have insisted that an oral command of the foreign language is imperative. Professor Fife points out that American colleges offer scant facilities to major students in a modern language for acquiring oral ability and that, with an entire lack of logic, most language departments nevertheless demand of future teachers an ability to speak. The same writer remarks that the teachers themselves lay the neglect of oral and aural training to their large classes and the amount of ground to be covered, as well to the lack of this ability on the part of the teachers. "In the opinion of three-fourths of the college teaching body, the last named is the chief cause." [1]

Unfortunately, only one German University, Munich, has at present a Junior-year course accredited by American colleges. Zürich in Switzerland is to be added for 1939–1940.[2]

In other countries school authorities have gone much further in the preparation of language teachers. The authors of *Modern Foreign Languages in France and Germany* state:

> The importance of the study of the life and thought of the foreign people in modern language instruction requires a far different type of scholarship than that gotten by the average teacher of modern

[1] Fife, *op. cit.*, p. 60.
[2] Compare Max Diez, "Junior Year in Munich," *Modern Language Journal,* XXI, 6 (March, 1937), pp. 452–53. The Announcement of the Junior year in Zürich is mailed from year to year. Its Director is Dr. Edmund E. Miller, Münsterhof 20, Zürich, Switzerland. Cf. Chapter II, p. 47, note 1.

language in America, who frequently has but poor command of the written and spoken language and knows practically nothing of the country whose language is being taught. The principle that the modern language teacher should teach France and England rather than French and English is very fundamental to a true conception of the place of modern languages in education. Language becomes a vehicle rather than a destination.[1]

The inference is obvious: No one can teach what he does not know.

9. A properly qualified representative of the modern language department should be placed in charge of the training of its prospective teachers with respect to the subject-matter courses and should serve as a liaison officer with the department of education. His duties would be:

   (a) To examine the academic history of candidates with a view to judging their fitness for specialization in a modern foreign language, and to test their progress at regular intervals.

   (b) To advise candidates in the proper choice of courses.

   (c) To give the course in the technique of teaching the subject, and either to conduct personally or to keep in close touch with the work in observation and practice teaching.

   (d) To be chiefly responsible for recommending the candidates for teaching positions, and to maintain close contact with the placement bureau.

This recommendation is closely connected with certain very important and far-reaching developments in some institutions of higher learning. Universities are becoming more and more conscious of their duty toward the community and the country as a whole. At the University of Chicago, for instance, a committee appointed by the President has been in operation since 1932, consisting of members of various departments concerned with the preparation of teachers for all levels of service.

The main features of the University's plan are to provide for special and unified programs of study designed to lead to proficiency in teaching in secondary schools and junior colleges. To students who pursue appropriate programs and who give evidence of satisfactory attainments, as defined by the particular Division or departments involved, the University will grant a Master's degree and, in

---

[1] McMurry, Mueller, and Alexander, *op. cit.*, p. 493.

addition, a Secondary-School Certificate. Upon the completion of such additional requirements by prospective junior-college teachers as have been set by the respective Divisions or departments, the University will grant a Junior-College Certificate.[1]

The last-named committee, feeling that a definition of the personal qualifications of a representative of the modern language department is quite difficult and involved, has not made a definite statement in regard to such a personality, but hopes to specify such desirable qualifications later. It seems reasonable to expect that the representative shall have: (1) broad scholarship; (2) an established reputation as a superior teacher at the levels for which he prepares his students; (3) a keen interest in pertinent educational research; (4) a membership in regional and national organizations or committees concerned with instructional problems; (5) a genuine interest in the problems and the welfare of his students.

Recently a study was undertaken to help administrative officers of teacher-training institutions in the selection of staff members, and to guide higher institutions of learning in preparing candidates for positions in teacher-training institutions.[2] More than one hundred experienced teachers were asked to characterize their best and their poorest instructor. More than 160 personal traits were proposed, and three different plans were followed to find the most frequent characteristics. Three lists resulted. The following characteristic traits were found to be in all three lists for the best and the poorest teacher respectively:

The best teacher:
- Mastery of subject matter
- Pleasing personality
- Keen sense of humor
- Sympathetic
- Fair in measuring results
- Patient
- Neat in personal appearance

[1] Quoted from Announcements, The University of Chicago, *The Preparation of Teachers*, Sessions of 1938–1939, Volume XXXVIII (April 25, 1938), number 11, p. 7.

[2] O. E. Peterson, *A Study of Desirable Qualifications of Staff Members of Teachers Colleges*, p. 12, Northern Illinois State Teachers College, De Kalb, Ill.

The poorest teacher:
$\begin{cases} \text{Sarcastic} \\ \text{Lack of interest in his student's needs} \\ \text{Unfair in grading} \end{cases}$

10. Each language department, together with the department of education, should make adequate provision for observation and practice teaching extending over at least one semester.

One single semester of observation and practice teaching is adequate, perhaps, for the most gifted. For a teacher engaged in his first experience it is best to widen his meager training of one semester by teaching a year or two in a larger city where he can profit from the experience and advice of older colleagues. However, a longer probationary period such as is used in the New York School system seems far superior.

11. Courses in tests and measurements, psychology of high-school subjects and the technique of teaching modern languages should be included among the courses in education required of teaching candidates, since these seem to bear an especially close relationship to problems involved in teaching modern foreign languages.

The first two courses mentioned are an important part of the early offerings of most schools of education. As to a course in the technique of teaching a language there are several possibilities. We may give a course in the general principles underlying all language teaching, or we may offer a course for each specific language. Since each language is different from every other one, since each has its own laws and its own secrets and "teacher craft" one may say: A course in the technique of language teaching is effective to the exact extent to which certain definite principles are used to illustrate and clarify specific problems in specific languages. For we speak about definite and specific points with far more competence than about general principles, which are often difficult to illustrate effectively in several languages, even though modern. Personal experience has convinced me that as a rule students are less interested in general principles of teaching than in the specific devices and techniques of teaching one definite language.

The success of teacher practice and observation courses depends entirely on the qualifications of the high-school teacher, whose good example will deeply impress the young teaching candidate.

12. Efforts should be made to induce educational officers to give up any form of certificate for secondary-school teachers that does not specify the subject or subjects that the candidate is qualified to teach.

It is a definite practice of institutions engaged in the preparation of teachers to direct the program of the teaching candidate in such a way that he may be able to teach one major subject and one or two minor ones, satisfying at the same time the requirements of accrediting agencies such as the North Central Association. We quote advice given by the University of Chicago in regard to spread of individual programs [1]:

Inasmuch as school authorities regularly require most teachers to teach more than one subject or field, the prospective teacher is strongly advised to pursue a program of study at the divisional level in a second subject or field, including a course relating to the problems and techniques of teaching that subject. Advice concerning such programs may be obtained from subsequent sections of this bulletin and should be supplemented through conferences with departmental and divisional counselors. In the main, it is hoped that the academic requirements for the primary subject will be so flexible that the prospective teacher, as a part of his divisional program in preparation for the Master's degree, will be able to make the necessary preparation in a secondary subject or field.

13. Graduation from a four-year college and the fulfillment of a major or minor requirement in a modern foreign language should be regarded as necessary to receive a license to teach that subject in a secondary school.

Even a first reading of the book by Woellner and Wood (cf. p. 231, note 1) shows that there is no reason for complacent acquiescence in the present status of the preparation of language teachers. By far the most hopeful sign is that some states have high requirements. The District of Columbia insists on a Master's degree as a prerequisite for a high-school certificate; California demands

[1] Announcements, The University of Chicago, *The Preparation of Teachers*, Volume XXXVIII (April, 1938), Number 11, p. 13.

one year, and Washington and Oregon thirty and ten semester hours respectively, of graduate work, for the privilege of teaching in high schools.

Requirements change in some states from year to year, but the general tendency is upward. Higher professional standards are certain to prevail in the end. More and more states will follow the splendid example set by the District of Columbia, and soon low professional requirements and standards will serve as horrifying examples of times fortunately past.

14. To promote further the professional development of modern language teachers in service, local school boards should seek through bonuses, salary increases, or leaves of absence, to encourage teachers to attend summer courses or regular sessions at centers offering special opportunities for modern language work, and to travel and study abroad.

This problem has long been and probably will continue to be very difficult. Even in France and Germany no permanent and quite satisfactory solution has been found.[1] Perhaps our most important single contribution will be to give encouragement to the teacher in service and provide for him every opportunity for further professional growth. There are many effective ways of encouraging postgraduate study here or abroad. The most obvious and simple ones seem to be:

(1) The person or committee in charge of promotions has a definite understanding with all teachers to the effect that salaries depend on superior teaching and on scholarship. Records are kept on performance and on all work done toward higher degrees.

(2) A bonus, however small, is granted for all graduate work done with a grade of A or A+.

(3) Salaries are raised for distinguished teaching, higher degrees, and years of satisfactory service.

(4) A major increase is granted on attainment of a Master's or Doctor's degree.

(5) A leave of absence is granted for study abroad as soon as the teacher's salary reaches a point where it may be divided tempo-

[1] McMurry, Mueller, and Alexander, *op. cit.*, pp. 146 ff. and 478 ff.

rarily, the larger part going to the regularly appointed teacher, the other to an able substitute who takes over his work.

These and many other ways have probably been tried before. The main point is not only to promote the superior teacher, but also to eliminate the ineffective one. A merit system administered strictly but tempered by kindness will do much to keep a body of competent and loyal teachers on the permanent staff of the school.

15. In so far as possible, modern foreign language instruction in high schools should be supervised and inspected by experts in foreign languages.[1]

This point, seemingly quite clear and beyond controversy, involves one basic problem: Who is an expert?

Take for instance the one fundamental recommendation of the *Study*, namely, that reading ability should be our first concern in brief courses. Is he an expert who insists that reading cannot be learned at all by the reading method, that everything depends on a certain degree of oral command, or he who believes that while a certain oral command is highly desirable it is not absolutely necessary for reading, and that vocalization and guided exercises toward speaking are sufficient?

However this may be, my experience is that the result of teaching corresponds point for point to that which has been carefully taught, fully understood, and thoroughly assimilated, or, to express the same thought in other words: we get out of teaching at best what we put into it, never more, and usually from 2 to about 40 per cent less.

The teacher who neglects reading in favor of speaking has no right to expect reading ability. He who never talks to his students in the foreign language and never engages in oral practice as a preparation for speaking must not deplore the lack of aural and oral ability. And so it is in regard to each and every skill and each and every question implying simple information: from the various skills (aural comprehension, reading, speaking, and writing) to the

[1] A chapter on "Problems in the Supervision of Modern Language Instruction" is contained in Cole-Tharp, *Modern Foreign Languages and Their Teaching* (Appleton-Century Company, 1937), pp. 456–516.

knowledge gained through these skills; from the knowledge of the physiology of the lingual *r* to the skill of uttering this sound flawlessly; from the knowledge of Brugmann's theory of the gender of nouns to the skilful use of nouns with correct genders and cases; from the knowledge of a movement in literary history to the skill and art of imitating the style of a specific author in this movement.

Though it is impossible to enumerate all problems about which experts might quarrel, something can perhaps be gained if experts will agree on two simple points:

(1) Language learning is specific in regard to information and knowledge as well as to skills.
(2) The more complete the knowledge of the teacher, the greater is the student's confidence in him and the better the student's chances for success.

In the last part of our discussion we have enumerated and briefly commented on the 15 points advanced by the Committee on Investigation of the *Study*. We have noted that these points represented the result of a compromise between ideal preparation and preparation possible under prevailing conditions. We also have noted the strong interest of institutions of higher learning in the preparation of teachers as an integral part of their duty toward the community.

The latest and perhaps most encouraging development in teacher training is that the American Association of University Professors has made this problem its own. In 1938 a committee (Committee Q) on the Preparation and Qualification of Teachers was formed under the chairmanship of Dr. Dinsmore Alter who, since then, has directed the reorganization of this committee. Each subject connected with the secondary-school field is to be carefully studied and to receive consideration. Professor F. H. Reinsch was elected chairman for the modern foreign languages. After a meeting held in December, 1938, in which Reinsch represented the American Association of Teachers of German (AATG), he issued a report to the Executive Council of this association, suggesting for approval a statement concerning the preparation of teachers of German. Unfortunately the report cannot be printed in full:

A. Minimum preparation (The minor)
1. Historical, literary, and cultural backgrounds of the German language and people with particular reference to American life.
2. Grammar and composition sufficient to provide reasonable facility in reading, speaking, and writing the language.
3. Professional study including educational orientation, curriculum development, teaching procedures in the modern language field, and practice teaching.

B. Adequate preparation (The major)
1 to 3 inclusive as listed under A above.
4. Sufficient advanced work to provide reasonable fluency in writing and speaking the language.
5. Familiarity with the major literary movements with particular reference to the interests of secondary students.

C. Complete preparation (Junior College credential)
1. Completion of all requirements under B above.
2. A Master's or Doctor's degree with a major in German. The graduate program should include the fields of bibliography, literature, and linguistics. The graduate program should, in general, stress breadth of scholarly achievement rather than intensive specialization within a limited field, and should be evaluated by a comprehensive examination rather than a thesis.
3. Recommended: At least a summer of study or travel in Germany.

For the first time in the history of language teaching in this country there arises the possibility that an agreement may be reached in regard to the organization and the content of teacher courses. It is sincerely to be hoped that the modern language group of Committee Q will succeed in preventing in method courses most if not all weaknesses and inconsistencies which naturally arise in a country as large as ours as a result of sharply differing conditions and needs.

Professor Reinsch is correct in stating:

I believe the problem of teacher training is one which will never be adequately or completely solved. There are too many variable factors beyond the control of any planning or regulating body ... As our needs change, as our school 'public' changes, and as we ourselves change from decade to decade, the problem will present different aspects.[1]

All human problems finally yield to persistent, intelligent work, clear thinking, and exact experimentation. The individual language teacher can do most toward raising the standard of his profession by beginning at home. In the final analysis, higher professional standards are not only the result of ably given courses in content and method, but quite as much the outcome of work done in the quiet of the study and in the stimulating atmosphere of the classroom. In short, the student of today through his own preparation is certain to play an important role in determining the standards of tomorrow.

BIBLIOGRAPHY

ARON, A. W. "The Linguistic Background of the Modern Language Teacher." *Modern Language Journal* (Nov. 1922), pp. 75–83.

CHURCHMAN, PHILIP H. "Wanted: The Graduate School of Teacher Training." *Modern Language Journal* (Oct. 1926), pp. 1–11.

DANTON, GEORGE H. "Training German Teachers for the New Era." *Monatshefte* (Jan. 1931), pp. 1–11.

—— "An Experiment in a Methods Class." *Monatshefte* (Nov. 1934), pp. 223–30.

HAGBOLDT, PETER. "Elements of Art and Science in Modern Language Teaching." *Modern Language Journal* (Dec. 1928), pp. 192–96.

JOCKERS, ERNST. "Lehren als schöpferische Tätigkeit." *German Quarterly* (March, 1937), pp. 60–67.

JOHNSON, LAURA B. "Teacher Training Through Participation." *Modern Language Journal* (Oct. 1922), pp. 28–37.

KENISTON, HAYWARD. "The Role of the Graduate School in the Training of the Modern Language Teacher." *Modern Language Journal* (Oct. 1922), pp. 1–4.

MANKIEWICZ, F. "Training of Teachers in Service." *German Quarterly* (May, 1938), pp. 142–52.

McMURRY, RUTH EMILY; MUELLER, MAX; and ALEXANDER, THOMAS. In cooperation with the Modern Foreign Language Study. *Modern Foreign Languages in France and Germany. The Training of Teachers and the Methods of Instruction.* (New York: Bureau of Publications, Teachers College, Columbia University, 1930), viii + 566 pp.

---

[1] Quoted from a personal letter of May 30, 1939.

PURIN, CHARLES M. *The Training of Teachers of the Modern Foreign Languages*, Vol. XIII, Publications of the American and Canadian Committees on Modern Languages. (New York: The Macmillan Company, 1929), xvi + 112 pp., 75 cents.

STROEBE, LILIAN L. "Self-Improvement and Inexpensive Books for the Teacher of German." *Modern Language Journal* (Jan. 1932), pp. 289–98.

STUART, HUGH. *The Training of Modern Foreign Language Teachers for the Secondary Schools in the United States*. "Teachers College Contributions to Education," No. 256. Ph.D. thesis (New York: Teachers College, Columbia University, 1927), x + 111 pp., $1.50.

Volume II of *Modern Language Instruction in Canada*. Vol. VII of the Study (Toronto: The University of Toronto Press, 1928). Contains articles dealing with the training of teachers, *i.e.*, "The History of the Training of Modern Language Teachers in Ontario," pp. 311–27, and "The Training of Modern Language Teachers in Canada," pp. 545–602.

SUPPLEMENTARY READINGS

GAEDE, WM. R. "Die Neuorganisation der höheren Schule in Deutschland." *German Quarterly*, X, 4 (Nov. 1937), pp. 182–87.

—— "Neuerungen im deutschen Bildungswesen." *German Quarterly*, XI, 2 (March, 1938), pp. 71–77.

—— "Neuerungen im deutschen Bildungswesen. III. Die neuen Lehrpläne der höheren Schulen." *German Quarterly*, XI, 4 (Nov. 1938), pp. 178–84.

HAESSLER, LUISE. "Das Ideal eines Lehrers des Deutschen in Amerika." *German Quarterly*, X, 4 (Nov. 1937), pp. 188–93.

PORTERFIELD, ALLEN W. "Gothic as an Undergraduate Study." *German Quarterly*, XI, 2 (March, 1938), pp. 78–86.

REINSCH, F. H. "Goethe's Interpretation of Language Mastery." *German Quarterly*, XI, 3 (March, 1938), pp. 115–25.

SUGGESTIONS FOR DISCUSSIONS AND REPORTS

1. Secure information in regard to the status of the "Junior Year Abroad" from the German Service Bureau of the University of Wisconsin.
2. Report on Chapters X and XI, pp. 464–500, of the book by McMurry et al.
3. Report on your personal experience with observation. Mention briefly the school, the student body, the supervisor, the main aim of

instruction, and the typical errors of pupils. Suggest remedies for the prevention or the correction of the latter.

4. Read and summarize the main points of the various articles on graduate training.
5. Enumerate the requirements for a Bachelor's (Master's, Doctor's) degree at a standard American university.
6. Discuss critically "Ideal preparation" as outlined by the Committee of Twelve.
7. A class discussion of minimum, adequate, and complete preparation as stated on p. 241.
8. Report on Hagboldt's *Language Learning*, Chapter III, pp. 100–56.

CHAPTER ELEVEN

TESTING

THE NECESSITY AND VALUE OF TESTING by objective measurements has long been recognized throughout our country. In 1905 Thorndike and several of his students constructed a number of tests and scales for measuring purposes, and ever since that time interest in standardized measures for achievement in school subjects has grown by leaps and bounds. Today testing at regular intervals is considered to be as important in nearly all school subjects as teaching itself.

The year 1926 marks the beginning of a new era in teaching languages. It was in that year that the *Study* began its careful and far-reaching investigation of teaching results in the modern foreign languages by the use of standardized tests. Since 1926, problems in the field of tests and measurements have become more and more the concern of specialists. In the construction of tests it is no longer possible to rely merely on a thorough knowledge of one's subject. Experts in the intricate problems of measurement must supplement our knowledge of the foreign language with their technical information and skill.

We shall discuss some basic and elementary notions of testing and devote our attention in the main to the three volumes of the *Study* which deal specifically with the problem of tests.[1]

It seems presumptuous, and indeed impossible in a short chapter, to attempt to do justice to three volumes so bristling with im-

---

[1] These three volumes are briefly and lucidly summarized and described by Professor Robert Herndon Fife in *A Brief Summary of Reports on the Modern Foreign Languages*, issued by the Modern Foreign Language Study and the Canadian Committee on Modern Languages (The Macmillan Company, 1931), pp. 98–141.

Quotations from the various volumes of the *Study* are reprinted by special permission of The Macmillan Company and of Professor Fife.

portant information as these. Before trying, nevertheless, to give some of the high points of these books, I must express my appreciation to Professors Fife, Henmon, and Wood for permitting me to quote freely from their writings. All I can hope to accomplish here is to introduce the prospective language teacher to the pioneer work in the field, to encourage him to study carefully these books for himself, and to help break down the widespread prejudices against standardized tests on the part of conservative teachers, young and old.

Since the topical arrangement of the Henmon volume appears to lend itself readily for a first introduction to the problems of testing, we begin with this book.[1]

I. THE HENMON REPORT

Henmon starts out by stating that valid, reliable, comprehensive, and administratively feasible tests may be expected to be of permanent value in

1. Setting standards of accomplishment at different levels of training in objective, realistic, and comparable terms.
2. Making possible more accurate comparisons of attainment in different schools and classes under different methods and conditions.
3. Serving as a means of classification and placement to secure homogeneity in classes in terms of actual achievement in the languages rather than in terms of time spent in study.
4. Furnishing instruments of analysis for investigation of the effects of varying ages, intelligence levels, methods, curricula, and objectives.
5. Diagnosing deficiencies and locating them for definite remedial exercises.
6. Defining in more specific terms the immediate objectives of instruction.[2]

It may be said without exaggeration that all of the six values mentioned were actually realized even in the first standardized

[1] V. A. C. Henmon, *Achievement Tests in the Modern Foreign Languages*, prepared for the Modern Foreign Language Study and the Canadian Committee on Modern Languages (The Macmillan Company, 1929).

[2] *Ibid.*, p. 1.

tests.[1] The American Council Tests, Alpha as well as Beta, do set definite standards, they make possible accurate comparisons of attainment, and they emphasize achievement rather than time spent in class for any teacher willing to examine carefully the distribution of the scores made. They furnish instruments of analysis for various investigations, they diagnose deficiencies for remedial exercises, and they encourage a close definition of immediate objectives. This is clear to everyone who has administered these tests over a period of years.

Henmon informs us that the construction of tests in modern foreign languages involves four separate steps:

1. The analysis of achievement in modern languages into the specific abilities or elements of which it is composed.
2. The selection of a testing technique and a test length to give objective and reliable results.
3. The selection and gradation of test items.
4. Standardization on a basis of a wide administration at different levels to establish accurate norms of performance.[2]

The author then enumerates nine different abilities in modern languages which may be tested: vocabulary, silent reading or comprehension, translation into English, translation into the foreign language, written composition, grammar, aural comprehension, pronunciation, and oral composition or speaking. Of these nine abilities only four were finally selected for special study, namely: vocabulary, grammar, silent reading, and written composition.[3]

[1] American Council Alpha German Test. By V. A. C. Henmon, B. Q. Morgan, and Stella M. Hinz, C. M. Purin, and Elizabeth Rossberg. Forms A and B. Two booklets. Part I, Vocabulary and Grammar, 12 pages; Part II, Silent Reading and Composition, 12 pages, with Class Record, Keys, and Manual of Directions, including Composition Scale. Yonkers-on-Hudson, New York: World Book Company.
American Council Beta German Test. By C. M. Purin and Ben D. Wood. Forms A and B. Part I, Vocabulary; Part II, Comprehension; Part III, Grammar. Each forms a 12-page booklet, with Class Record, Keys, and Manual. World Book Company. [2] Ibid., p. 2.
[3] Besides the tests mentioned in note 1 above, the American and Canadian Committees have sponsored and developed a German Reading Scale. By M. J. Van Wagenen and Sophia Hubman-Patterson. Forms A and B. Bloomington, Ill.: Public School Publishing Company.

Before proceeding with our discussion, let us define carefully some of the terms ordinarily used in discussions of standardized tests. Authorities agree that a test, to be of permanent value, must be valid, reliable, comprehensive and comparable, and administratively feasible.

BASIC TERMS [1]

Valid

"We have tried to make our tests valid by basing our questions on materials which word-counts and analysis of textbooks and of syllabi have shown to be important, if not in fact indispensable, common essentials; and by making our sampling of the common essentials adequate not only as to the extent of materials, but also as to variety and depth of the learning-units tapped." (Wood)

"To be valid, the test must measure what it purports to measure." (Henmon)

Reliable

"We have tried to make our tests reliable by insisting on large numbers of relatively independent questions, the answers to which involve few irrelevant activities on the part of the student, and which can be scored objectively, accurately, and expeditiously." (Wood)

"To be reliable, the test must yield consistent results with a minimum of error when administered to different groups or the same group at different times." (Henmon)

Manuals of directions usually furnished with the tests are often confusing. The young teacher fails to see a clear relationship between validity and reliability. He does not understand why a valid test is always reliable, and why a reliable test is not necessarily valid. Perhaps the following statement will help:

Validity includes reliability as a necessary and concomitant quality, but not vice versa.

A test is valid: (1) when it measures what it intends to measure, that is, indispensable, common essentials arrived at by a thorough

[1] The following definitions are given in two volumes: Ben D. Wood, *New York Experiments with New-Type Modern Language Tests*, Publications of the American and Canadian Committees on Modern Languages. Volume I of the *Study* (The Macmillan Company, 1928), p. 95, and Henmon, *op. cit.*, p. 2.

analysis of materials; and (2) when it is consistent with itself in measuring the same elements two or more times.

A test is reliable when it is consistent with itself. Reliability is not concerned with validity in not ascertaining whether or not it is based on common essentials.

Therefore, a valid test is always reliable, but a reliable test is not necessarily valid.

Validity = basic content + consistency.
Reliability = consistency.

Comprehensive and comparable

"We have tried to make our tests yield comparable measurements by making valid and reliable tests adapted to the whole range of achievement in the first three or four years of modern language work, and by constructing several equivalent Forms at the outset in such a way that additional Forms equivalent in difficulty and variability may be made as needed." (Wood)

"It must be comprehensive enough to give comparable measures at different stages or levels of achievement." (Henmon)

Administratively feasible

"And finally, we have tried to make our tests administratively feasible by putting the questions in such a way that the tests are largely self-administered, and by arranging spaces for students' answers such that the scoring is not only objective, but accurate and expeditious." (Wood)

"To be administratively feasible, it must be reasonable in cost and in length of time required, objective, and largely self-administering." (Henmon) [1]

Validity, reliability, comprehensiveness and comparability, and administrative feasibility are the basic requirements of good tests. Some other terms often confusing to persons untrained in statistical methods may be explained here:

Correlation is the degree of relationship of correspondence between two or more series of data. The degree of correlation is

[1] For further discussion of reliability and validity, comprehensiveness and comparability, see Henmon, *op. cit.*, pp. 81–104, and Wood, *op. cit.*, pp. 39–44.

established by the correlation coefficient. We take a hypothetical case: If we measure a number of persons first in feet and then in inches, the correlation between the height in feet and the height in inches is 1.00, is perfect; or if we weigh a series of articles first in pounds and then in kilograms, the correlation between their weight in pounds and their weight in kilograms is 1.00, is perfect; 1.00 denotes a perfect correlation coefficient. Perfect correlations do not exist in testing. Supposing we give the American Council Alpha Vocabulary Test to the same group of students twice, the correlation coefficient between the scores made by this same group of students will not be perfect, it will be less than 1.00.

The relationship between two Forms of a standardized test is called the "reliability" of the test.

Percentile curve

"A percentile curve is a smooth line having a horizontal length representing 100 per cent of the scores of any group of individuals and so drawn that any point on the curve has the height representing the amount of a given score and horizontal position on the graph representing the per cent of scores of the group that is exceeded by the given score. A percentile curve shows at a glance not only the median score of a class but also the range and variability of scores. It shows at a glance just what per cent of the scores of a class is exceeded by the score of any given individual and just what per cent of the class attains or exceeds any given score. Two or more curves on the same graph show very vividly the amount of overlapping of the scores of different classes." [1]

Median is used in statistics to designate a number in a series arranged in order of size, such that the numbers which are greater are as many as the numbers which are smaller. In the series 1, 2, 3, 4, 5, the median number is 3. Median may be defined as the middlemost number in a series.

Mean denotes the arithmetic average or the sum computed by dividing the sum of several quantities by their number. "Mean"

[1] This description of the percentile curve is that of A. S. Otis; it is quoted as the simplest and most effective by Wood; cf. *op. cit.*, pp. 19 ff. For illustrations see Wood, pp. 23, 25, 29, etc.

is preferred to "average" because the latter term has been rendered vague by popular use.[1]

The Selection of Testing Techniques [2]

Vocabulary. The words for the vocabulary test were taken from a compilation of a count of nearly eleven million running words in Kaeding's *Häufigkeitswörterbuch*, which is the basis of Morgan's *German Frequency Word Book.* One hundred German words were taken at random from successive frequency groups, which thus represented an ascending scale of difficulty according to the frequency of use. The vocabulary test follows the so-called "alternative response," "multiple choice," "selection," or "recognition" technique. The student is required to select the one correct English translation out of five translations, one or two of which are confusion words resembling the foreign word. Henmon's studies and experiments with vocabulary testing techniques finally led to the adoption of the "multiple-choice" form, which proved to be more objective and easier to score and, besides, gave the maximum student response in the shortest time.[3] Henmon refutes various objections raised against the vocabulary test, the main one, perhaps, being that vocabulary must always be tested in context, and never in isolation.[4]

Here is an example taken from the American Council Alpha Test, Part I, Form A. We reproduce every twentieth vocabulary item of the test.[5]

[1] Technical terms in statistics are elusive and often defy close definition. The only way of understanding such terms completely is to live and experience them in actual statistical work with tests and their administration.

[2] The captions of the pages now following are mostly those of Fife's Summary. Cf. Fife, *op. cit.,* pp. 109–128.

[3] Henmon, *op. cit.,* p. 16.

[4] *Ibid.,* pp. 9 ff. Compare W. C. Decker, "Tests and Examinations," *German Quarterly* (Feb. 1928), pp. 74–80. Compare also William Kurath and John M. Stalnaker, "Two German Vocabulary Tests," *Modern Language Journal* (Nov. 1936), pp. 95–102. The authors reach the conclusion that the two tests, one based on recognition, the other on recall, measure very nearly the same ability. The tests are reproduced and the norms given.

[5] This illustration and those following below are reproduced by permission of the World Book Company. For the authorship of the test, see p. 247, note 1.

Directions: One of the five English words or phrases in each line is a correct translation of the German word. Draw a heavy line under it as in Examples A and B.

(Two examples are given.)

Time allowed: Eighteen minutes.

1. Während	keeping	smiling	during	ending	truly
20. Eigentum	property	quality	selfishness	simplicity	imagination
40. Berechnung	report	building	respect	calculation	sale
60. Wurzel	twist	dice	angle	design	root
80. Gespenst	expense	vegetables	broom	appetite	ghost
100. Klause	claw	secret	clover	hermitage	glue

Grammar.[1] An experimental administration of two types of French tests, one based on the "multiple-choice" technique, the other on "completion" or "recall," led to the conclusion that no superiority can be claimed for either technique. Experiments with German showed similar results. Yet statisticians have pointed out that from the standpoint of reliability the "recall" method is more advantageous.

We give an illustration of the technique used in the American Council Alpha German Test in grammar.

Directions: Only one translation is correct in each case. Put a cross mark (×) between the parentheses that follow the correct form.

Time allowed: Twenty-two minutes.

1. Father has often wanted to see this town.

Vater hat oft wollen diese Stadt zu sehen.......... ( )
Vater hat diese Stadt sehen oft wollen............ ( )
Vater hat diese Stadt oft sehen wollen............ ( )
Vater hat oft diese Stadt wollen zu sehen.......... ( )

Silent reading.[2] Henmon gives six reasons for preferring the paragraph-question technique. In briefed form they are these: (1) The paragraph-question technique is the most natural. (2) Comprehension is revealed in the student's ability to select what is relevant to the questions and to eliminate the irrelevant. (3) In the classroom we are not so much concerned with completeness of comprehension as we are with taking samples of understand-

---

[1] Fife, *op. cit.*, p. 110; Henmon, *op. cit.*, pp. 10 f.
[2] Cf. Fife, *op. cit.*, pp. 110 f. Henmon, *op. cit.*, pp. 11 ff.

ing here and there. (4) The paragraph-question technique is more interesting to students than other techniques. (5) It is best adapted to measure reading power at higher levels. (6) Other techniques are not so useful for measuring classroom achievement or individual achievement and progress.

The question as to which technique is best — paragraph-questions in the foreign language or in English, true-false questions or questions requiring a correct choice among four answers — is unsolved. Fife remarks:

The paragraph-question technique was retained by the Committees because of the greater familiarity of modern language teachers with this form, which is of course traditional in modern language usage.[1]

The American Council Alpha German Test, Part II, gives as its silent reading test seven paragraphs with a varying number of questions in German, the total number being forty. Again we give an example:

Directions: Read the first passage attentively, twice if necessary. Then answer the questions in English. Your answer should be brief but should show that you have understood the passage. Treat each passage the same way.

Time allowed: Thirty-two minutes.

Reading Selection 1

Einer von den Jungen lief und holte Wasser im Kessel (kettle). Zwei andere sammelten trockene Holzstückchen, steckten ein Streichholz an und machten Feuer. Die Mädchen taten etwas Tee in die Teekanne und gossen das kochende Wasser darauf. Unser Tee war fertig, und wir aßen Brot und Butter und Marmelade dazu. Tante Marie hatte uns einen Kuchen mitgegeben, der sehr gut schmeckte. Wir waren sehr fröhlich und sangen und spielten. Als wir die Sonne im Westen untergehen sahen, packten wir die Teekanne, den Kessel und die Teller in die Körbe (baskets) und fuhren in einem Ruderboot nach Hause.

Answer in English:
1. Wer brachte das Wasser? ....
2. Wie war das Holz? ....

[1] Note that Wood uses the "completion" and the "true-false" form in several of his tests; see Wood, *op. cit.*, pp. 55 ff., 62 ff., 73 ff., 80 ff. In the American Council Beta German Test he uses the techniques employed also in the alternative form.

3. Was tat man in die Kanne? ....
4. Von wem war der Kuchen? ....
5. Wie verbrachte (*spent*) man den Nachmittag? ....
6. Wann ging man nach Hause? ....
7. Wohin packte man die Teller? ....
8. Wie fuhr man heim? ....

Henmon digests carefully and at length various comparative studies of testing techniques,[1] and finally gives a special section devoted to a detailed discussion of the

Composition scales.[2] Many teachers are convinced that free composition reveals most adequately the student's knowledge in a foreign language. We have briefly described the composition scales in dealing with the active phases of language study (see Chapter VIII). What remains to be done is to give illustrations of the various qualities of composition. We quote from the American Council Alpha German Test, Part II, Form A, Quality 0, 7, and 14, that is, the lowest, the middlemost, and the highest:

Quality 0

Die Knob sie moschend eine Hous sie in ein baum est. Sie arbeitet ich sehe drie Knabe. Sie sind in einer Groß Baum.

Quality 7

Ein Tag wunschen drei Knaben, Fritz, Hans und Martin, ein Haus bauen. Sein Vater sagte „Ihr konnet die Holz haben, daß ich hatte nicht wünschen für unser neues Gebäude.

So die drei Knaben erwiederten „Wir wollten bauen unser Haus in dem großen Eich Baume hinter unserem Haus. Sie arbeiteten jedes Tag und ein Tur, sieben Fenster, ein Boden und ein (*roof*) machten.

Die Vögel songen während die Knaben arbeiteten, die Eichkätzer liefen auf und hinter, und die oder Knaben und Mädchen komen oft zu sehen die kleinen Haus.

Quality 14

Heinrich, Karl und Georg sind Kinder eines Zimmermannes. Der Vater sprach oft mit seine Söhne von seiner Arbeit. Manchmal haben die Kinder dem Vater geholfen; sie konnten ihm Nägel bringen, oder den Hammer halten.

Einst gab der Vater den Knaben einige Bretter und eine Leiter. Georg sagt er möchte ein Vogelhaus bauen. Heinrich wollte eine Scheune bauen. Nach vielem Plaudern wählte Karl eine Idee die den Brüdern auch gefiel. Eine Leiter wurde

---

[1] Henmon, *op. cit.*, pp. 13–33.   [2] *Ibid.*, pp. 34–62; Fife, *op. cit.*, pp. 111 f.

gegen den Baum getragen, und die Arbeit war begonnen. Oben, unter große Ächste, wurde ein kleines Spielhaus gebaut.

Jeden Tag, nach der Schule, haben die Kinder da gelesen, gesungen oder geschrieben. Auch luden sie die Mutter und den Vater ein ihn zu besuchen.

Henmon describes most carefully the statistical method which finally led to the selection of the different quality groups for the composition scales.

The Difficulty of Individual Testing Items [1]

"In order to be most useful for testing purposes," Henmon states, "the individual test items should show uniform increases in difficulty with successive years of training or uniform increases in the percentage of correct responses." Then he proceeds to a close analysis of each individual item in the vocabulary, grammar, and silent reading tests.

In the case of the vocabulary test, he finds a wide spread between the order in which the words were given in the test and the order in which they were answered by the students, the spread being widest in German. Vocabulary items of low frequency, such as Bleistift, Kreide, Pult, are overlearned, while items of high frequency, such as Heer, Gedanke, wegen, are imperfectly learned. Henmon attributes this fact in part to an imperfect classification of students and to inequalities in achievement in home and school training. Another reason may be the strong emphasis on so-called "environmental" words and on oral exercises with a corresponding neglect of reading.

As to grammar, the test scores reveal that grammar is poorly learned even after three or four years of study. It was found that third-year students may be superior to fourth-year students in grammar. In Fife's words: "When instruction in grammar ceases at the end of the third year, what has been learned does not hold."

The silent reading tests were better graded than any other. The difficulties of the paragraph-question technique were finally overcome by several careful revisions. Henmon states: "The German reading test shows a uniform gradation and a close equivalence in the two forms."

Variations in achievement between school and school and be-

[1] Fife, *op. cit.*, pp. 112 f.; Henmon, *op. cit.*, pp. 63–80.

tween class and class even of the same school were found to be extraordinarily great.

THE RELIABILITY OF THE ALPHA TESTS [1]

Henmon first discusses the meaning of reliability and points out a method by which to indicate reliability in case two equivalent form of a given test are not available. He states that a reliability coefficient of .90 is generally regarded as necessary for reasonably accurate individual measurement. Then he describes the statistical steps by which the coefficient measuring reliability is obtained. In five tables (22–26) he sets forth the reliability data for the Alpha Tests. He concludes that the Alpha Tests meet the accepted standards of reliability in educational testing for group or class measurement and for individual diagnosis as well.

The German grammar test was found to have the lowest reliability. Fife remarks that "the modern language teacher will doubtless be surprised to learn that in the opinion of psychologists grammar tests have in general less reliability, *i.e.*, less consistency as measuring devices, than vocabulary tests." Henmon points out that the reliability of a test can within limits be improved by increasing the length of the test. He adds:

> If we gave more time to accurate diagnosis of achievement and less to training, we should not have the bad classification of pupils which we now have and which is perhaps the greatest source of weakness in modern language instruction.[2]

As a proof for the reliability of the American Council Tests, Henmon refers to the Ford experiment, in which the American Council Tests were compared with the two-and-a-half-hour matriculation examination in Canadian universities. The American Council Tests, even though requiring half as much time, showed a much higher reliability.

THE VALIDITY OF THE ALPHA TESTS [3]

Henmon begins with a clarification of terms. Reliability and validity are discussed as to their mutual relationship. A test may

---

[1] Fife, *op. cit.*, pp. 113 f.; Henmon, *op. cit.*, pp. 81–91.
[2] Henmon, *op. cit.*, p. 89.   [3] Fife, *op. cit.*, pp. 114 ff.; Henmon, *op. cit.*, pp. 91–104.

be quite reliable in yielding consistent results and still may not be valid since it measures very inadequately what it is intended or claims to measure. The author points out that there is no absolute criterion of validity and that the nearest approach to validity might be teachers' marks if they were not highly unreliable. Then he shows in eight tables (27–34) the intercorrelations of the various linguistic abilities — vocabulary and grammar, vocabulary and silent reading, vocabulary and composition, etc. He concludes that in general the results of the various studies of interrelationships show that any of the Alpha Tests are valid instruments.

Henmon continues by making a thorough study of teachers' grades in relation to the validity of the Alpha Tests. In four tables (35–38) he shows that grammar plays a dominant part in determining teachers' marks and that vocabulary grows in importance with increasing amounts of training.

RESULTS OF ADMINISTERING ALPHA TESTS IN THE SCHOOLS AND COLLEGES OF THE UNITED STATES [1]

Nearly one third of Henmon's volume is devoted to a minute analysis of statistics based on the extended testing campaign in American schools and colleges. Fife states:

> Here, for the first time in the history of American Education, students in a given curriculum subject are measured with the same yardstick and their achievement recorded on the basis of a sampling at all levels throughout every section of the country. The co-operation of more than two hundred secondary schools located in thirty states and of fifty-seven colleges, almost as widely distributed, with the devoted service of hundreds of teachers, made this vast sampling possible.[2]

Henmon shows in twenty-four tables (39–62) the distribution of scores, percentile ranks, and norms of the Alpha Tests in French, German, and Spanish. These tables reveal an amazing range of achievement at every semester level and in every ability tested. The range of performance of high-school pupils after two years of study is from zero to a perfect score. Eleven figures (3–14) show at a glance the overlapping of classes, the variability of achieve-

[1] Fife, *op. cit.*, pp. 116 ff.; Henmon, *op. cit.*, pp. 105–214. [2] Fife, *op. cit.*, p. 116.

ment, and the curves of growth from semester to semester. The overlapping of classes is presented in three tables, showing for each test in an upper line the percentage of each semester group reaching or exceeding the median of the next higher semester group, and showing in a lower line the percentage of each semester group failing to reach the median of the next lower group. Figures 15–38 show graphically the percentile curves for each test in each language for both high school and college, and the amount of overlapping. Henmon points out that a score in a given test has little or no significance in itself and that scores have meaning only in relation to the percentile rank and the norms established by the test.

Henmon recommends the conversion of test scores into percentile ranks so as to make the scores comparable and commensurable. In Table 66 he presents the conversion of the scores made on the Alpha German Tests into percentile ranks. In Table 67 he gives another illustration.

Tables 68–70 give the class medians for different schools and classes, and Figures 39–47 show at a glance the variations in class medians for different schools and classes in the various languages and abilities tested. Further tables and figures give statistical proof of the defects in the organization of modern language instruction in the United States, the startling overlapping of classes, and the wide variations of school standards.

Fife writes:

> As a broad but demonstrable statement it may be said that approximately one-half of all the students tested in the three modern foreign languages were erroneously classified by one semester or more . . . No wonder that discontent and discouragement with modern language teaching are voiced by teachers, administrators, and pupils . . . Under such circumstances, pupils and principals could not fail to ask the teachers nor the teachers to ask themselves why they require two years to accomplish what some of their colleagues do in one year.[1]

In summing up the merits of the Henmon volume, Fife states:

> The work is for the future as well as for the present. The uses of objective tests for a restudying of the whole scheme of modern language teaching: its curriculum making, its class organization and its

[1] Fife, *op. cit.*, pp. 117–19.

methods are analyzed, and while no immodest claim to finality is made either as regards the form of the tests or the manner of their use, the demonstration of the indispensable character of such instruments if our subject is to make progress is so thorough that the foreign language teacher would be blind indeed if he should refuse to draw the inevitable inferences for his practice ... No member of the profession who has his work really at heart will be deterred by the difficulties from making ready for a full use of the equipment which this report furnishes.[1]

II. THE WOOD REPORT

Professor Ben D. Wood, helped by various grants from different sources as well as the American and Canadian Committees, undertook the gigantic task of testing in two successive years, 1925 and 1926, all modern language pupils of New York City, and in the state of New York all high-school pupils who presented themselves for the Regents' examinations in 1925. City and state authorities lent their full support to make possible this extensive and important experiment with new-type tests. Approximately 19,000 students of French were tested in two successive years, while the Spanish test was administered to 6500 pupils in 1925 and to about 4000 pupils in 1926. The Regents' examinations were given to more than 31,000 students in French, German, and Spanish.

Wood developed the new-type tests with experiments carried out at the Columbia Educational Research Bureau over a period of four years. Placement examinations in modern foreign languages for college Freshmen formed their basis. Also the French and Spanish examinations used in the New York experiments were based on placement forms, which were later revised in coöperation with the Committee on Investigation. One of the members of the Committee prepared the German test, which was then standardized by the Committee. The tests in vocabulary, grammar, and silent reading were revised and standardized by being administered to small groups of students until the tests had proved to be valid, reliable, comparable, and easily scorable.[2]

---

[1] Fife, *op. cit.*, p. 123. Lack of space prevents giving even the briefest summary of the remaining part of Henmon's report. See Fife, *op. cit.*, pp. 119–23, and Henmon, *op. cit.*, pp. 215–363.   [2] Fife, *op. cit.*, pp. 100 ff.

Since the new-type tests prepared by Wood had proved to be comprehensive and comparable they could be given to all grades and they made possible the comparison of the achievement of any school with any other school and any student with any other student.

Fife fittingly states:

> In case of students who took the Regents' examinations, the new-type examinations were administered to two-, three- and four-year classes in French, German, and Spanish. Here, in addition to the possibility of comparison of student with student and school with school, another field of comparison was opened. At the same time that the new-type tests were administered, the traditional old-type examinations were also given to the same students. The results of the administration permitted a conclusive comparison of the two types of examinations as to their ability to meet the requirements of a good examination with respect to validity, reliability, comparability of results and ease of objectivity of scoring.[1]

The First Test Administration in the Junior High Schools of New York City

In Part I, pp. 3–103, of the Wood volume the results of the first administration of the tests are graphically presented in numerous tables and charts, and carefully analyzed. The author finds that in 1925 over 2000 pupils out of nearly 19,000 in the French classes of the junior high schools of New York were misplaced by one whole semester or more, and that approximately 10,000 of them were nearer to a higher or lower class average than to the average of the class in which they were reciting.[2] In the Spanish classes the misplacement of students was even worse. More than one in ten of the Spanish pupils of New York City junior high schools were misplaced by one semester or more, and considerably more than half of the students were nearer in achievement to the average of the class above or below them than to the average of their own class.[3]

The standards in individual schools showed wide variations. In one school a fourth-semester class showed an average achieve-

---

[1] Fife, *op. cit.*, p. 101.   [2] Wood, *op. cit.*, p. 26.   [3] *Ibid.*, p. 27.

ment little better than a third-semester class. In another school actual achievement in terms of norms varied by one full year.[1]

The author then goes on to analyze with utmost care the validity and reliability of the American Council Beta Tests (pp. 39–44). He defines reliability, discusses the reliability of old- and new-type examinations, the standard and probable error estimate, the validity of tests in general, and the intercorrelations of the three parts of the new-type tests.

Wood then analyzes individual questions in the new-type tests (pp. 45–93). Among other problems he discusses the experimental validation of individual questions, he gives a definition of a "good" question, explains the possible causes of "inverted" questions, and presents a graph of "good" and "bad" questions.

Wood concludes Part I of his volume with a chapter called "Summary and Recommendations" (pp. 94–103). In less than ten pages he makes recommendations so vital and important that they will not fail to impress deeply every progressive teacher of language. Here we find discussed under ten topics in a forceful and crisp style all the problems of testing and, by implication, many problems of instruction with which we should be thoroughly familiar. We find also a highly welcome indictment of the evil "time-serving" conception which is so closely connected with opposition to new-type tests.

Wood is convinced, rightly so I believe, that this opposition is due to a complex of causes: "a too great sensitivity to tradition"; "a too careless acceptance of the theory that examinations have a miraculous power to create and raise standards"; "too much emphasis in the early years upon literature and what is called 'cultural content'"; and "too much faith in the reality and measurableness of an octoplasm called 'spirit of the language.'" Wood continues:

> Some of those who use "spirit of the language" as conclusive argument against new types of tests have been intemperate enough to say that they were not interested in vocabulary, and have insisted on measuring the spirit of the language in students who did not yet know its "dry bones," i.e., its words . . .
>
> If we continue our present practice of trying to make unprepared

[1] Wood, *op. cit.*, p. 35.

students sense the native beauties of a Goethe, a Molière, a Cervantes, or a Dante in the original tongues when they have to look up every tenth word in the dictionary, and must have every other idiom or poetic expression explained by the teacher, our students will continue to leave the modern language classes with feelings toward the great masters as ardent as the feelings of many high-school students who have unwillingly toiled over Shakespeare, or who have memorized Milton's sonnets as penances for rebellion against class exercises which seemed to them supreme folly . . .

There can be no doubt about the necessity of sweeping away, completely and for all time, the time-serving conception which has thus far so largely dominated the organization and administration of modern language instruction. The continuance of this indefensible iniquity would be a crime against both teachers and students . . . It puts a premium on stupidity and laziness, and penalizes intelligence and industry . . . It is precisely the highest 15 or 20 per cent of first-year students who, in spite of our almost malicious and invidious efforts to stultify and misrepresent them, will ultimately contribute 70 per cent of the successful students in our advanced courses.[1]

THE SECOND TEST ADMINISTRATION IN THE JUNIOR HIGH SCHOOLS OF NEW YORK CITY was undertaken one year after the first. Naturally it had been hoped that in view of the startling misplacements revealed in the 1925 testing, the classes would be grouped far more homogeneously in 1926. However, when the results of the second administration were analyzed, the situation on the whole had not improved. Wood reports that "the relation between the rate or amount of progress of the same group of individuals in the same school in the second year of its modern language work is very nearly a pure chance relation, under the present organization of modern language work in the junior high schools of New York City." [2] A little below he adds:

So long as the real potentialities of individual students and of classes are masked by being made the sport of chance in the chaos of school and classroom situations uncovered by these charts, the effective educational guidance of students will remain a pious hope.[3]

THE ADMINISTRATION OF THE NEW-TYPE AND OLD-TYPE EXAMINATIONS BY THE REGENTS is described and analyzed in Part II of the Wood Report (pp. 106–319).

[1] Wood, *op. cit.*, pp. 100–02.   [2] *Ibid.*, p. 329.   [3] *Ibid.*, p. 339.

We cannot possibly do justice to this careful and detailed report by a mere summary, and must confine ourselves to Wood's statement: "The general conclusions from the data of this experiment are that the new-type examinations are roughly twice as reliable and valid as the old-type examinations of equal time allowance." Wood finds the old-type examinations defective and unworthy of the confidence reposed in them, but he also finds the principle of centrally administrated examinations quite sound. He urges that the duties of examining agencies should include research and information services, and, coming back to the time-serving conception as an evil and indefensible practice, he gives a typical example from his own experience during the testing campaign:

> The retention in a French II class of the 300-odd students who in actual achievement are above the fourth-year average is a clear example of the evil workings of the old time-serving conception of education which has persistently ignored the fact of individual differences. It is only one of many examples that might be cited wherein the rules of examining agencies put a premium on stupidity and laziness and a penalty on intelligence and industry. Regents rules, like those of the College Entrance Examination Board, prejudice every modern language student without trial by jury or any other of the amenities which law accords to criminals, and sentences them to a fixed number of years in modern language classrooms [1] . . .

In fact, so strong and repeated is the appeal for a thorough revision and a radical change in our testing practices that one of Wood's own sentences might serve as a *Leitmotiv* for the entire volume:

> Let us not punish these capable young students because they are not stupid enough to require four semesters for what they have achieved in one.[2]

On the same page Wood points to the one fundamental necessity in all successful instruction. "The most important thing," he says, "is that classes should be kept homogeneous, and that each student be kept busy, constantly stimulated and mentally challenged by the class work and progressing at a maximum rate."

[1] Wood, *op. cit.*, p. 317.   [2] *Ibid.*, p. 17.

Paying tribute to the Wood volume, Fife writes on page 107 of his Summary:

Wood's experiments and report are a valuable and in many respects a remarkable piece of pioneer work ... The value of the study lies chiefly in the careful manner in which these experiments with relatively tremendous numbers of students are unfolded before the reader and the penetrating analysis of the tests themselves and the results of their administration ... The author is frankly a strong partisan of the new-type test and it must be said that the reader who has an objective mind will find his arguments convincing ...

III. PROGNOSIS TESTS

We have very briefly discussed two volumes of the *Study* dealing with testing. We now come to a third and last volume: *Prognosis Tests in the Modern Foreign Languages* by V. A. C. Henmon.[1]

With the influx of vast numbers of students into our high schools and colleges shortly after the World War the problem of curriculum construction became more and more important. It was keenly felt that a new principle of selection had to be found in order to guide the enormous masses of students into courses which would fill their future needs. Intelligence tests had demonstrated their usefulness, and psychologists began to consider the possibility of constructing a test which would have value in predicting success in special subjects. Prognosis tests have offered interesting and important problems ever since. Modern language teachers in particular are much interested in this question because nothing could serve them better than a test which would safely select out of large numbers of students only those gifted in language or those certain not to fail. The trial-and-error method, which every pupil weak in language and every experienced language teacher knows to his regret, is of course wasteful and costly in terms of time and energy.

Modern language teachers in general are convinced that a linguistic aptitude exists apart from general intelligence. From the

[1] Volume XIV of the *Modern Foreign Language Study* (The Macmillan Company, 1929), xviii + 182 pp. For a summary see Fife, *op. cit.*, pp. 123–41.

standpoint of the psychologist, prognosis in modern languages centers around four questions:

"(1) Is there a general intelligence level below which success in modern language study is improbable? (2) Is there a general scholarship level below which success is doubtful? (3) Can special abilities and disabilities involved in learning a foreign language be determined and tested so as to predict future success in this subject? (4) Can achievement and progress at the end of a semester's work or a year's work be measured so accurately as to predict whether the pupil has the capacity to profit from further work?" [1]

Fife in concluding his summary of the Henmon volume on prognosis states that as a whole it is a very impressive contribution to the subject. He expresses the hope that the psychological abilities involved in language learning will some day yield up their secrets. Discussing the negative results of Henmon's findings he writes that the highest relationship obtained as yet between predictive tests and foreign language achievement does not rise to a coefficient of correlation of more than .60 to .70 when measured by teachers' marks, and that the high-water mark reported for all measurements of achievement has not yet reached a correlation coefficient of .75, which is only about forty per cent better than a pure guess as a basis for predicting success or failure. He concludes:

It may indeed be long before a special aptitude test in languages will be found which will work in this field as well as a general intelligence test does in a wider field. Possibly this will not come until some of the dynamic factors which condition scholastic success, such as will power and motivation, the capacity for sustained attention, etc., can be tested. The present work at least has defined more clearly the intellectual functions which are concerned in modern language learning. It has also made clear that before the modern language teacher can be relieved of his defective pupils, if linguistic defectives really exist, he must himself assist in removing the variables which now obstruct a clear view of linguistic abilities through an improvement in the materials and forces of teaching and a greater objectivity and exactness in judging achievement.[2]

[1] Fife, *op. cit.*, p. 125.   [2] *Ibid.*, p. 141.

In 1931 Professor Walter V. Kaulfers published a comprehensive survey on the "Present Status of Prognosis in Foreign Languages." This survey was the last article in a series of ten,[1] all of which were based on experimental data with the exception of two, numbers 6 and 10. In the last named article (no. 10) Kaulfers states that seven years previous to 1931, as shown by the 51 studies he had analyzed, 48 investigators had correlated achievement in the various abilities of language — grammar, reading, vocabulary — with 67 different bases, including such elements as ability to think in abstract terms, memory span for visual and non visual material, general intelligence, etc. One of his main conclusions was that because of the lack of standardization in foreign language teaching and because of the variety of abilities involved, it was doubtful whether any basis of prediction would be found applicable.

Two years later, in 1933, the same author completed his doctor's dissertation and with it one of the most comprehensive and detailed studies on foreign language prognosis concerning Spanish in the

[1] (1) "Mental Selection in Foreign Languages," *Hispania*, XI, 6 (Dec. 1928), pp. 505–10.

(2) "Intelligence and Spanish Failures," *Modern Language Journal*, XIII, 7 (April, 1929), pp. 550–54.

(3) "Prognostic Values of the IQ in Spanish," *Modern Language Forum*, XIV, 3 (June, 1929), pp. 5–9.

(4) "Effect of IQ on Grades of 1000 Students of Foreign Languages," *School and Society*, XXX, 762 (Aug. 1929), pp. 163–64.

(5) "Value of English Marks in Predicting Foreign Language Achievement," *School Review*, XXXVII, 7 (Sept. 1929), pp. 541–46.

(6) "Why Prognosis in the Foreign Languages?" *Modern Language Journal*, XIV, 4 (Jan. 1930), pp. 269–301.

(7) "Comparative Study of Intelligence of Beginners in College Foreign Languages," *School and Society*, XXXI, 805 (May, 1930), pp. 749–54.

(8) "A Guessing Experiment in Foreign Language Prognosis," *Ibid.*, XXXII, 825 (Oct. 1930), pp. 535–38.

(9) "Intelligence Factor in Foreign Language Achievement," *School Review*, XXXIX, 1 (Jan.), pp. 42–48.

(10) "Present Status of Prognosis in Foreign Languages," *Ibid.*, XXXIX, 8 (Oct. 1931), pp. 585–96.

These articles are briefed in *An Analytical Bibliography of Modern Language Teaching, 1927–1932*, compiled for the Committee on Modern Language Teaching by Algernon Coleman with the assistance of Agnes Jacques (The University of Chicago Press, 1933), pp. 233–34.

junior high schools.[1] Kaulfers found that the two best prediction bases or factors of comparison were prognosis tests and tests on ability in English.   In 1930 and 1932 he experimented with 461 eighth- and ninth-grade pupils, and with 209 ninth-grade pupils in various junior high schools in California.   As achievement measures he used five criteria: reading, vocabulary, grammar, total scores on the Columbia Research Bureau Spanish Test, Form A, and teachers' marks.   As a prediction battery he used eleven different bases or factors of comparison, among them the Luria-Orleans Prognosis Test scores and the Stanford Word Meaning scores which latter proved to yield the highest forecasting efficiency for the five criteria of achievement mentioned above.

In a short but significant article published in 1939,[2] Kaulfers restated some of his findings.   He repeats that he had selected from the vast numbers of investigations reported between 1900 and 1930 those bases or factors of comparison which seemed to yield the most promising correlations with subsequent success in the several phases of foreign language work, and combined them into a multiple correlation with scores from the best standardized tests available at that time, as well as with teachers' grades.   The results showed that the highest degree of accuracy in predicting foreign language achievement would be only thirty per cent better than pure guess — i.e., far too unreliable a basis on which to risk the exclusion of pupils from language work.   Kaulfers explains that "even if a perfectly valid test of foreign language aptitude existed, there would still be no way of knowing how effectively a pupil would use such language talent as it revealed."   He points to the irrefutable fact that a mere possession of ability does not give the slightest indication as to how effectively a given student will use this ability.   He argues that a test designed to predict achievement in a course following a strictly "direct method" can-

[1] Walter V. Kaulfers, *The Forecasting Efficiency of Current Bases for Prognosis in Spanish.* Unpublished Ph.D. dissertation (Stanford University, California, 1933), 381 pages and appendix. This dissertation is briefed in *An Analytical Bibliography of Modern Language Teaching, 1932–1937* by Algernon Coleman with the assistance of Clara Breslove King (The University of Chicago Press, 1938), pp. 427–30.

[2] "Prognosis and Its Alternatives in Relation to the Guidance of Students," *German Quarterly* (March, 1939), pp. 81–84.

not be expected to predict success equally well in a course following a so-called "eclectic method"; and that a prognosis test designed to forecast success in a beginning course featuring grammar cannot be expected to forecast success in a course which features the "reading approach" or the "cultural approach" or any of the many potential "approaches." Kaulfers argues further that all his studies had indicated

> that a twelve-minute test of English vocabulary is almost as good for purposes of homogeneous grouping as the most expensive and time consuming foreign language prognosis test. Moreover, it was found that several of the so-called tests of "linguistic aptitude" predicted ability in science and mathematics as well as (or better than) work in foreign languages . . .
>
> All the evidence from objective investigations tends to show that nothing can be depended upon to predict success or failure as reliably as an actual try-out in the foreign language.

By a twelve-minute test of English vocabulary Kaulfers means the "Word Meaning" section in the Stanford Achievement Test,[1] of which we give an example below:

> Direction: In each sentence draw a line under the word that makes the sentence true.
>
> To mitigate means to   contrive   extinguish   extol   lessen   revere

By actual try-out with the foreign language, Kaulfers has in mind types of courses which have been developed in various parts of this country.

> The first semester is made as rich an experience as possible without sacrificing the development of ability in the language. Then at the end of ten weeks or a semester those pupils who give evidence of serious maladjustment are transferred to a culture course, to a course in the foundations of language, or to a class in world literature, carrying college entrance credit as electives, but not as credit in lieu of foreign language. Some schools are successfully experimenting with orientation courses in general language. Although some of these offerings are as yet little more than courses in "baby philology" — a mere ride on the language merry-go-round — the marked im-

[1] *Stanford Achievement Test*, by Truman L. Kelley, Giles M. Ruch, and Lewis M. Terman. World Book Company, 1922; revised since.

provement in textbooks and materials published in recent years gives promise of really significant future developments in this field.[1]

In 1937 William Mark Taylor and James B. Tharp made an analysis of the situation of courses in general language, and found that "there is a definite lessening of stress on prognosis in favor of orientation and terminal purposes, regardless of superior or inferior capacities." [2] Kaulfers, in his article of 1939, shares the opinion of Taylor and Tharp. Kaulfers is convinced that in order to avoid radical reductions in enrollments, definite provisions must be made for pupils unable to learn a foreign language in terms of abstract grammatical concepts. "It is important in considering any basis for selecting pupils," he says, "to realize that the inevitable outcome is always fewer pupils, fewer classes, and fewer teachers, unless some provision is made for those students

---

[1] Kaulfers refers to abstracts of discussions dealing with orientation courses in foreign cultures in Volume II of Coleman's *Analytical Bibliography*, pp. 332–53, mentioning especially abstracts 742, 744, 747, 753, and 755.

For courses in general language see:

Ella B. Adams, "General Language in High-School Courses," *School Review*, XLIII, 9 (Nov. 1935), pp. 664–71.

Wilton W. Blancké, *General Principles of Language and Introduction to Foreign Language Study* (D. C. Heath and Company, 1934), xiv + 459 pp.

E. C. Cline, *Your Language* (Appleton and Company, 1930), xiv + 256 pp.

Helen S. Eaton has prepared general language courses for the International Auxiliary Language Association in the United States, Inc., 525 W. 120th Street, New York City.

Estelle Edith Feldman, *Introductory Course in Foreign Language* (New Haven, Conn.: Board of Education, 1931), vii + 132 pp.

Beth Hughson and Olga Gostick, *In Foreign Lands* (D. C. Heath and Company, 1934), xvi + 362 pp.

Walter V. Kaulfers, "The Prognostic Value of General Language Courses," *School and Society*, XXVII (Nov. 1928), pp. 662–64.

Lilly Lindquist, *Laboratory Courses in General Language*, Book I: *English and Modern Foreign Languages*. Book II: *Latin and Greek*. Manual and Key to the above. (Henry Holt and Company, 1929), 83 pp.; also "A General Language Course as a Prerequisite to Foreign Language Study," *Modern Language Journal* (Jan. 1930), pp. 285–89.

For other titles see Oliver, *The Modern Language Teacher's Handbook* (D. C. Heath and Company, 1935), and Taylor and Tharp (see below).

[2] William Mark Taylor and James B. Tharp, "An Analysis and Evaluation of General Language; The Language Art Survey Course," *Modern Language Journal* (Nov. 1937), pp. 83–91. Compare also Wilton W. Blancké, "General Language as a Prognosis of Success in Foreign Language Study," *German Quarterly* (March, 1939), pp. 71–80.

who are rejected." He closes his article with a plea for the strengthening of the foreign language departments. "Having tried rather vainly for three decades to fit our students to our courses," he concludes, "we might profitably try for a time to fit our courses to our students."

It should be noted that Kaulfers' article was first presented to the Tenth Annual Meeting of the Association of Teachers of German in New York City, on December 27, 1938, and that C. M. Purin, who reported on the meeting in the *Monatshefte* (Jan. 1940), pp. 54–56, says: "Kaulfers' paper was discussed by Professor Reinsch and many others. The general tenor of the discussion was highly complimentary to the author. He seemed to have convinced the audience that the ghost of prognostication has been irrevocably laid."

Among the sixteen contributions on prognosis listed by Coleman in the *Analytical Bibliography, Volume II* (pp. 423–40), there is besides Kaulfers' dissertation a Master's thesis by Sister Virgil Michel.[1] Coleman praises it as one of the best studies of this puzzling problem. Sister Virgil Michel's study is based on German. Two years after her Master's thesis she restated some of her findings in a Journal article.[2]

> In general, the experiment corroborates the findings of the majority of investigators in foreign language prognosis in so far as the correlations are rather low, in so far as predicting success in any subject is much more difficult than prognosis of success in all subjects in high school or in college, and in so far as it points with increasing insistence to the need for further research in order to secure more efficient predictive measures than those that exist at present.[3]

It is impossible to predict the future of prognosis tests. Certain it is that our best efforts have so far failed to develop a test by which we may predict quickly and reliably future success in language work. Certain it is also that the task of developing a prognosis test will continue to tempt teachers and scholars, for, in Fife's words, "nothing can be more important or more fascinat-

---

[1] *Prognosis in the Modern Foreign Languages.* Unpublished Master's thesis (University of Minnesota, 1934), 106 pp. + .

[2] "Prognosis in German," *Modern Language Journal* (Feb. 1936), pp. 275–87.

[3] Compare Coleman, *Analytical Bibliography, Volume II*, pp. 433–35.

ing than an exploration of the psychological functions which underlie success in language study." Prognosis by means of a probationary period appears to be the most reliable procedure in existence. Yet Rome was not built in a day. It is quite conceivable that some day someone will discover a combination of two or three prediction bases which will eliminate all uncertainty and yield a correlation coefficient of .90 or better.[1]

CONCLUSION. We have discussed some of the basic points set forth in the three volumes of the *Study*. We have seen in these volumes how conscientiously the pioneers, Henmon and Wood, considered every minute detail in order to produce adequate and valid testing instruments, and with what meticulous care they reported their results. The facts proved by the administration of the standardized tests stand out in bold relief. The destructive effect of the "time-serving" conception, which is at the bottom of all our evils, the startling overlapping of classes, and the wide variations of school standards can be eliminated only if each individual teacher works conscientiously and consistently toward a permanent elimination of these evil and harmful factors. So long as our classes remain heterogeneous, our standards uncertain, and our procedures a matter of controversy and strife, so long there will be no justified hope for further important progress in our field of endeavor.[2]

BIBLIOGRAPHY

COLE, ROBERT D. *Modern Foreign Languages and Their Teaching.* Revised and enlarged by James Burton Tharp (New York: Appleton-Century Company, 1937), Chapters XII and XIII, pp. 385–455.

COLEMAN, ALGERNON. *An Analytical Bibliography of Modern Language Teaching, 1927–1932.* Compiled for the Committee on Modern Language Teaching with the assistance of Agnes Jacques (Chicago: The University of Chicago Press, 1933), numbers 389–491.

——— *An Analytical Bibliography of Modern Language Teaching, Volume II, 1932–1937.* Compiled and edited for the Committee on

---

[1] In a personal note of November 18 Professor Henmon curbs my optimism. He writes: "Your standard of .90 is higher than has ever been thought possible. I should say between .70 and .80 as a degree of forecasting efficiency would be eminently useful."

[2] For a list of standardized tests see pp. 290 ff.

Modern Language Teaching with the assistance of Clara Breslove King (Chicago: The University of Chicago Press, 1939), numbers 832–933 and 1057–60.

FIFE, ROBERT HERNDON. *A Summary of Reports on the Modern Foreign Languages* (New York: The Macmillan Company, 1931), pp. 98–141.

FRANTZ, ADOLF I. "The Reading Knowledge Test in the Foreign Languages: A Survey." *Modern Language Journal*, XXIII, 6 (March, 1939), pp. 440–46.

HAWKES, HERBERT E.; LINDQUIST, E. F.; MANN, C. R. *The Construction and Use of Achievement Examinations*. Prepared under the auspices of the American Council on Education (Boston: Houghton Mifflin Company, 1936). Chapter VI, "Examinations in the Foreign Languages" by Algernon Coleman, pp. 264–336.

HENMON, V. A. C. *Achievement Tests in the Modern Foreign Languages*. New York: The Macmillan Company, 1929.

—— *Prognosis Tests in the Modern Foreign Languages*. New York: The Macmillan Company, 1929.

KAULFERS, WALTER V. "Present Status of Prognosis in Foreign Languages." *School Review*, XXXIX, 8 (Oct. 1931), pp. 585–96.

—— *The Forecasting Efficiency of Current Bases for Prognosis in Spanish*. Unpublished Ph.D. dissertation (Stanford University, California, 1933). See Coleman's *Analytical Bibliography, Volume II*, pp. 427–30.

—— "Prognosis and Its Alternatives in Relation to the Guidance of Students." *German Quarterly* (March, 1939), pp. 81–84.

SISTER VIRGIL MICHEL. *Prognosis in the Modern Foreign Languages*. Unpublished Master's thesis (University of Minnesota, 1934), 106 pp. + . See Coleman's *Analytical Bibliography, Volume II*, pp. 433–35.

—— "Prognosis in German." *Modern Language Journal* (Feb. 1936), pp. 275–87.

TAYLOR, WILLIAM MARK and THARP, JAMES B. "An Analysis and Evaluation of General Language; The Language Art Survey Course." *Modern Language Journal* (Nov. 1937), pp. 83–91.

WOOD, BEN D. *New York Experiments with New-Type Modern Language Tests*. New York: The Macmillan Company, 1928.

SUGGESTIONS FOR DISCUSSIONS AND REPORTS

1. Discuss briefly each of the following terms: (*a*) valid; (*b*) reliable; (*c*) comprehensive and comparable; (*d*) administratively feasible; (*e*) correlation; (*f*) percentile rank; (*g*) median; (*h*) mean.

2. Select a reader and prepare a vocabulary test of 25 items with the

multiple choice technique. Use Morgan's *German Frequency Word Book* in checking all words outside the frequency range of 2000.

3. Prepare a grammar test with 25 items on the model of the American Council Alpha German Test. In absence of a syntax count, take as a basis the grammar you are now using in class.

4. Prepare a silent reading test by the paragraph-question technique. Choose ten reading selections and try to grade them in difficulty. Take into consideration vocabulary, idioms, and grammar.

5. In evaluating the written work of your students, make use of the German Composition Scale as given in the Manual of Directions for the American Council Alpha German Test (World Book Company) and in *Modern Language Instruction in Canada*, Vol. VI of the *Study*, pp. 514 ff.

6. Study carefully the testing techniques in the tests prepared by the Cooperative Test Service. Then prepare a short test using the same techniques.

7. Enumerate the main findings of Wood and Henmon in regard to the overlapping of classes and the wide variations in standards.

8. Report on the "time-serving" conception. See Wood, *op. cit.*, pp. 94–103.

9. Report on the present status of prognosis tests; use as a basis the references given in this chapter.

10. Report on the articles by Taylor and Tharp, and by Blancké (see p. 269, note 2).

11. Report on Coleman's chapter on "Examinations in the Foreign Languages." See bibliography under Hawkes, Lindquist, and Mann.

A NOTE ON SYLLABI

In planning this book, I first intended to include a number of course outlines which might be representative of courses in various parts of the country: the East, the Middle West and South, and the Pacific Coast. Thus I hoped to present to the reader a fairly clear picture of the nature and content of average courses offered during the first four years of high-school or college instruction. However, in trying to gather such course outlines I found that they existed in very few institutions. The dearth of such official statements is evidently due to the reluctance of department heads and administrators to go on record with a printed statement which has to be amended as soon as conditions change. Besides, many if not most administrative officers are frankly sceptical in regard to syllabi. They know that more often than not syllabi do not present reality, but an idealized version of ambitions and hopes. Recently I received a letter from the chairman of the Department of Germanic Languages and Literatures in a large and important university. It read: "I did, some years ago, formulate such a syllabus for graduate courses, but when I read it over now I see how definitely it 'glorified' the actual situation." No doubt the same might be said of most statements concerning undergraduate courses.

The main difficulty with syllabi appears to be that they always describe the means and devices by which certain results are supposedly achieved, and that they always fail to justify these means by stating actual outcomes or results. A syllabus should show clearly in terms of norms of standardized tests (the American Council Tests or those of the Cooperative Test Service) what has really been achieved at the end of a definite period of time in vocabulary, grammar, silent reading and, possibly, in composition. For the means and devices are interesting only in the light of these results and have no independent value as such.

Let me give an illustrative example from actual experience. At the end of three quarters (one year or two semesters) of German a group of thirty students were given the American Council

Alpha German Test. The result showed medians of 55 in vocabulary, 36 in grammar, and 33 in silent reading. If we compare these medians with the national norms of high-school pupils after six semesters and of college students after four semesters, as given in the Manual of Directions, we have the following:

MEDIANS AT THE END OF	VOCABULARY	GRAMMAR	SILENT READING
3 quarters (experimental group)	55	36	33
6 semesters H. S. (national norms)	52	29	24
4 semesters college (national norms)	46	27	26

Therefore, the experimental group of 30 students had achieved in three quarters of college German considerably more than high-school pupils normally achieve in six semesters and college students in four. In the light of such results the methodical features of syllabi are seen in an entirely new light. Now they seem indeed interesting and important.[1]

Hence, ideally speaking, a syllabus should be a carefully reasoned statement of methodical features which, according to valid, reliable, and standardized tests, have actually been proved to be highly effective. The outcome of tests should throw light on and justify the means employed, but methodical features should not be considered as having value independent of results.

What we urgently need, then, are course outlines seen in the light of reality, of actual outcomes, and not based on preconceived notions or wishful thinking.

Some time in the future, when we know better how to evaluate and test results of courses, one of the great universities may perhaps issue a carefully reasoned statement, outlining all required courses leading up to the Master's degree, thus furnishing a model for other universities to follow.

The only printed course outlines known to me are those which originated in the City of New York:

Modern Foreign Languages, A Syllabus of Minima. High Schools and Junior High Schools of the City of New York. Adopted by the

[1] Compare my article, *Modern Language Journal*, II, 2 (March, 1929), pp. 33–43.

Board of Education, May 27, 1931. First printing 1931. Reprinted 1934 and 1936. Prepared by a committee of high-school department heads under the chairmanship of Lawrence A. Wilkins, Director of Foreign Languages. Acting Director, Dr. Theodore Huebener. 150 pages.

This *Syllabus of Minima* is supplemented by the *Auxiliary Syllabus in Modern Foreign Languages.* Board of Education of the City of New York. Adopted by the Board of Superintendents, September 30, 1937. 268 pages.

While these syllabi, to my knowledge, have not been tested and evaluated in terms of the norms of standardized measurements, they seem reasoned and clear.

After a brief and lucid preliminary statement regarding aims and general considerations the *Syllabus of Minima* sets forth clearly similar accounts on the following topics: reading, pp. 8–18; translation, p. 20; aural comprehension, pp. 21–22; dictation, pp. 22–23; concert work, p. 24; memory work, pp. 24–25; grammar, p. 26; composition, pp. 27–38; tests and testing, pp. 28–37; bibliography on modern language testing, pp. 45–48; teaching how to study a language, pp. 49–50; homework and supervised learning, pp. 52–54; *realia* and informational material, pp. 54–56; general bibliography on modern language teaching, pp. 58–66; detailed syllabus of minima, pp. 67–106; junior high-school syllabus, pp. 107–150.

Unfortunately, space does not allow the reprinting of the pages of the *Syllabus of Minima* (pp. 75–85) dealing specifically with German, but I wish to thank Dr. Theodore Huebener of the Board of Education of the City of New York for granting permission to do so.

SPECIAL BIBLIOGRAPHIES

1. THE MODERN FOREIGN LANGUAGE STUDY

In Chapter I (pp. 19–24) we have quoted Professor Robert Herndon Fife who gives a brief summary of the seventeen volumes of the *Study* which appeared between 1927 and 1930 under the general title *Publications of the American and Canadian Committees on Modern Languages.* To these must be added:

> *A Summary of Reports on the Modern Foreign Languages.* Issued by the Modern Foreign Language Study and the Canadian Committee on Modern Languages, with an Index to the Reports by Robert Herndon Fife (New York: The Macmillan Company, 1931), viii + 261 pp. Pages 209–61 represent a thorough General Index prepared by M. E. Anstensen. Compare Professor Fife's letter to the *Modern Language Journal* (Feb. 1931), pp. 372–75.
>
> *Experiments and Studies in Modern Language Teaching.* Compiled for the Committee on Modern Language Teaching by Algernon Coleman (Chicago: The University of Chicago Press, 1934), ix + 367 pp.
>
> *An Analytical Bibliography of Modern Language Teaching, Volume I, 1927–1932.* Compiled for the Committee on Modern Language Teaching by Algernon Coleman with the assistance of Agnes Jacques (Chicago: The University of Chicago Press, 1933), xiii + 296 pp.
>
> *An Analytical Bibliography of Modern Language Teaching, Volume II, 1932–1937.* Compiled and edited for the Committee on Modern Language Teaching by Algernon Coleman with the assistance of Clara Breslove King (Chicago: The University of Chicago Press, 1938), xviii + 561 pp.

It is expected that a third volume now being compiled for the committee by Clara Breslove King under the supervision of Robert Herndon Fife will be issued for the years 1938–1942 at the end of this five-year period.

2. PRONUNCIATION

BARKER, MARIE L. *A Handbook of German Intonation for University Students.* New York: Appleton-Century Co., 1926. 102 pp.

DRACH, ERICH. *Deutsche Aussprachelehre für den Gebrauch im Ausland.* Frankfurt am Main: Diesterweg, 1931. 82 pp.

MEYENBURG, PHIL. ERWIN. *Kleine Phonetik für Ausländer.* Schriften des deutschen Instituts für Ausländer an der Universität Berlin. Berlin C 2.: Universität, Verlag des akademischen Auskunftsamts. Paper bound. 20 pp. and 4 pp. of bibliography. 1 mk.

PROKOSCH, EDUARD. *Sounds and History of the German Language.* Part One: German Phonetics. Part Two: History of the German Language. New York: Henry Holt and Company, 1916. xvi + 212 pp. $1.75.

SIEBS, THEODOR. *Deutsche Bühnenaussprache-Hochsprache.* Auf Veranlassung des deutschen Bühnenvereins und der Genossenschaft Deutscher Bühnenangehöriger bearbeitet. 14th edition. Köln: Albert Ahn, 1927. 264 pp.

VIËTOR, WILHELM. *Wie ist die Aussprache des Deutschen zu lehren?* Marburg: 1928. 25 cents.

—— *Kleines Lesebuch in Lautschrift.* Leipzig: B. G. Teubner. 1 mk.

—— *Deutsches Lesebuch in Lautschrift.* 5th edition. Leipzig: B. G. Teubner, 1914. 3 mks.

For further titles see footnotes in Chapter IV and Oliver, pp. 493 ff. and 541 ff.

3. DICTIONARIES

BELLOWS, MAX. *German-English and English-German Dictionary.* New York: Henry Holt and Company, 1912. $2.50.

DE VRIES, LOUIS. *A German-English Science Dictionary.* New York: McGraw-Hill Book Company, Inc., 1939.

Der Große Duden, Rechtschreibung der deutschen Sprache und der Fremdwörter bearbeitet von Dr. Theodor Matthias. Zehnte Auflage. Leipzig: Bibliographisches Institut AG., 1932.

Der Große Duden, Bildwörterbuch der deutschen Sprache herausgegeben von Dr. Otto Basler. Mit 342 Tafeln in Strichätzung und 6 Farbentafeln. Leipzig: Bibliographisches Institut AG., 1935; Boston: D. C. Heath and Company.

Der Sprach-Brockhaus, Deutsches Bildwörterbuch für jedermann. Richly illustrated. Leipzig: F. A. Brockhaus, 1935.

Der Volks-Brockhaus, Deutsches Sach- und Sprachwörterbuch für Schule und Haus mit etwa 3500 Abbildungen und Karten im Text und auf 68 einfarbigen und bunten Tafeln- und Kartenseiten sowie 35 Übersichten und Zeittafeln. Sechste, verbesserte Auflage, A–Z. Leipzig: F. A. Brockhaus, 1938.

Heath's New German and English Dictionary, with a phonetic key to the pronunciation of German words, by Karl Breul. Thoroughly revised and enlarged. Boston: D. C. Heath and Company, 1939. $3.75.

JAMES, WILLIAM. *Dictionary of the German Language.* In two parts. Fourth edition. New York: The Macmillan Company, 1929.

KLUGE, FRIEDRICH. *Etymologisches Wörterbuch der deutschen Sprache.* Elfte Auflage. Berlin und Leipzig, 1934.

Knaurs Konversationslexikon A–Z. 35,000 Stichwörter, 2600 Illustrationen, 70 einfarbige und bunte Tafeln und geographische Karten, 18 Übersichten, 115 statistische Schaubilder im Text. Berlin: Verlag von Th. Knaur Nachf., 1932.

Lang's German-English Dictionary of terms used in medicine and the allied sciences with their pronunciation. Fourth edition enlarged. By Milton K. Meyers, M.D. Philadelphia: P. Blakiston's Son & Co., Inc., 1932.

LINDEMANN, HERMANN. *Taschenwörterbuch* der englischen und deutschen Sprache mit Angabe der Aussprache nach dem phonetischen System der Methode Toussaint-Langenscheidt. First part English-German. Second part German-English. Revised by Edmund Klatt. Berlin-Schöneberg: 1929. Both parts, $2.00.

MURET-SANDERS. *Encyclopaedic English-German and German-English Dictionary.* First part, English-German. Second part, German-English. Berlin: Langenscheidt. About $5.00 each volume.

PATTERSON, AUSTIN M. *A German-English Dictionary for Chemists.* Second edition. London: John Wiley and Sons, Inc., 1935.

PINLOCHE, A. *Etymologisches Wörterbuch der deutschen Sprache,* enthaltend: Ein Bilder-Wörterbuch mit erklärenden Legenden zu 5,700 Abbildungen, ein Verzeichnis der Eigennamen und eine grammatische Übersicht, unter Mitwirkung von Theodor Matthias. Paris and Leipzig: 1922.

PURIN, C. M. *A Standard German Vocabulary* of 2932 words and 1500 idioms illustrated in typical phrases and sentences. The Heath-Chicago Series. Boston: D. C. Heath and Company, 1937.

Schlag nach! Wissenschaftliche Tatsachen aus allen Gebieten. Ein umfassendes Nachschlagewerk mit 982 Übersichten und Tabellen, 387 Textabbildungen und 12 farbigen Tafeln herausgegeben von den Fachschriftleitungen des Bibliographischen Instituts. Leipzig: Bibliographisches Institut AG., 1938.

VIËTOR, WILHELM. *Deutsches Aussprachewörterbuch.* Vierte und fünfte durchgesehene und durch einen Anhang erweiterte Auflage besorgt von Dr. Ernst A. Meyer. Leipzig: O. R. Reisland, 1931.

WADEPUHL, WALTER and MORGAN, BAYARD QUINCY. *Minimum Standard German Vocabulary* in dictionary form prepared for the American Association of Teachers of German. New York: F. S. Crofts & Co., 1936.

WASSERZIEHER, ERNST. *Woher?* Ableitendes Wörterbuch der deutschen Sprache. Achte Auflage. Berlin und Bonn: Dümmlers Verlag, 1930.

WEBEL, A. *Technical and Scientific German Dictionary.* New York: E. P. Dutton & Co., 1930. 887 pp.

WHITNEY, W. D. *Compendious German and English Dictionary.* New York: Henry Holt and Company, 1905. $2.50.

WICHMANN, K. *Pocket Dictionary.* London: Routledge; New York: E. P. Dutton & Co., 1933.

Compare:

HANDSCHIN, C. H. "French, German, Spanish, and Italian Service Dictionaries for Students and Teachers." *Modern Language Journal,* XXIII, 8 (May, 1939), pp. 602–07.

4. GRAMMARS

For Reference:

CURME, GEORGE O. *A Grammar of the German Language.* Revised and enlarged. New York: The Macmillan Company, 1922. Is generally considered the best reference grammar on the subject.

MATTHIAS, THEODOR. *Sprachleben und Sprachschäden.* Leipzig: 1930.

SANDERS, DANIEL. *Wörterbuch der Hauptschwierigkeiten in der deutschen Sprache.* Neubearbeitet von Julius Dumcke. Berlin-Schöneberg: Langenscheidt, 1908.

SÜTTERLIN, LUDWIG. *Die deutsche Sprache der Gegenwart.* Ihre Laute, Wörter, Wortformen und Sätze. Leipzig: 1910.

THOMAS, CALVIN. *Practical German Grammar.* Revised. New York: Henry Holt and Company, 1925.

WHITNEY, WILLIAM D. *A Compendious German Grammar.* 6th edition. New York: Henry Holt and Company, 1888.

For Historical and Philological Study:

BEHAGHEL, OTTO. *Die deutsche Sprache.* Leipzig: 1911. An earlier edition was translated by Trechmann under the title, *Short Historical Grammar of the German Language.* New York: The Macmillan Company.

—— *Geschichte der deutschen Sprache.* 5th edition. Berlin and Leipzig: Walter de Gruyter & Co., 1928. Also in Vol. III of Hermann Paul's *Grundriss der germanischen Philologie.*

DIEKHOFF, T. J. C. *The German Language. Outlines of Its Development.*
New York: Oxford University Press, 1914.

KLUGE, FRIEDRICH. *Deutsche Sprachgeschichte. Werden und Wachsen
unserer Muttersprache.* Leipzig: Quelle & Meyer, 1920.

PRIEBSCH, R., and COLLINSON, W. E. *The German Language.* New York:
The Macmillan Company, 1938.

PROKOSCH, EDUARD. *Sprachgeschichte und Sprachunterricht.* A reprint
from *Monatshefte für deutschen Unterricht,* Vols. XX–XXII, *i.e.*, 1928–
1930, is available at the University of Wisconsin. 35 cents.

SCHNEIDER, KARL. *Was ist gutes Deutsch? Ein Führer durch Schwierig-
keiten und Zweifelsfälle.* München: C. H. Beck, 1930.

TONNELET, E. *Histoire de la langue allemande.* Paris: Colin, 1928.

WILMANNS, WILHELM. *Deutsche Grammatik.* 3 vols. Straßburg:
Trübner, 1897–1911.

WRIGHT, JOS. *Historical German Grammar.* New York: Oxford University Press, 1907.

For fuller bibliography see Oliver, *The Modern Language Teacher's
Handbook* (Boston: D. C. Heath and Company, 1935), pp. 230–32.

5. PERIODICALS

Periodicals for Students and Class Use:

Das deutsche Echo. G. Kartzke and Wilhelm Rumpf, Editors. Published
monthly in two sections. Section I: Texte; Section II: Anmerkungen
und Vokabeln zu sämtlichen Texten. Does not appear in July and
August. B. Westermann Co., Inc., 18–20 West Forty-eighth Street,
New York City. Subscription price, $1.00 a year. Representatives for
the American schools: F. S. Crofts & Co., Inc., 41 Union Square West,
New York City. Agents in Johannesburg, South Africa; Chastswood,
Australia; London, England; and Tokyo, Japan.

Jugendrotkreuz Zeitung. 75 cents a year; for reduced block subscriptions
write to Dr. Wilhelm Viola, 1 Stubenring, Vienna, Austria.

For other titles see Oliver, *op. cit.,* p. 458–61; for periodicals written
for students, see Chapter IX, p. 213, note 2.

Periodicals Devoted to the Study and the Teaching of Modern
Languages (cf. Oliver, pp. 461–65):

The Modern Language Journal. Eight numbers a year. October through
May. $2.00. Vol. I was 1916–1917. Organ of the National Federation
of Modern Language Teachers. Indispensable publication because of

its able articles, reviews, and lists of new books in the field of modern language teaching. For subscriptions address the Business Manager.

Books Abroad: An International Quarterly of Comment on Foreign Books. Roy Temple House, University of Oklahoma, Norman, Okla., Editor-in-chief. A periodical of value and importance. $2.00 a year.

Bulletin of High Points (since July, 1931, officially shortened to *High Points*). Editor, Lawrence A. Wilkins. Monthly, except for July and August. Published by the Board of Education, High School Division, 500 Park Avenue, New York City.

Publications of the Modern Language Association of America. Edited by Percy Waldron Long, Secretary of the Association. Executive Offices, 100 Washington Square East, New York City. Appears quarterly. $5.00 a year. A subscription includes membership in this important organization which holds annual meetings alternately in the East and the Middle West during the Christmas holidays.

The Modern Language Forum. Organ of the Modern Language Association of Southern California. Published quarterly. $1.50 per year. Address 1240 South Main Street, Los Angeles, California.

Periodicals for German Instruction:

Monatshefte für deutschen Unterricht, formerly *Monatshefte für deutsche Sprache und Pädagogik* (founded 1898). Its *Jahrbuch* was issued during the first World War. Official Organ of the German Section of the Modern Language Association of the Central West and South. Editor-in-chief: R. O. Röseler. Published by the University of Wisconsin under the auspices of the Department of German, Madison, Wis. 8 issues a year. $2.00.

Deutschunterricht im Ausland. Zeitschrift des Goethe-Instituts der Deutschen Akademie, herausgegeben von Dr. Kurt Derleth und Dr. Wolfhart Klee. Excellent. 6 issues a year. 2.20 mks.

The German Quarterly. Published by the American Association of Teachers of German in January, March, May, and November at George Banta Pub. Co., 450 Ahnaip Street, Menasha, Wis. Editor: Frank Mankiewicz. Treasurer of the Association: Günther Keil, Hunter College, Kingsbridge Station, New York City. $2.00 a year. Membership fee including the Quarterly, $2.50.

For further titles, see Oliver, *op. cit.,* pp. 465–66.

Periodicals of more General Cultural or Literary Scope:

Die Literatur. Monatsschrift für Literaturfreunde. (Formerly *Das Literarische Echo,* Vols. 1–25.) Editor: W. E. Süskind, München.

Deutsche Verlags-Anstalt, Stuttgart. Appears monthly. 20 mks. a year. Address: Berlin W 30, Mackensenstr. 17.

Die deutsche Rundschau. Monthly. 22 mks. a year. Editor: Rudolf Pechel. Berlin, Deutsche Rundschau.

Velhagen und Klasings Monatshefte. 2.40 mks. an issue. Editors: Paul Oskar Höcker and Paul Weiglin. Berlin (Velhagen and Klasing). Superbly illustrated.

Die Woche. Weekly. $8.50 a year. Berlin (Verlag Scherl). Copiously illustrated and quite popular.

Daheim. Illustrated weekly. 2 mks. a month. Leipzig (Velhagen and Klasing).

Leipziger Illustrierte Zeitung. Weekly. 13.50 mks. quarterly. Edited by J. J. Weber, Leipzig. The leading German illustrated journal.

Die Kunst. Monthly. 7 mks. quarterly. Munich (F. Bruckmann). The leading German art journal devoted to modern productions in all fields.

Das deutsche Buch. Monatsschrift für deutsche Neuerscheinungen. 6 issues a year, 50 pfs. each. Leipzig (Verlag des Börsenvereins der deutschen Buchhändler).

Reclams Universum. Popular illustrated weekly. 8.20 mks. quarterly. Edited by Friedrich Zillhoefer. Leipzig (Ph. Reclam Jr.).

The American-German Review. Managing Editor: Wilbur K. Thomas. Published by the Carl Schurz Memorial Foundation, Inc. Issues six numbers a year. Excellently printed and illustrated. $2.00 a year.

6. POLITICAL HISTORY

ANGELL, JAMES W. *The Recovery of Germany.* New Haven: Yale University Press, 1929. 325 pp. Based upon a year's residence and study in Germany. Authorized translation: *Der Wiederaufbau Deutschlands.* Munich: Duncker and Humblot, 1930. 323 pp. 17 mks.

BARKER, J. ELLIS. *Modern Germany: Her Political and Economic Problems. Her Policy, Her Ambitions, and the Causes of Her Successes and Failures.* 5th edition. New York: E. P. Dutton & Co. Also the same author's *The Foundations of Germany's Strength.* New ed. New York: E. P. Dutton & Co.

BITHELL, JETHRO, editor. *Germany; A Companion to German Studies.* New York: Dial Press, 1932. xii + 423 pp. Maps.

DANTON, GEORGE H. *Germany Ten Years After.* Boston: Houghton, Mifflin Company, 1928. Reviewed by B. Q. Morgan, *Monatshefte,* XX, 125–26 (April, 1928).

FIFE, ROBERT HERNDON. *The German Empire between Two Wars: A Study of the Political and Social Development of the Nation between 1871 and 1914.* New York: The Macmillan Company, 1916. xi + 400 pp. Very favorably reviewed *Modern Language Journal*, I (Jan. 1917), pp. 143–46.

GOOCH, G. P. *Germany.* New York: Charles Scribner's Sons, 1925. 358 pp. Now translated into German: *Deutschland* (Berlin: Wasmuth). 12 mks. Very interesting book showing especially the development in the post-war period.

HALLER, JOHANNES. *The Epochs of German History.* New York: Harcourt, Brace & Co., 1930. 247 pp. English translation of the German original. Stuttgart: Cotta, 1924. xii + 375 pp. 6.50 mks.

—— *France and Germany: The History of a Thousand Years.* Translated by Dora von Beseler. London: Constable, 1932. xii + 312 pp. 7s. 6d.

HENDERSON, ERNEST FLAGG. *A Short History of Germany.* New York: The Macmillan Company, 1906. Also in an enlarged, revised edition, 2 vols. in one, 1916. The Macmillan Company.

PINNOW, HERMANN. *Deutsche Geschichte. Volk und Staat in Tausend Jahren.* Berlin: Frankfurter Verlags-Anstalt, 1929. 392 pp. 12.50 mks. English translation. New York: The Macmillan Company, 1932.

PRIEST, GEORGE MADISON. *Germany since 1740.* Boston: Ginn and Company, 1915. xvi + 199 pp. Reviewed favorably *Modern Language Journal*, I (Jan. 1917), pp. 143–46.

SCHEIDEMANN, PHILIPP. *The Making of New Germany.* New York: Appleton-Century Company, 1929. English translation by J. E. Mitchell. 2 vols. 367 pp.; 372 pp.

SCHEVILL, FERDINAND. *The Making of Modern Germany.* Chicago: A. C. McClurg & Co., 1916. Six public lectures delivered in Chicago in 1915. Reviewed *Modern Language Journal*, II (Nov. 1917), pp. 86–87. Best brief survey in English.

THOMPSON, JAMES WESTFALL. *Feudal Germany.* Chicago: The University of Chicago Press, 1930. 700 pp.

WUESSING, F. *Geschichte des deutschen Volkes.* Berlin: 1925. $1.80. Excellent.

These titles are reprinted with the permission of D. C. Heath and Company from Oliver, *The Modern Language Teacher's Handbook*, pp. 260–64.

7. LITERARY HISTORY

AMMON, HERMANN. *Deutsche Literaturgeschichte in Frage und Antwort.* I. Von den Anfängen bis Luther. 2nd ed. 4.80 mks. bound, 1930.

II. Von Luther bis zur Gegenwart. 2nd ed. 1929. Berlin and Bonn: Ferd. Dümmler.

ARNOLD, ROBERT F., general editor. *Das deutsche Drama.* München: Beck, 1925. x + 816 pp. 24 mks.

—— *Allgemeine Bücherkunde zur neueren deutschen Literaturgeschichte.* 3rd ed. Berlin and Leipzig: Walter de Gruyter, 1932. xxiv + 362 pp. 16 mks. Valuable reference bibliography. Reviewed *Monatshefte*, XXIV (Oct. 1932), pp. 205–06.

BIESE, ALFRED. *Deutsche Literaturgeschichte.* 3 vols. München: Beck, 1907. 16.50 mks. Excellent. Treats 19th century. 24th ed. 1930. Favorably reviewed *Monatshefte*, XXIII (March, 1931), pp. 86–89.

FRANCKE, KUNO. *History of German Literature as Determined by Social Forces.* Fourth edition, enlarged, of the author's *Social Forces in German Literature.* New York: Henry Holt and Company, 1907. 595 pp. Highly praised.

—— *Die Kulturwerte der deutschen Literatur in ihrer geschichtlichen Entwicklung.* Berlin: Weidmann. Was to be published in four volumes of which two have appeared. This is a revision of previous works by the late Professor Francke.

HEWITT-THAYER. *The Modern German Novel.* Boston: Marshall Jones Co., 1924.

KLUGE, HERMANN. *Geschichte der deutschen National-Literatur.* 50th edition revised by Besser and Oertel, 1920. 280 pp. The first edition of this popular work was in 1869.

KOCH, MAX. *Deutsche Literaturgeschichte.* Numbers 31 and 783 of the *Sammlung Göschen.* Berlin, W 10, and Leipzig: Walter de Gruyter & Co. Each 1.50 mks. Vol. I: to 1748; Vol. II: 18th–20th centuries.

KOISCHWITZ, OTTO. *Deutsches Geistesleben der Gegenwart.* New York: Alfred A. Knopf. xxiv + 164 pp. An introduction to contemporary German literature.

KÜRSCHNER's *Deutscher Literatur-Kalender*, published annually by Göschen in Leipzig. 5 mks. An indispensable bibliographical reference work for German writers since 1888.

MAHRHOLZ, WERNER. *Deutsche Literatur der Gegenwart. Probleme. Ergebnisse. Gestalten.* Revised and enlarged by Max Wieser. Berlin: Sieben Stäbe-Verlag, 1931. 528 pp. 2.85 mks. Several plates.

MORGAN, B. Q. *Critical Bibliography of German Literature in English Translation.* Stanford University, California: Stanford University Press, 1938. $10.00.

NAUMANN, HANS. *Die deutsche Dichtung der Gegenwart.* Vom Naturalismus bis zur neuen Sachlichkeit. 5th revised and enlarged ed. Stuttgart: I. B. Metzler, 1931. 415 pp. 9.75 mks. Reviewed *Monatshefte*, XXIII (Oct. 1931), pp. 189–90.

PORTERFIELD, ALLEN WILSON. *An Outline of German Romanticism, 1766–1866.* Boston: Ginn and Company, 1914. xxx + 263 pp.

PRICE, LAWRENCE MARSDEN. *English-German Literary Relations; Bibliography and Survey.* Berkeley, California: University of California Publications in Philology, Vol. IX. 1919–1920. 616 pp. Reviewed by R. H. Fife, *Modern Language Journal*, VI (Jan. 1922), pp. 225–28.

PRIEST, GEORGE MADISON. *Brief History of German Literature.* Based upon Gotthold Klee, *Deutsche Literaturgeschichte.* New York: Charles Scribner's Sons, 1909.

ROBERTSON, JOHN G. (1) *History of German Literature.* New and revised edition. New York: G. P. Putnam's Sons, 1931. A rather detailed history; best in English; excellent for reference. (2) *Outlines of the History of German Literature.* New York: G. P. Putnam's Sons, 1911. Brief but good manual. (3) *The Literature of Germany.* Home University Library. New York: Henry Holt and Company. Still briefer.

RÖHL, HANS. *Wörterbuch zur deutschen Literatur.* 8th enlarged and completely revised ed. (1st ed. 1914). Berlin: Teubner, 1931. 382 pp. 5.20 mks. Very favorably reviewed *Monatshefte*, XXIV, 117–19 (March–April, 1932). A revision of this edition for use in the United States was prepared by Arpad Steiner and published by the Johnson Publishing Company (1931), viii + 279 pp. See favorable reviews *Monatshefte*, XXIII (Dec. 1931), pp. 261–62, and XXIV (May, 1932), pp. 163–65. G. Bell of London has an edition edited by F. Norman (1931), viii + 279 pp. An earlier edition is in the series: Teubner's *Kleine Fachwörterbücher*, No. 14. 3.60 mks.

SCHERER, WILHELM. *Geschichte der deutschen Literatur.* Berlin: Weidmann. 10 mks. 2nd ed. xviii + 732 pp. Berlin: Askanischer Verlag, 1918. 15 mks. "Mit einem Anhang: *Die deutsche Literatur von Goethes Tod bis zur Gegenwart*, von Oskar Walzel." English translation of the first edition by F. C. Conybeare. Oxford: Clarendon Press. Two vols.

SOERGEL, ALBERT. *Dichtung und Dichter der Zeit. Eine Schilderung der deutschen Literatur der letzten Jahrzehnte.* Leipzig: R. Voigtländer, 1928. xii + 1062 pp. 377 illustrations. Half leather, 32 mks.; cloth, 26 mks. Also *Dichtung und Dichter der Zeit. Neue Folge.* Same publishers, 1927. xi + 896 pp. 340 illustrations. Half leather, 30 mks.; cloth, 24 mks. These delightful books have been deservedly popular, 76,000 of the first, and 20,000 of the second having been printed.

VOGT und KOCH. *Deutsche Literaturgeschichte.* Leipzig und Wien: Bibliographisches Institut. $5.00. Two richly illustrated volumes. 4th enlarged edition, 1918. A superior work for general reference and advanced study.

These titles and comments are reprinted by permission of D. C. Heath and Company from Oliver's *The Modern Language Teacher's Handbook,* pp. 372–78.

8. SCIENTIFIC READERS

For science readers, see Oliver, pp. 592 ff. Most of the recent scientific German Readers are named and briefly discussed by A. B. Ernst in the *Monatshefte* for May, 1938, pp. 277–80.

BURKHARD, OSCAR. *Readings in Medical German.* New York: Henry Holt and Company, 1930. $2.50.

CURTS, P. H. *Readings in Scientific and Technical German.* New York: Henry Holt and Company, 1935. $1.90.

—— *Einführung in die Chemie.* New York: Henry Holt and Company, 1938.

FIEDLER and SANDBACH. *A First German Course for Science Students.* New York: Oxford University Press, 6th edition, 1936. $1.25.

—— *A Second German Course for Science Students.* 3rd edition. New York: Oxford University Press, 1935. $1.25.

FIEDLER and DE BEER. *A German Reader for Biology Students.* New York: Oxford University Press, 1933. $1.25.

FOTOS and SHREVE. *Intermediate Readings in Chemical and Technical German.* New York: John Wiley and Sons, Inc. $1.25.

HORN, H. *Der menschliche Körper* (Mohme). Boston: D. C. Heath and Company, 1938. 40 cents.

KOISCHWITZ, OTTO. *Introduction to Scientific German.* New York: F. S. Crofts & Co., 1936. $1.25.

NOCK, F. J. *An Introduction to Scientific German.* New York: The Macmillan Company, 1937. $1.25.

SOKOL, A. E., and NYE, H. M. *Berühmte Forscher und ihre Beiträge.* New York: American Book Company, 1938.

VAIL, CURTIS C. D. *Scientific German for Science and Premedical Students.* New York: F. S. Crofts & Co., 1938. $1.80.

WILD, H. *An Introduction to Scientific German.* New York: Oxford University Press, 1937.

—— *An Anthology of Scientific German.* New York: Oxford University Press, 1937. $1.95.

YOE and BURGER. *German for Chemists.* New York: Prentice-Hall, Inc., 1938. $4.50.

ZIPFEL, H. *Bakterien und ansteckende Krankheiten* (Mohme). Boston: D. C. Heath and Company, 1939. 40 cents.

A stimulating article on "Scientific German" by William Diamond is to be found in the *Jahrbuch* of the *Monatshefte* for 1925, pp. 24–29. See also:

COFFMAN, BERTHA REED. "Motivation of a Course in Scientific German." *German Quarterly*, XI, 1 (Jan. 1938), pp. 1–3.

NOCK, FRANCIS J. "The Teaching of Scientific German." *German Quarterly*, XI, 2 (March, 1938), pp. 106–10.

VAIL, CURTIS C. D. "The Scientific German Course." *Monatshefte*, XXVIII, 6 (Oct. 1936), pp. 250–54.

For other titles see Oliver, *The Modern Language Teacher's Handbook*, pp. 592–93.

9. CULTURAL READERS

ALBRECHT, ERICH. *Deutschland im Umbruch.* Philadelphia: J. B. Lippincott Company, 1938.

BAERG, GERHARD. *Deutschland*, Kulturlesebuch mit Übungen. New York: Henry Holt and Company, 1938.

Cambridge German Contact Readers. General Editors: E. K. Bennett and G. F. Timpson.

Series I: Medieval Epics. Stories, with exercises and vocabulary, by Professor and Frau Dr. W. Fröhlich. Cambridge, 1936. Each volume, 64 pp. limp cloth.
Das Nibelungenlied.
Die Gudrunsage.
Dietrich von Bern, and Tannhäuser.
Parzival, and Lohengrin.

Series II: Biographies of the Great Germans. With vocabularies, by the Baroness Seydewitz. Cambridge, 1937. Each volume, limp cloth.
Schiller. 78 pp.
Martin Luther. 94 pp.
Bismarck. 80 pp.

Series III: German Stories of Today. Edited, with vocabularies, by Georg Schnöckelborg, Haileybury College, Hertford. Cambridge, 1936. Limp cloth.

Förster und Wilddieb, by Paul Ernst; *Eis,* by Alfred Karrasch, and *Der Kopf im Fenster,* by Wilhelm von Scholz. 70 pp.

Herr Reineke Fuchs, by Werner Jansen. 94 pp.

Series IV: Yesterday and Today in Germany. Material on actual life in Germany, with vocabularies. Cambridge, 1937. Limp cloth.

Im Frieden und im Krieg, by G. F. Timpson. 93 pp.

Der Weg ins Leben, by Ernst Heller. Edited by F. R. H. McLellan. 79 pp.

Des Deutschen Vaterland, I, by Dr. G. Kamitsch. Edited by E. K. Osborn. 79 pp.

Des Deutschen Vaterland, II, by Dr. G. Kamitsch. Edited by F. R. H. McLellan.

DODGE and VIERECK. *Das neue Deutschtum.* New York: Henry Holt and Company, 1934.

EVANS, M. B. and ROESELER, R. *Das Rheinland.* New York: F. S. Crofts & Co., 1934.

FLEISSNER, O. S. and FLEISSNER, E. M. *Deutschland von heute und gestern.* New York: F. S. Crofts & Co., 1930.

FRIEDERICH, WERNER P. *Kurze Geschichte des deutschen Volkes.* New York: F. S. Crofts & Co., 1939.

GAEDE, WILHELM R.; REUNING, KARL; and HUBBEN, WILHELM. *Germany Past and Present.* A series of cultural readers. New York: Cordon Company. 64–68 pages each. 45 cents each.

HAGBOLDT, PETER. *Inductive Readings in German, Book II.* An Introduction to the Spirit of German Life and Literature. The Heath-Chicago Series. Boston: D. C. Heath and Company, 1927.

—— *Land und Leute.* Book XI of the Graded German Readers. Total vocabulary, 1528 words and 278 idioms. The Heath-Chicago Series, 1936. 28 cents.

—— *Aus deutscher Vergangenheit.* Book XII of the Graded German Readers. Total vocabulary, 1671 words and 286 idioms. The Heath-Chicago Series, 1936. 28 cents.

—— *Von deutscher Sprache und Dichtung.* Book XIII of the Graded German Readers. Total vocabulary, 1815 words and 301 idioms. The Heath-Chicago Series, 1938. 28 cents.

HANDSCHIN, CHARLES H. *An Introduction to German Civilization, An Outline.* New York: Prentice-Hall, Inc., 1937.

See also the Oxford Rapid Reading Texts, Oxford University Press.

JOCKERS, ERNST. *Die Deutschen, ihr Werden und Wesen.* Richmond: Johnson Publishing Company, 1929.

JORDAN, EMIL L. *Kultur-Geographie von Deutschland.* New York: F. S. Crofts & Co., 1935.

KAUFMANN, F. W. and BALDUF, E. W. *Inductive Readings in German, Book III.* Introduction to German Political and Cultural History. The Heath-Chicago Series, 1929. $1.15.

KOISCHWITZ, OTTO. *Deutsche Fibel.* New York: F. S. Crofts & Co., 1932.

―― *Bilderlesebuch.* New York: F. S. Crofts & Co., 1933.

KRAUSE, CARL A. *Deutschkunde.* An Introduction to the Study of Germany and the Germans. New York: Charles Scribner's Sons, 1929.

LEOPOLD, WERNER. *Reise durch Deutschland.* A Cultural First Reader. The Heath-Chicago Series, 1934. $1.60.

―― *Ein Sommer in Deutschland.* Book X of the German Graded Readers. Total vocabulary, 1375 words and 273 idioms. The Heath-Chicago Series, 1940. 20 cents.

MANKIEWICZ, F. and BRANDT, W. *Deutscher Alltag.* Richmond: Johnson Publishing Company, 1931.

NEUSE, WERNER. *Wege zur deutschen Kultur.* Philadelphia: J. B. Lippincott Company, 1937. $1.50.

PURIN, CHARLES M. and ROSE, ERNST. *Deutsche Kulturkunde.* A Cultural Reader. Richmond: Johnson Publishing Company, 1928.

STEINHAUER, H. *Deutsche Kultur.* New York: Oxford University Press, 1939.[1] $1.85.

For a much fuller bibliography, see Otto Springer, "German Kulturkunde," *Monatshefte für deutschen Unterricht* (Oct. 1933), pp. 168–75; also Mariele Schirmer, "The Place of Civilization in Modern Foreign Language Teaching," *Modern Language Journal* (April, 1938), pp. 489–99.

10. STANDARDIZED TESTS

American Council Alpha German Test, Forms A and B. By V. A. C. Henmon, B. Q. Morgan, Stella M. Hinz, C. M. Purin, and Elisabeth

―――――

[1] Henry Grattan Doyle in an important article points out that "the study of foreign languages should stress things that bind men together, not those that divide them." Cf. "Foreign Politics in the Classroom: A Problem for the Modern Foreign Language Teacher," *Modern Language Journal,* XXIV, 2 (Nov. 1939), pp. 91–98. In the same issue of the Journal see comment on a cultural reader by Paul G. Graham, pp. 153 f.

It is interesting to note that the *German Quarterly,* in order to secure in the future only the most carefully prepared book reviews, has introduced a change in the method of handling new books. See "Report of the Committee on Book Reviews," *German Quarterly,* XII, 2 (March, 1939), pp. 108–09.

Rossberg. Yonkers-on-Hudson, New York: World Book Company, 1926.

American Council on Education German Reading Scales, Scales A, B, C, D. By M. J. Van Wagenen and Sophia Hubman-Patterson. Bloomington, Illinois: Public School Publishing Co., 1927.

Columbia Research Bureau German Test, Forms A and B. By C. M. Purin and Ben D. Wood. Yonkers-on-Hudson, New York: World Book Company, 1926.

Lundeberg-Tharp Audition Test — German. By Olav K. Lundeberg and James B. Tharp, 1932. (To be published)

Cooperative German Test. By Miriam Van Dyck Hespelt and E. Herman Hespelt, New York University, and Geraldine Spaulding, Bureau of Collegiate Educational Research, Columbia College. Forms 1933, 1934, 1935, 1936, 1937.

Cooperative German Test. Junior Form. By Emma Popper and Alice Miller, Junior High Schools, New York City, and Lucy M. Will, University of Minnesota. Forms 1933, 1934, 1935.

Cooperative German Test. Advanced Form. By Miriam Van Dyck Hespelt and E. Herman Hespelt, New York University, and Geraldine Spaulding, Bureau of Collegiate Educational Research, Columbia College. Revised Series: Forms N, O, and P available.

Cooperative German Test. Elementary Form. By Emma Popper and Alice Miller, Junior High Schools, New York City, and Lucy M. Will, University of Minnesota. Revised Series: Forms N, O, and P available.

American Council on Education German Reading Test. By E. P. Appelt, University of Rochester, and V. A. C. Henmon, University of Wisconsin. Forms A and B.

For an excellent bibliography of books and articles on tests see T. E. Oliver, *The Modern Language Teacher's Handbook*, D. C. Heath and Company, 1935, pp. 654–61.

The Cooperative Test Service of the American Council on Education was established in 1930 through a subvention from the General Education Board to render a significant type of service to the secondary schools and colleges. The Advisory Service Office, the Distribution, and the Editorial Office are at 15 Amsterdam Avenue, New York City. The Director is Ben D. Wood. This Advisory Service Bureau is of inestimable value to all teachers and administrators. On request they will send a booklet describing the high-school and college tests and giving other information. The 1940 announcement has just been issued. A more complete statement is given in *The Cooperative Achievement Tests, A Handbook Describing Their Purpose, Content, and Interpretation.* October, 1936. 36 pp.

A Bibliography of Tests in the Modern Language Field, compiled by V. A. C. Henmon is found in Coleman's *Analytical Bibliography, 1927–1932*, pp. 245–56. The items listed comprise French, German, and Spanish tests. They give in turn: 1. Content; 2. Reliability; 3. Validity; 4. Time; and 5. References to articles dealing with the specific test, each written by a master in the field of testing.

The last six items (486–91, pp. 254–56) describe in the same manner five prognosis tests.

A Foreign Language Prognosis Test, Forms A and B. By Percival M. Symonds. New York: Bureau of Publications, Teachers College, Columbia University, 1930.

Handschin Predetermination Test. By C. H. Handschin. Washington, D. C.: U. S. Bureau of Education, April 25, 1921.

Iowa Placement Examinations — Foreign Language Aptitude Series FA–I, Revised. By G. H. Stoddard and G. E. Vander Beke. Iowa City, Iowa: Extension Division, State University of Iowa, 1925.

Luria-Orleans Modern Language Prognosis Test, Form A. By Max A. Luria and J. S. Orleans. Yonkers-on-Hudson, New York: World Book Company, 1930.

Wilkins Prognosis Test in Modern Languages, Preliminary Tests (visual-motor, aural-motor, memory, grammar concepts) and Elimination Tests after Four Weeks of Study. By L. A. Wilkins. Yonkers-on-Hudson, New York: World Book Company, 1920.

A large part of Coleman's *Analytical Bibliography, Vol. II, 1932–1937*, is devoted to Examinations and Tests. See pp. 381–472, sections 832–952.

INDEX

INDEX

Numbers refer to pages of the text on which names and topics are mentioned. Names and topics on pages 189–91 have been omitted as too numerous. The topics are cross-referenced as far as possible.

A supplementary Index of names mentioned in the footnotes and the bibliographies follows on pp. 302–306.

SUPPLEMENTARY INDEX

This Index comprises names appearing in the footnotes and the bibliographies. No attempt has been made to list names mentioned in the Suggestions for Discussions and Reports.